Mastery Through Quizzing

An Active Learning Approach for Today's Classroom

Stan Skrabut, Ed.D.

Stan Skrabut

Editing by Wendy Picard, WPC.
Cover design by Bernadette van der Vliet, BMTPhotos.com.
Special thanks to beta readers Alan Adams, Camille Napier Bernstein, Jenn Buckley, Amanda Gibson, Kathleen Gradel, Nikki Vassallo, and Dawn Walker-Elders.

Paperback ISBN: 979-8-9928544-0-4

eBook ISBN: 979-8-9928544-1-1

Please share about this book with your friends.

Contents

Introduction

"Clear your desks. You have a quiz!" The words slice through the quiet classroom, stirring a sudden rustle of papers and tense glances between students. For many, these words summon a familiar wave of dread, a tight stomach that clenches as the teacher walks the aisles, handing out sheets of crisp white paper with ominous black print. Eyes widen, breaths grow shallow, and fingers gripping pencils tight. The silence in the room feels heavier, punctuated only by the faint scratches of pencils on paper and the occasional sigh as students grapple with nerves that can feel as overwhelming as the quiz itself.

For some students, the pressure of the test is enough to bring on a headache, others squirm in their seats, while fighting the wave of anxiety that has become as routine as the quizzes themselves. But it doesn't have to be that way. I used to feel that same stress whenever I sat down for an exam, the tension creeping up my spine. Everything changed, however, when I discovered the power of mastery quizzing—a shift that transformed my experience from dread to confidence. Mastery quizzing emphasizes learning through repeated assessments until achieving mastery.

For example, learners preparing for upcoming SAT or ACT exams elect to complete practice exam questions. Thousands of learners voluntarily quiz themselves to study for these assessment exams. These exams are not happening in the traditional classroom but in the comfort of home. Are these learners in search of anxiety? No, they search for question banks because they recognize the value of this preparation method.

This book aims to transform how educators, administrators, and instructional designers view quizzing, moving it from a source of stress to a powerful tool for fostering deep learning and long-term retention. By embracing the mastery quizzing approach, you'll see how thoughtfully designed, low-stakes assessments can alleviate test anxiety, reinforce student engagement, and ultimately strengthen learning outcomes.

This book guides those committed to creating supportive, growth-focused educational environments moving quizzes from being sources of apprehension to stepping stones of mastery.

Quizzing is more than testing what a student knows. It's a valuable active learning tool that helps students tap into their prior knowledge and practice emerging understanding.[1] Tapping into prior knowledge is crucial for understanding new concepts, making quizzing an indispensable part of learning.[2]

Quizzing is not limited to classrooms; it is significant in complex fields like medicine. In the medical profession, nurses and doctors actively employ mastery quizzing to bolster their knowledge and improve their ability to retrieve critical information.[3] These low-stakes quizzes prepare them for high-stakes assessments integral to their careers.

Quizzing is a versatile and potent learning tool that goes beyond mere assessment. It fosters active learning, critical thinking, and long-term retention. By understanding its benefits and embracing its challenges, students and professionals can leverage the power of quizzing to excel in their respective fields. In the following chapters, we will explore different learning theories and effects related to quizzing.

You will learn about various strategies for maximizing the impact of questions, question banks, and quizzes. Finally, you will discover a strategy you can use to scaffold student knowledge. Here is a quick look at the mastery quizzing strategy.

The Mastery Quizzing Strategy

The mastery quizzing strategy I recommend is a straightforward and effective method for helping students master course content. This approach helps students understand the material deeply and encourages active participation in their learning journey.

The strategy consists of 9 steps:

- Start with learning objectives.

- Create questions.

- Add real-world context.

- Provide detailed feedback.

- Build a flexible test bank.

- Create an exam blueprint.

- Build short quizzes.

- Deploy the quizzes.

- Build and deliver midterm and final exams.

That's it. This strategy will help students develop their knowledge. Mastery quizzing will also help them become better students by reducing their test anxiety, increasing class attendance, and improving their performance.

While this strategy addresses formative (low-stakes quizzes) and summative assessments (high-stakes exams), it primarily focuses on formative quizzes, aligning with educational principles and providing a comprehensive approach to student learning.

You can find more details on this strategy in chapter 13.

What to Expect

This book offers a comprehensive guide to mastery quizzing, blending personal insights with practical strategies to enhance learning outcomes. Each chapter builds upon the last, moving from foundational concepts to advanced techniques. Through stories, explanations, and actionable advice, you'll discover how to leverage quizzes as powerful tools for student engagement, retention, and mastery.

In the following chapters, you'll find both theory and practice: from understanding the core principles of mastery quizzing to exploring advanced strategies that foster long-term success. Whether you're new to this approach or looking to refine your skills, this journey will equip you with the tools to incorporate mastery quizzing as a central part of the learning experience.

Chapter One: My Story with Quizzes. Discover how mastery quizzing shaped my journey from high school to the Air Force and influenced my career and understanding of effective learning strategies. This chapter introduces my firsthand experiences with quizzes and exams and their role in achieving mastery.

Chapter Two: Key Concepts. Dive into the core principles of mastery learning and quizzing, highlighting their benefits for all learners. This chapter demonstrates how mastery quizzing enhances understanding and reduces student anxiety through clear learning objectives, assessments, and feedback.

Chapter Three: Why Quizzing. Explore the transformative power of quizzing, from boosting performance to identifying knowledge gaps. This chapter shows quizzing as a tool for engagement, motivation, and real-time feedback, which in turn supports teaching and learning goals.

Chapter Four: Technology. Learn how digital tools and platforms streamline mastery quizzing, offering instant feedback, flexibility, and accessibility. This chapter guides educators in using learning management systems, student response systems, and game-based apps to enhance quiz effectiveness.

Chapter Five: Question Design. Dive into crafting effective quiz questions. This chapter explains how well-designed questions align with learning objectives, assess comprehension, and promote mastery. It also covers different question types and best practices for clarity and relevance.

Chapter Six: Feedback. Explore the role of feedback in the quizzing process. This chapter emphasizes timely and constructive feedback as a key component in helping students identify areas for improvement, guiding them toward mastery, and fostering a positive learning experience.

Chapter Seven: Test Banks. Discover the importance of test banks in supporting mastery quizzing. This chapter details developing, organizing, and maintaining a comprehensive test bank to provide students with diverse questions, ensuring thorough preparation and skill reinforcement.

Chapter Eight: Quiz Design. Learn the essentials of quiz design, from structuring quizzes for different learning outcomes to creating balanced assessments that challenge students while supporting their learning. This chapter highlights techniques to design quizzes that are both fair and effective.

Chapter Nine: Quiz Delivery. Review the various methods for delivering quizzes to maximize engagement and accessibility. This chapter explores delivery options, such as in-person, digital, and hybrid formats, ensuring quizzes are accessible and adaptable for diverse learning environments.

Chapter Ten: Mastery Quizzing Considerations. Uncover key considerations for implementing mastery quizzing effectively. This chapter covers the balance between rigor and flexibility, the frequency of assessments, and practical tips for maintaining student motivation and integrity in a mastery-based system.

Chapter Eleven: In-Class Activities. Discover how in-class activities like concept checks, exam wrappers, and brief writing assignments enhance student engagement and retention. This chapter explores practical strategies to integrate these activities seamlessly into your teaching to support mastery learning.

Chapter Twelve: Strategies. Explore a range of strategies to integrate quizzing into your teaching toolkit. This chapter provides actionable tips for embedding quizzes in different instructional models, from traditional to flipped classrooms, to create an interactive, mastery-focused learning experience.

Chapter Thirteen: The Mastery Quizzing Strategy. Delve into the comprehensive mastery quizzing strategy, a structured approach that ensures students achieve deep understanding before advancing. This chapter combines all elements, from question design to feedback, offering a step-by-step guide to implementing mastery quizzing successfully.

As you turn the pages of this book, you'll discover a new way of approaching learning—one that transforms quizzes from sources of stress into powerful tools for mastering knowledge. Embrace the journey ahead, and let each quiz become a stepping stone for students to develop confidence, increase retention, and gain genuine understanding.

---

1. Ingrid AE Spanjers et al., "The Promised Land of Blended Learning: Quizzes as a Moderator," *Educational Research Review* 15 (2015): 59–74.

2. Lukas K. Sotola and Marcus Crede, "Regarding Class Quizzes: A Meta-Analytic Synthesis of Studies on the Relationship between Frequent Low-Stakes Testing and Class Performance," *Educational Psychology Review* 33, no. 2 (2021): 407–26.

3. Monir M. Almotairy et al., "Comprehensive Licensure Review and Adaptive Quizzing Assignments for Enhancement of End-of-Programme Exit Examination Scores in Saudi Arabia: A Quasi-Experimental Study," *BMJ Open* 13, no. 7 (2023): e074469.

Chapter One

My Story with Quizzes

In my journey through life, mastery quizzing has evolved and gained significance. Here is a glimpse into my experiences and insights into the world of quizzes and exams and their pivotal role in my life. These insights have profoundly impacted my understanding of its effectiveness.

Objective

- Recognize the impact of mastery quizzing on professional and personal growth through the author's experiences in the Air Force and higher education.

Air Force: Uncovering the Value of Quizzes

Quizzes and exams were a routine part of my high school education. I didn't fully grasp their purpose and how they were interconnected until my time in the Air Force. During this period, I realized the tremendous power of quizzes and exams in discerning knowledge and shaping one's career.

In the Air Force, career advancement relied on rigorous practical, oral, and written exams, pushing us to continuously study and stay sharp. In security forces, we faced demanding requirements that tested our competence, with 50 written questions, 20-25 oral questions, and practical scenarios annually. This commitment to maintaining high standards was central to my 20-year service.

Later in my career, I had the opportunity to lead quality control and training efforts. In these roles, I developed and administered assessments. These experiences gave me a deep understanding of creating clear learning objectives and effective questions at varying difficulty levels. I also learned strategies to help airmen prepare and succeed with these rigorous requirements.

The Air Force Academy Prep School: A Lesson in Continuous Testing

I had the fortune to attend the United States Air Force Academy Preparatory School[1], a place that further shaped my perspective on quizzes and exams. There, we faced a relentless schedule of quizzes. We received a quiz for each course every other day. With four courses daily, we often took up to twelve weekly quizzes. The curriculum designers use the Thayer method,[2] an instructional approach that emphasizes active, student-centered learning, as a guiding architecture. The core principle of the Thayer Method is that students must come to class prepared to engage actively with the material, typically by studying assigned readings and problems before the lesson. Quizzing and recitation played prominent, active, student-centered role in learning.

This constant exposure to quizzes proved instrumental in preparing us for the midterm and final exams. For ten months, I discovered the benefits of repetitive testing, which helped me maintain high academic performance. Additionally, regular quizzing helped to reduce test anxiety. I will discuss this more in a later chapter.

We also tackled standardized exams on alternate weekends during the first eight weeks. This constant testing resulted in a significant uptick in my scores for both exams.

According to the CollegeBoard, "1.9 million students in the class of 2023 took the SAT in high school."[3] Students preparing for the SAT spent $50 to $3,000 on study guides, online courses, and tutors.[4] Test takers can see a score increase of a hundred or more points through diligent preparation. One of the most common ways to prepare for the SAT is to take practice tests. These tests mimic what a test taker will see on the actual SAT.

Returning to the Air Force: Testing for Advancement

Upon leaving the prep school, I resumed my career in the Air Force, where I encountered tests crucial for earning promotions. These tests encompassed both career-specific knowledge and leadership skills. I relied on third-party study guides to prepare for these assessments. Similar to preparation test banks for the Law School Admission Test (LSAT) or Medical College Admission Test (MCAT). These guides contained thousands of questions, providing a comprehensive resource for study.

My successful approach involved rigorous practice, where I completed hundreds of questions nightly. I reviewed and studied the topics I struggled with, identified through missed questions, and steadily reduced the number of errors. This method consistently led to promotions throughout my military career.

Quality Control and Training: Utilizing Test Banks

In my quality control (QC) and training roles, I learned to capitalize on learning objectives, operational objectives, and test banks to assess individuals' knowledge and skills. The QC section conducted the assessments, whereas the training section developed the assessment materials that QC and trainees used. QC drew random questions from extensive test banks and evaluated individuals through examinations. While working in QC, we used computers to streamline our process by automating assessment development. Using computers accelerated our ability to scale and adapt to changing needs.

The training section prepared individuals for quality control exams and supplied comprehensive training materials. Each assigned duty assignment required annual qualification, involving major exams covering all aspects of the role. The training section developed and provided access to extensive test banks containing thousands of questions to assist airmen in their preparation. QC also used the same questions and scenarios. This active study engagement proved more effective than passive reading, resulting in highly skilled professionals.

Higher Education: A Lack of Mastery Quizzing

While pursuing my various degrees in higher education, I noticed a need for formative quizzes. Bachelor's and master's programs primarily relied on midterm and final exams with limited preparation support. This deficiency in preparatory resources prompted me to recognize an opportunity to improve higher education by implementing mastery quizzing.

My journey has illuminated the power of mastery quizzing as an active learning strategy. It has been pivotal in my personal and professional growth, shaping my perspective on education and assessment. Let's look at mastery quizzing and its transformative potential.

The concept of mastery lies at the heart of the strategy I want to share with you. Developing strong foundations shaped my experiences. My knowledge and skills were, in large part, honed through mastery quizzing. Learn why this is such a powerful active learning method in the next chapter.

Quick Quiz

Please take this quick quiz to wrap up this chapter and get into the spirit of mastery quizzing.

1.1. What role did quizzes play in the author's experience at the Air Force Academy Preparatory School?

a) They were used occasionally to assess knowledge retention.

b) They were a primary method for regular assessment and preparing for exams.

c) They were used only for midterms and final exams.

d) They focused mainly on leadership skills.

1.2. Which of the following best describes the author's preparation for advancement exams in the Air Force?

a) Relying solely on knowledge from previous courses.

b) Participating in weekly study groups without additional materials.

c) Using test banks and answering hundreds of questions nightly.

d) Focusing only on oral questions without written tests.

1.3. What deficiency did the author observe in higher education regarding quizzes and exams?

a) A lack of final exams.

b) Insufficient formative quizzes for practice.

c) Too many ungraded quizzes.

d) Exams that focused only on multiple-choice questions.

---

1. The United States Air Force Academy Preparatory School, often called the "Prep School," is a military academy located at the U.S. Air Force Academy in Colorado Springs, Colorado. Its primary mission is to prepare selected candidates for admission to the U.S. Air Force Academy. The Prep School offers a 10-month program designed to strengthen cadet candidates academically, physically, and militarily, with a focus on building skills necessary for success at the Academy.

2. The Thayer Method, developed at the U.S. Military Academy at West Point by Colonel Sylvanus Thayer in the early 19th century.

3. "SAT Suite of Assessments – Reports," CollegeBoard, 2024, https://reports.collegeboard.org/sat-suite-program-results.

4. Nicole Spector, "How Much Does It Cost for College Test Preparation and Is It Worth It?," Yahoo Finance, August 12, 2022, https://finance.yahoo.com/news/much-does-cost-college-test-180001346.html.

Chapter Two

Key Concepts

Maya, a first-year college student, had always struggled with math. When she enrolled in Calculus 101, she dreaded the complex equations and theoretical concepts she would face. However, her professor, Dr. Williams, used a mastery learning approach in her course, combined with mastery quizzing techniques, which soon changed Maya's perspective.

Dr. Williams broke the calculus curriculum into manageable modules, each with clearly defined objectives. He required students to pass a quiz for each module before moving on to the next. These low-stakes quizzes allowed for multiple attempts. Immediate feedback guided students on where they went wrong and what concepts they needed to review.

Maya found herself stuck on the first module: limits. After her first quiz attempt, she received a "not yet" grade with detailed feedback pointing out her misunderstandings. Initially discouraged, Maya noticed the feedback included links to video tutorials and practice problems. The next evening, she revisited her notes, worked through the practice problems, and consulted a peer in her study group.

On her second attempt, Maya improved but still hadn't mastered the material. This time, her professor encouraged her to think about how limits applied to real-life problems, such as calculating the speed of a car at a specific moment. The contextual application clicked with Maya, and on her third attempt, she earned her "go" grade and progressed to the next module.

Over the semester, Maya repeated this process with derivatives, integrals, and advanced applications. While the multiple attempts required extra effort, Maya noticed something remarkable: the concepts stuck with her far better than they had in previous math classes. She could recall and apply the material during exams and even unrelated courses.

By the end of the semester, Maya passed Calculus 101 and developed confidence in her ability to tackle challenging subjects. The mastery learning approach transformed her struggle into a rewarding journey of discovery, reinforcing her understanding and building her resilience.

Let's look closer at mastery learning, mastery quizzing, and the psychology making this all work.

Objectives

- Recognize the principles of mastery learning and its application in educational contexts.

- Explain the key elements and benefits of mastery quizzing, including its alignment with active learning principles.

- Analyze the psychological theories and principles that underpin the effectiveness of mastery quizzing, such as the testing effect, spaced repetition, and active recall.

Mastery Learning

Benjamin Bloom, an American educational psychologist best known for creating *Bloom's Taxonomy*, introduced the concept of mastery learning in 1968. Mastery learning centers on the idea that students must demonstrate proficiency in a skill before progressing to the next topic.[1] Struggling students receive additional support to close learning gaps. For example, instructors provide students with additional opportunities to redo assignments. The core premise of mastery learning is that students can achieve a higher level of understanding if given ample time. This approach allows students to work independently, ensuring they master each concept before moving forward. Understanding the fundamentals of mastery learning is crucial to appreciating the effectiveness of mastery quizzing.

Key Features and Implementation Strategies

The core elements and implementation strategies of mastery learning emphasize well-defined objectives, measurable standards, and structured feedback. Mastery learning's foundational aspects include clear learning objectives, assessments for measurement, feedback and reassessment, skill application, and mastery-based standards.[2] Each component plays a role in fostering student success by ensuring learners meet specific benchmarks before advancing. Assessments, especially quizzes, gauge progress toward objectives, often incorporating formative and summative elements to monitor and reinforce learning. Constructive, timely feedback and reassessment opportunities enable students to refine their understanding and approach mastery iteratively.

Consider practical strategies that adapt these principles to your course structure for effective implementation. Begin with clearly defined learning objectives and reshape the course layout to accommodate time for multiple assessment rounds.[3] Utilize an additive grading system to reward progress without penalty, providing students with clear feedback, possibly through weekly emails and tools like a burn-down chart to track progress. Allow reasonable opportunities for reassessment, establishing a clear passing score aligning with course goals while maintaining rigor. A tiered progress system can provide structure without overly complex grading schemes. Through these steps, mastery learning fosters an environment where students can achieve competency at their own pace, focusing on skill acquisition and application, just like Maya was able to do

Benefits of Mastery Learning

Implementing mastery learning into a course provides many benefits.[4]

- **Improved performance for weaker students**. Mastery learning significantly benefits students with lower grade point averages, helping them to excel and improve their GPA.

- **Fair grading**. Students find mastery learning grading fairer than traditional methods due to its clear standards and assessments.

- **Higher grades and confidence**. Mastery learning often leads to higher grades and improved performance across the entire course, including final exams. Students also develop greater confidence in their abilities.

- **Preferred grading method**. After experiencing mastery learning, students often prefer this method over traditional approaches, especially once students understand how mastery grading works.

- **Immediate feedback**. Students appreciate the immediate feedback provided by mastery learning assignments, which aid their understanding and allow them to self-assess their progress.

- **Reduced test anxiety**. Mastery learning, with its frequent assessments, significantly reduces test anxiety. A key benefit of the method is supporting students' emotional well-being. Students become accustomed to taking quizzes and gradually become less sensitive to them through repeated exposure.

- **Lower motivation to cheat**. Mastery learning allows students to improve their understanding through reassessment, thus reducing motivation to cheat.

- **Self-paced learning**. Mastery learning empowers students with the flexibility to work at their own pace, continuously focusing on mastering content until they succeed. This student-centered approach fosters a sense of empowerment and ownership over their learning journey.

- **Mastering content**. Mastery learning encourages a shift in student mindset from earning a grade to truly understanding and mastering the content. This promotes a deeper understanding of the subject matter, a key educational goal.

Mastery Quizzing as Part of Mastery Learning

Mastery learning offers numerous benefits for all students when paired with mastery quizzing, a subset of mastery learning. Instructors can implement this highly flexible activity as a standalone graded element or integrate it into weekly course activities. Regardless, it will result in a positive outcome. While it presents challenges such as time constraints and student resistance, the rewards of improved understanding, fairness, and reduced anxiety make it a valuable strategy to consider in your educational approach.

Mastery quizzing, focusing on multiple assessments and immediate feedback, can be a powerful tool to implement in a course. Let's learn more about mastery quizzing.

Mastery Quizzing

Instructors can apply many powerful active learning strategies in a classroom. Mastery quizzing is one of the best, as it complements mastery learning.

Mastery quizzing represents a shift in educational assessment, focusing on proper understanding rather than just passing exams. It requires careful planning regarding assignment load, grading fairness, and maintaining student integrity. Mastery quizzing can significantly enhance learning outcomes and reduce student anxiety when implemented effectively.

Mastery-based quizzing is a unique approach often used for quizzes and exams.[5] Mastery quizzing can vary in format. One method allows students to try multiple times until they reach a satisfactory grade, which could be a perfect score or another set standard.[6] Another strategy is to have students complete a set number of questions perfectly with no partial credit.

Quizzes can cover various levels of Bloom's Taxonomy, a framework for categorizing educational goals.

Key Elements of Mastery Quizzing

Mastery learning and mastery quizzing have many similarities, as you will see. The key mastery quizzing elements include:[7]

- **Frequent testing**. Regular quizzes help students stay engaged and understand their progress.

- **Immediate feedback**. Providing instant responses helps students immediately identify what they need to improve.

- **Multiple attempts**. Allowing students to try more than once ensures they genuinely understand the material before moving on.

- **Tied to learning objectives**. Each quiz directly relates to what the students need to learn.

- **Low-stakes**. These quizzes are usually not high-pressure situations, which helps students focus on learning rather than the grade.

- **Pacing**. Mastery quizzing allows students to work at their own pace.[8]

Mastery quizzing is an effective way to ensure students understand their subjects thoroughly. It emphasizes learning and comprehension over just passing tests.

The "go" or "no-go" (not yet) system is at the heart of emphasizing learning and comprehension over grades.[9] Once a student reaches a certain level of mastery, they earn a "go." Otherwise, they receive a "no-go" or "not yet." This means the learner has not yet mastered the content and needs to conduct additional learning and assessment. There is no room for partial scoring in a go or no-go grading system.[10] Students either meet the standard or they do not. You increase the rigor of a course because of the ability for students to retake quizzes. However, too many retakes come at a cost. The primary cost is time. Students must allocate time to retake a quiz, which can cut the time available to learn new content. Educators may also be impacted by time if they have to manually grade quiz retakes or track student progress.

When implementing mastery quizzing, balancing the number of assignments is crucial.[11] Overloading students can be counterproductive since they need time to retake quizzes. Assignments should be weighted equally and not resemble traditional exams too closely. Completing quizzes should become routine for students. To change the focus from getting a grade to one of learning, students need to approach quizzing differently. Student integrity plays a vital role in this system. They have to understand how completing these quizzes will help them achieve mastery.

Mastery quizzes might seem challenging, but they are helpful for learning. Mastery quizzing is excellent for students because it helps them feel less stressed and understand the subject more deeply. If teachers and students see quizzes differently and use them well, everyone can improve. With more practice, improved testing, and a focus on learning, mastery quizzing can change how students learn in school.

Active vs. Passive Learning

When we talk about learning, we can think of it in two main ways: passive learning and active learning.

Passive learning. Imagine sitting in class, listening to the teacher talk, and taking notes without doing much else. That's passive learning. Passive learning is an educational approach in which students receive information from the instructor without actively engaging in the learning process. This method typically involves traditional lecture-based teaching styles, where the teacher talks and the students listen, take notes, and hopefully absorb information. Other examples of passive learning include reading textbooks and watching educational videos without engaging in discussions, question-and-answer sessions, or other interactive elements. The student's role is more of a recipient of knowledge rather than an active participant in creating and understanding the material.

Passive learning often presents a significant challenge in education. The main issue is that studying passively does not effectively build connections between the new information and what students already know.[12] This lack of connection makes it difficult for students to recall and apply the information later. While passive learning can be effective for certain types of information dissemination, it is generally considered less effective than active learning in promoting deep understanding and retention of material.

Active learning. Now, let's switch gears and talk about active learning. This is where things get exciting! Active learning is like being a detective in a learning adventure. Instead of just listening or reading, learners get to dive in and play with the information. This could be through quizzes, group projects, discussions, or solving problems that makes one think hard and connect the dots. Active learning is more fun and helps learners understand and remember things better. It turns learning into a two-way street, where students receive information and actively engage with it, making it stick in their brains more effectively.

There are two main types of active learning:[13]

- **Behavioral active learning**. This involves a physical response from the student. However, these responses might only sometimes lead to meaningful learning.

- **Cognitively active learning**. This learning activates prior knowledge and requires cognitive processing. It leads to more meaningful learning than merely memorizing facts (rote learning).

Active learning, particularly in science, technology, engineering, and mathematics (STEM) courses,[14] offers numerous benefits, including heightened student engagement, as it sustains their involvement for extended durations within the class[15]. These strategies also foster improved learning outcomes by facilitating a deeper comprehension of the subject matter.

Quizzing is a form of active learning known as retrieval practice. Students actively engage with the content during a quiz, attempting to recall and provide correct answers.[16] Whether they answer correctly or not, quizzes offer the opportunity for targeted feedback, addressing specific questions and reinforcing knowledge. Retrieval practice helps activate students' prior knowledge and strengthens neural connections, making learning more effective.

Despite its merits, active learning encounters several challenges, notably student resistance, whereby certain individuals may perceive their learning efficacy to be compromised by such methods.[17] Additionally, the time-consuming nature of active learning activities, like answering questions or engaging in interactive exercises, poses a hurdle as they demand more time compared to passive studying approaches, deterring some students from embracing it wholeheartedly.

Educators often view quizzes mainly as a tool for assessing learning, not realizing their potential as an active learning strategy.[18] Because of this underestimation, they neglect quizzes in the classroom. Students, too, often see quizzes as a negative experience rather than an opportunity to enhance their learning.[19]

Psychology That Makes Mastery Quizzing Work

Quizzing, more than a simple test, is a powerful tool for deepening understanding and strengthening memory through strategic learning practices. This section will uncover how quizzing taps into core learning theories and harnesses key psychological principles to fuel lasting knowledge. We'll explore the motivational aspects that drive quizzing's effectiveness, from retrieval practice that strengthens memory to spaced intervals that embed learning more firmly over time. By examining theories like the testing effect, backward and forward testing, and the cognitive benefits of multimedia learning, we'll see how each element contributes to a richer, more engaging learning experience. Additionally, we'll dive into metacognitive approaches and the role of a growth mindset, as well as practical strategies to motivate students and foster genuine engagement. These insights will reveal how quizzing connects new information with prior knowledge, creating an environment where learning flourishes.

Let's start with the testing effect and build layer by layer from there.

Testing Effect

Jacob, a sophomore majoring in history, struggled to retain dates and events for his exams. His usual study method of rereading his notes failed him repeatedly. Inspired by advice from his professor, Jacob switched to self-quizzing. He wrote questions for himself based on lecture notes and forced himself to recall answers without looking.

Initially, it was tough because he couldn't answer many questions correctly. However, trying to recall the answers reinforced the material in his mind. How much he remembered when the exam rolled around surprised Jacob. Not only did he score higher, but he also found he retained the information for future classes, proving the power of the testing effect and active recall.

The **testing effect**, a powerful phenomenon, highlights the benefits of regular self-quizzing. Students who regularly quiz themselves retain information better than those who only review the material.[20] Testing strengthens memory through active retrieval, making it more effective than passive reviewing. Regardless of the academic subject, the types of questions asked (closed or open-ended), and the distribution modality (on paper, online, or as a clicker quiz), the testing effect remains consistently beneficial.[21] This effect applies across various academic levels and subject areas, such as mathematics, humanities, and technical subjects, making quizzing a universally effective learning tool.

Backward and Forward Testing Effects

Quizzing reinforces previously learned material and prepares the mind for learning new content. The **backward testing effect** suggests that taking quizzes or tests on previously learned material can help individuals remember and understand that material more effectively.[22] Quizzing taps into prior knowledge and neural connections. It helps them recall information they've learned before and reinforces those connections. It also makes it easier to grasp new concepts.

The **forward testing effect** occurs when testing on familiar material helps learners prepare for and absorb new information more easily.[23] Quizzing can prime the brain for learning by activating existing knowledge. Quizzing's ability to strengthen existing knowledge and pave the way for new learning makes it a versatile educational strategy.

Here is a collection of learning theories related to the testing effect.

Integration theory. Integration theory proposes individuals create connections between previous knowledge and new content through testing.[24] These connections help learners relate new information to what they already know, deepening understanding.

Test potentiated new learning theory. The test potentiated new learning (TPNL) theory suggests taking tests improves memory for previously learned material and makes the brain more receptive to acquiring new information.[25] Testing enhances the learning process itself.

Active Recall

The goal of learning is to acquire new information to build knowledge. Then, one must be able to recall the information and apply the knowledge in varying situations. Ideally, once someone learned something, they could recall it forever. Unfortunately, that is not the case; we are also working to counteract Ebbinghaus' Forgetting Curve. **Ebbinghaus' Forgetting Curve** is the rate at which one forgets information over time if there is no effort to retain it. A combination of active recall and spaced learning can serve as an effective method for increasing the retention of information.

One can take a passive or active learning approach when learning new information. **Dual memory theory** differentiates between **study memory**, or the encoding of information, and **testing memory**, or the recall of information through the use of cues.[26] Quizzing enhances both aspects by actively engaging the memory systems. Encoding alone (study memory) does not ensure successful retrieval unless paired with opportunities to practice recall (testing memory). Techniques like retrieval practice leverage this understanding by encouraging active recall during learning, strengthening both the memory trace and the use of cues.

This book focuses on using quizzing for active recall. **Active recall**, an intentional strategy for responding to questions or solving problems, is more effective than passive learning.[27] Answering questions through quizzing is an active recall strategy.

Active recall strategies strengthen the neural connections in the brain. According to researchers, memories are associations between cues and targets.[28] These associations are the role of a **mediator**, a cognitive tool or process that helps connect cues (triggers or prompts) with targets (the desired information). Mediators act as mental bridges, making recalling and retrieving learned material easier. Examples include mnemonic devices, associations, or visualizations.

The **mediator effectiveness hypothesis** suggests that a learning strategy's success depends on how well it encourages the creation of effective mediators. Strong mediators lead to better retention and recall, while weak or ineffective mediators result in poorer learning outcomes.

Repeated quizzing strengthens these cue-target connections by testing the mediators created during the learning process. Learners might use strategies such as taking notes, creating diagrams, or using acronyms to generate effective mediators. Quizzing, however, provides a unique advantage: it evaluates how well these mediators work in facilitating recall.

This concept naturally leads to the **mediator shift hypothesis**, which explores how mediators' effectiveness evolves and adapts throughout the learning process.

According to the mediator shift hypothesis, individuals create mediators while testing, and if a mediator doesn't work effectively, they seek new ones.[29] Continuous testing ensures effective mediators are in place. When I prepared for promotion tests in the Air Force, I would run through a bank of quiz questions. I would look up the ones I got wrong in my study materials and highlight the correct answers. Before going through another quizzing round, I would review the information I previously got wrong. I would use different strategies to remember the content better.

The **elaborative retrieval hypothesis** suggests that individuals can do so through multiple connections or trigger points when answering a question.[30] Creating diverse pathways to recall information makes learning more robust. Instructors can help build multiple trigger points by developing comprehensive test banks with questions of varying difficulty levels and perspectives. For example, when quizzing on vocabulary, one could ask for a term and, in other cases, a definition. Working on the same vocabulary, you could create questions for learners to apply the correct term in a sentence. Individuals then have multiple pathways to provide a correct answer.

Context theory explains that quizzing helps individuals build a contextual framework around the tested material.[31] Context aids in recalling information because it provides a mental structure for retrieval. For example, if you, as the instructor, use specific examples or case studies during your lessons, you should use similar examples in the quizzes or exams. These similar contexts can help students recall the correct information. Students are often frustrated when they take an exam and the questions do not resemble their practiced content.

Another thing you can do when developing quizzing to help with student recall is to show multiple questions at once. Seeing a group of multiple questions aids in performance because test takers can trigger recall, which helps to answer similar questions.[32]

Spaced Repetition

Sam, a communications student, was preparing for a debate tournament. He had to memorize facts and figures for his argument, but the information felt overwhelming. A friend introduced him to spaced repetition, which involves reviewing material at increasingly longer intervals between review sessions.

Sam created flashcards and spaced his reviews. At first, he reviewed them every day. Once familiar with the material, he shifted to every three days, then every week. By tournament day, Sam had such a firm grasp of the data that he could recite it effortlessly. He credited his success to the spaced repetition technique, which helped him retain information long-term.

Spaced learning, also known as **spaced repetition**, is a powerful addition to mastery quizzing. This method involves reviewing or interacting with content at set intervals. The timing of these intervals is crucial for remembering what you've learned.[33] Spaced learning is about revisiting information over time to enhance memory retention.

Research has shown that spaced learning can significantly improve academic performance.[34] For instance, in a calculus study, students who practiced spaced retrieval improved their grades by about half to a third of a letter grade. Spaced learning is not just about short-term gains; it also helps information stick for extended periods.[35] The skills

I learned using this method at the Air Force Academy Prep School stayed with me much longer than those from other courses.

The spacing effect is a key element of spaced learning. Learning is more effective over time rather than crammed into a short period.[36] In mastery learning, for instance, students might encounter questions from previous chapters in a quiz. This technique helps reinforce older material while learning new information.

Frequent low-stakes quizzing at spaced intervals reinforces memory pathways in the brain.[37] Retrieving information from memory and recalling it during quizzes helps strengthen these connections over time. Spaced learning works hand in hand with active recall.

Spaced practice works like scaffolding. It builds upon previous knowledge while continuously adding new information.[38] In contrast, massed practice (or cramming) might lead to better short-term performance, while spaced practice results in superior long-term retention. It's about studying in small, regular intervals rather than trying to learn everything at once. Short quizzing sessions can be enhanced with feedback clarifying misconceptions. This strategy is known as **additional exposure theory**, and it enhances learning.[39]

One of the challenges of spaced learning is determining the correct interval for review sessions. To effectively implement spaced learning, the interval between review sessions should be adjusted based on the student's familiarity with the content.[40] Extend the intervals as students become more knowledgeable of the material. Increasing the space between sessions can lead to more substantial long-term gains as their understanding improves. You control when students see one of your questions. If students struggle, shorten the intervals to reinforce the material more frequently. Balancing these intervals is crucial for maximizing the benefits of spaced learning. Remember, learning takes time, and it's often better to review content periodically than to try and absorb it all in one go.

The timing of quizzes can significantly impact their effectiveness. Administering pre- and post-instruction quizzes enhances the testing effect. Research indicates post-instruction quizzes have triple the impact of pre-class quizzes.[41] Furthermore, spaced intervals in quizzing reinforce memory pathways, allowing for longer intervals between reviews. This concept resembles the spaced repetition strategy used in language learning applications like Duolingo.

Students may find spaced questions more difficult than massed questions when it comes to immediate quiz performance. However, student performance improves significantly over time.[42] This is due to the concept of **desirable difficulty**, where a challenging learning process leads to better long-term retention.[43] Spaced practice also gives students a more accurate understanding of their abilities, as they get more comprehensive feedback over time.[44]

Motivation to Learn

Motivation plays a crucial role in a student's learning journey. Students motivated to engage with and benefit from quizzes are more inclined to do so.

The anticipation of an upcoming quiz motivates students to prepare, ensuring they are well-prepared for the assessment. Nobody wants to face a quiz unprepared, as the fear of failure is a powerful motivator. Therefore, the mere knowledge of an impending quiz encourages students to dedicate time to study and review the content. This preparation helps them feel confident and ready to succeed on the quiz.

A student's mindset can significantly impact their approach to learning. The growth mindset, which focuses on improvement through effort, aligns well with quizzing, encouraging students to leave their comfort zones and actively engage with the material.[45] In contrast, the fixed mindset may hinder learning, as students may believe they lack the aptitude to learn. Quizzing can help shift students toward a growth mindset by showcasing the benefits of effort and improvement. Developing a growth mindset can help with setting learning goals.

Goal-setting theory highlights that setting short-term goals and obtaining feedback on progress helps students detect gaps in their understanding and adjust their learning approaches effectively.[46]

Success helps breed more success. Students are more confident when tackling new material if they have confirmed their mastery of previous content through quizzing. Knowing that material will reappear on future quizzes motivates students to focus on learning it thoroughly.

Success in quizzes triggers the brain's reward system, releasing dopamine and creating a positive student experience.[47] This reinforcement of success motivates students to seek more learning opportunities. When students experience success in quizzes, they are more likely to actively engage in learning, fostering a cycle of improvement.

But what if a student is not successful in answering questions? For example, Natasha, a junior in a psychology course, hated statistics. She often guessed answers and got them wrong. Her professor, however, encouraged her to embrace the struggle by attempting problems before checking her notes.

Initially, Natasha found this frustrating. However, over time, she noticed that struggling to solve problems made her more likely to remember the correct methods once she looked up the answers. When the midterm came around, Natasha felt better prepared and performed significantly better than in previous assessments. The process of generating answers, even incorrect ones, had helped her internalize the material.

Some of the best learning occurs through failure. The brain becomes excited when working through problems. It wants to generate a correct answer. Struggling to generate an answer, even if wrong initially, has a lasting learning effect.[48] This is called the **generation effect**.

Liam, a pre-med student, illustrates another essential concept. Liam loved answering questions in class, but he often gave incorrect answers. Instead of discouraging him, his professor used those moments to teach. Whenever Liam confidently stated a wrong answer, the professor would provide the correct information and explain why.

Surprisingly, those corrections stuck with Liam more than the facts he had guessed correctly. He began actively volunteering answers, knowing he was learning something valuable even when he was wrong. By the end of the semester, Liam noticed that his corrected mistakes often became his strongest areas of knowledge.

Discovering the correct answer, even after confidently providing a wrong one, leads to better learning.[49] This is known as the **hyper-correction effect**.

You can also incorporate additional strategies to motivate students through quizzing, such as awarding tokens for course privileges or incorporating engaging elements like "Easter eggs" in quizzes.[50] An Easter Egg can be a hidden message or secret. For example, some instructors will give students extra points for correctly discovering the need to email a picture of a kitten to the instructor hidden deep in a syllabus.

Hannah, an education major, was in a course that used such a unique motivational system: tokens that could be redeemed for privileges like dropping a quiz or earning bonus points. At first, she only participated for the rewards. But as she engaged with quizzes and interactive lessons to earn tokens, she realized she was learning more deeply than ever.

The tokens motivated her initially, but the confidence and excitement she gained from her newfound understanding kept her engaged. By the end of the course, Hannah didn't need the external rewards—learning had become intrinsically motivating.

These engagement strategies boost motivation and lead to improved attendance, better preparation, and increased participation, ultimately enhancing the overall learning experience.[51]

Conclusion

In this chapter, we explored the transformative impact of mastery quizzing on student learning and retention. Educators can design courses fostering deeper understanding and long-term retention by understanding the core principles—frequent testing, immediate feedback, and low-stakes assessments. Quizzing, a powerful educational tool, blends motivation, retrieval practice, and key learning theories to strengthen memory, activate prior knowledge, and facilitate the acquisition of new concepts. Active learning strategies, particularly mastery quizzing, shift the focus from rote memorization to meaningful engagement, offering students multiple opportunities to succeed. By applying the principles and theories discussed, educators can harness the full potential of quizzing to enhance academic success, nurture a growth mindset, and foster a lifelong love of learning. Ultimately, mastery quizzing empowers both educators and learners, creating an environment where knowledge is not just acquired but retained and applied effectively.

Quick Quiz

It's time to take a short quiz on this chapter's content.

2.1. What is the primary goal of mastery learning?

a) To cover as much material as possible in a short time.

b) To ensure students achieve a high level of understanding before advancing.

c) To assess students' intelligence through standardized testing.

d) To limit feedback and focus solely on grades.

2.2. Which of the following is a key feature of mastery quizzing?

a) Low-stakes assessments.

b) Immediate feedback.

c) Multiple attempts to achieve mastery.

d) Pacing aligned with student learning.

2.3. What psychological principle explains why students retain information better when they quiz themselves regularly?

a) The generation effect.

b) The testing effect.

c) The hyper-correction effect.

d) The mediator effectiveness hypothesis.

2.4. How does spaced repetition improve learning outcomes?

a) By encouraging students to memorize information quickly.

b) By promoting massed practice in short, intensive intervals.

c) By reviewing material at increasingly spaced intervals to strengthen memory.

d) By focusing only on recent material to avoid confusion.

2.5. Which of the following describes active recall?

a) Encoding information passively through repetition.

b) Actively retrieving learned information to strengthen neural connections.

c) Using visual aids to absorb material passively.

d) Memorizing content without engaging in self-testing.

---

1. "Mastery Learning," in *Wikipedia*, March 1, 2023, https://en.wikipedia.org/w/index.php?title=Mastery_learning&oldid=1142187900 .

2. Carlos Perez and Dina Verdin, "Mastery Learning in Undergraduate Engineering Courses: A Systematic Review," in 2022 ASEE Annual Conference & Exposition, 2022

3. Nicolas Garzone, Tracey Howell, and Daniela Tirnovan, "Mastering Anxiety: The Effect of Mastery-Based Testing on Quantitative Literacy College Students' Anxiety Levels and Mindsets," *International Journal for Mathematics Teaching and Learning* 24, no. 1 (2023): 62–73; Ella Tuson and Tim Hickey, "Mastery Learning and Specs Grading in Discrete Math," in *Proceedings of the 27th ACM Conference on Innovation and Technology in Computer Science Education Vol. 1* (Dublin, Ireland, 2022), 19–25; Darryl Chamberlain Jr, "How One Instructor Can Teach a Large-Scale, Mastery-Based College Algebra Course Online," *PRIMUS*, 2023, 1–22.

4. Garzone, Howell, and Tirnovan, "Mastering Anxiety"; Perez and Verdin, "Mastery Learning in Undergraduate Engineering Courses"; Chamberlain Jr, "How One Instructor Can Teach a Large-Scale, Mastery-Based College Algebra Course Online."

5. Garzone, Howell, and Tirnovan, "Mastering Anxiety."

6. Carlos Rojas and Gina M. Quan, "Mastery Grading in a Software Engineering Course," in *2023 ASEE Annual Conference & Exposition* (Baltimore Convention Center, MD, 2023).

7. Justin J. Donato and Thomas C. Marsh, "Specifications Grading Is an Effective Approach to Teaching Biochemistry," *Journal of Microbiology & Biology Education* 24, no. 2 (2023): 1–9, https://doi.org/10.1128/jmbe.00236-22.

8. Chamberlain Jr, "How One Instructor Can Teach a Large-Scale, Mastery-Based College Algebra Course Online."

9. Rojas and Quan, "Mastery Grading in a Software Engineering Course."

10. Chamberlain Jr, "How One Instructor Can Teach a Large-Scale, Mastery-Based College Algebra Course Online."

11. Donato and Marsh, "Specifications Grading Is an Effective Approach to Teaching Biochemistry."

12. Lukas K. Sotola and Marcus Crede, "Regarding Class Quizzes: A Meta-Analytic Synthesis of Studies on the Relationship between Frequent Low-Stakes Testing and Class Performance," *Educational Psychology Review* 33, no. 2 (2021): 407–26, https://doi.org/10.1007/s10648-020-09563-9.

13. Abderrahim Mimouni, "Using Mobile Gamified Quizzing for Active Learning: The Effect of Reflective Class Feedback on Undergraduates' Achievement," *Education and Information Technologies*, no. Journal Article (2022), https://doi.org/10.1007/s10639-022-11097-2.

14. Donato and Marsh, "Specifications Grading Is an Effective Approach to Teaching Biochemistry."

15. Jeffrey S. Nevid and Casey E. Armata, "Paying Attention in Class: Using In-Class Quizzes to Incentivize Student Attention," *Teaching of Psychology*, 2023, 1–6, https://doi.org/10.1177/00986283231185136.

16. Sotola and Crede, "Regarding Class Quizzes."

17. John P. Marinelli et al., "Harnessing the Power of Spaced Repetition Learning and Active Recall for Trainee Education in Otolaryngology," *American Journal of Otolaryngology* 43, no. 5 (2022): 1–2, https://doi.org/10.1016/j.amjoto.2022.103495.

18. Chunliang Yang et al., "Frequent Quizzing Accelerates Classroom Learning," *In Their Own Words: What Scholars and Teachers Want You to Know about Why and How to Apply the Science of Learning in Your Academic Setting*, 2023, 190–99.

19. Yang et al., "Frequent Quizzing Accelerates Classroom Learning"; Chunliang Yang et al., "Do Practice Tests (Quizzes) Reduce or Provoke Test Anxiety? A Meta-Analytic Review," *Educational Psychology Review* 35, no. 3 (2023): 1–26, https://doi.org/10.1007/s10648-023-09801-w.

20. Sotola and Crede, "Regarding Class Quizzes"; Svitlana Mykytiuk et al., "Seamless Learning Model with Enhanced Web-Quizzing in the Higher Education Setting," *International Journal of Interactive Mobile Technologies* 16, no. 3 (2022): 4–19, https://doi.org/10.3991/IJIM.V16I03.27257.

21. Yang et al., "Frequent Quizzing Accelerates Classroom Learning."

22. Mykytiuk et al., "Seamless Learning Model with Enhanced Web-Quizzing in the Higher Education Setting."

23. Mykytiuk et al., "Seamless Learning Model with Enhanced Web-Quizzing in the Higher Education Setting"; Yang et al., "Frequent Quizzing Accelerates Classroom Learning."

24. Sotola and Crede, "Regarding Class Quizzes."

25. Ibid., 412.

26. Ibid., 411.

27. Marinelli et al., "Harnessing the Power of Spaced Repetition Learning and Active Recall for Trainee Education in Otolaryngology."

28. Sotola and Crede, "Regarding Class Quizzes."

29. Ibid., 411.

30. Ibid., 410.

31. Ibid., 412-413.

32. Keith B. Lyle et al., "Spaced Retrieval Practice Imposes Desirable Difficulty in Calculus Learning," *Educational Psychology Review* 34 (2022): 1–14, https://doi.org/10.1007/s10648-022-09677-2.

33. Marinelli et al., "Harnessing the Power of Spaced Repetition Learning and Active Recall for Trainee Education in Otolaryngology."

34. Ingrid AE Spanjers et al., "The Promised Land of Blended Learning: Quizzes as a Moderator," *Educational Research Review* 15 (2015): 59–74, https://doi.org/10.1016/j.edurev.2015.05.001.

35. Lyle et al., "Spaced Retrieval Practice Imposes Desirable Difficulty in Calculus Learning."

36. Ibid., 1800.

37. Robin Boyle-Laisure, "Didn't Cover That in Class? Low-Stakes Technique of Quizzing to the Rescue," *The Journal of the Legal Writing Institute* 27 (2023): 299–307.

38. Lyle et al., "Spaced Retrieval Practice Imposes Desirable Difficulty in Calculus Learning."

39. Mykytiuk et al., "Seamless Learning Model with Enhanced Web-Quizzing in the Higher Education Setting."

40. Marinelli et al., "Harnessing the Power of Spaced Repetition Learning and Active Recall for Trainee Education in Otolaryngology."

41. Yang et al., "Frequent Quizzing Accelerates Classroom Learning."

42. Lyle et al., "Spaced Retrieval Practice Imposes Desirable Difficulty in Calculus Learning."

43. David J. Epstein, *Range: Why Generalists Triumph in a Specialized World* (New York: Riverhead Books, 2019).

44. Lyle et al., "Spaced Retrieval Practice Imposes Desirable Difficulty in Calculus Learning."

45. Charlene Li, *The Disruption Mindset: Why Some Organizations Transform While Others Fail* (Oakton, VA: IdeaPress Publishing, 2019); Garzone, Howell, and Tirnovan, "Mastering Anxiety."

46. Sotola and Crede, "Regarding Class Quizzes."

47. Boyle-Laisure, "Didn't Cover That in Class?"

48. Epstein, *Range*.

49. Ibid.

50. Rojas and Quan, "Mastery Grading in a Software Engineering Course"; Lisa Michael and Irene-Angelica Chounta, "Quizzes and Eggs: Exploring the Impact of Course Design Elements on Students' Engagement," in *In Proceedings of the 15th International Conference on Computer Supported Education (CSEDU 2023)*, 2023, 25–34, https://doi.org/10.5220/0011745000003470.

51. Mykytiuk et al., "Seamless Learning Model with Enhanced Web-Quizzing in the Higher Education Setting."

Chapter Three

Why Quizzing

In this chapter, we'll explore the influential role that quizzing plays in learning. While quizzes are often seen as a way to grade students, quizzes offer much more to students and instructors. This section will help you understand how quizzes can be vital to teaching and learning, improving students' performance, finding gaps in their knowledge, and helping them stay motivated. Quizzes can be used in many different ways, from online quizzes that give instant feedback to game-based learning that makes review fun. We are going to explore the benefits along with the challenges of using quizzes.

Objectives

- Describe the benefits of quizzing in promoting mastery learning, retention, and engagement in the classroom.

- Identify challenges and limitations associated with using quizzes in educational settings.

Quizzing: A Powerful Learning Tool

Quizzing is more than just a way to assess students—it's a powerful strategy that helps improve learning in many ways. Let's examine the main benefits of quizzing.

Performance Enhancement

Quizzing can significantly boost how well students perform. Research shows that quizzes help students improve their understanding and scores. Whether it's low-stakes quizzes during the course or more extensive exams at the end, quizzing pushes students to engage with the material. It's invaluable for strengthening skills across different learning levels.

Low-stakes quizzing, which focuses on formative learning, has significantly impacted student performance more than high-stakes exams, often used for summative assessments.[1] Studies have shown that students who took quizzes outperformed those who only reread the material, demonstrating a 10% improvement in subsequent exams.[2]

Allowing for multiple attempts is particularly beneficial in subjects like math.[3] Students appreciate the opportunity to enhance their performance through repeated practice with multiple quizzes.[4] Students who pass many mastery quizzes tend to score higher on final exams; this active engagement in mastery quizzes is essential to their success.[5]

When students encounter questions in mastery quizzes that they see again in summative exams, their success rate increases.[6] This repetition is crucial, especially if students initially answer incorrectly. The idea is to align questions with learning objectives, ensuring the focus remains on mastering the material.

Daily quizzes have demonstrated effectiveness by increasing pass rates, especially among lower-performing students.[7] They also help reduce class performance variation.

Quizzing, especially mastery quizzing, lets students improve at their own pace while building confidence. Over time, students show improved performance, especially if they can retake quizzes. This method allows them to revise their work and focus on areas to improve.

Imagine Alex, a college student who is struggling with math. At first, Alex feels overwhelmed by new concepts. But instead of just reading the textbook, Alex's professor gives short quizzes every few days. These quizzes don't count much toward the final grade but help Alex practice regularly.

Each time Alex takes a quiz, the questions push him to recall what he's learned. If he gets questions wrong, he can retake the quiz. Over time, Alex starts to see patterns in the problems, making it easier to solve them on the final exam.

By the end of the semester, Alex's confidence has grown. He scored 10% higher on his final test than his classmates who only read the textbook. The regular practice and repeated exposure to quiz questions helped him master the material.

Quizzing isn't just about grades—it's about learning, building confidence, and improving step by step.

Knowledge Retention and Transfer

Quizzing helps with performance and helps students remember what they've learned. It forces students to recall information, strengthening their memory. Students actively retrieve information from their memory when answering quiz questions. This process stimulates thinking and creates new neural connections in the brain, facilitating the formation of fresh ideas.[8] Ultimately, this leads to a better understanding of the topic. The more often students retrieve this information through quizzing, the more likely they will remember it long-term.[9]

Regular quizzes, like those at the start of classes, can help students stay current on course content and prevent them from cramming at the last minute for exams. At the Air Force Academy Prep School, instructors gave quizzes every other day. Students spent time constantly learning, not just cramming for midterms or finals.

Through quizzing, learners build knowledge and develop the ability to apply this knowledge to solve problems in new situations.[10] This practical application of content makes quizzing a valuable learning strategy.

Motivation and Engagement

Students who are regularly assessed come to class more prepared and engaged.[11] Quizzes and exams drive students to prepare effectively, boost attentiveness, improve study habits, increase attendance, and participate more in class, creating a dynamic learning environment.[12] Regular quizzing keeps students engaged with course content and encourages proactive use of textbooks and materials, resulting in better note-taking than passive review methods.[13]

Quizzes can also be fun. Game-based quizzing, for example, makes learning more engaging.[14] This increased engagement makes the learning process more enjoyable, which can lead to better understanding and a greater connection to the material. Students enjoy the process and feel less stressed when quizzing is a regular part of class. They become more motivated to learn and prefer these methods over traditional testing.

Feedback and Identifying Learning Gaps

One of the best things about quizzes is how they help teachers and students spot learning gaps early. Quizzes give quick feedback so students immediately know where they need to improve.

When instructors use formative quizzes throughout a course, they help students develop their knowledge and identify knowledge gaps.[15] Formative quizzes are a key tool for active learning. Students might take several quizzes to determine their knowledge gaps and then work to address those gaps. Quizzes should be frequent and focus on the course learning objectives.

Instructors also benefit from seeing how well students understand the material. Quiz results are a goldmine of information for instructors.[16] Unlike waiting for a midterm exam, frequent quizzes provide a continuous stream of data that allows instructors to identify misconceptions, make course corrections, and provide targeted support. Regular quizzes allow for constant feedback, which is better than waiting until midterms or finals to discover problems.

Quizzes are also a great way to see what students know before a new lesson begins.[17] **Baseline quizzes** can identify areas where students struggle so that students and teachers know what to focus on moving forward. Baseline quizzes are often given before the start of the first class to identify what students already know.

Flexibility and Ease of Use

Quizzes are flexible and can be used in many ways. Instructors can use them before a lesson to checkpreparation, during a lesson to test understanding, or after a lesson to measure progress. Quizzes can even be part of flipped classrooms, where students learn new material at home and use class time for practice.[18] Quizzing also works well with different levels of learning, from simple recall to higher-level problem-solving.[19]

Many quizzes today are online, which makes them easy to set up and even easier to grade. Teachers save time with automated grading, while students get instant feedback.

Plus, the ability to retake quizzes gives students more opportunities to succeed, helping them feel more in control of their learning.

Benefits Summary

Quizzing is a powerful tool that helps students perform better, retain more, and stay engaged with the material. It provides valuable feedback and helps identify learning gaps early. With its flexibility and ease of use, quizzing can be integrated into any classroom environment, making it an essential part of effective learning.

Challenges and Limitations of Classroom Quizzing

Classroom quizzes also have their drawbacks. While they offer numerous benefits, like increased attendance, engagement, and continuous feedback, they also have limitations, particularly in assessing students' understanding. Teachers must balance the use of quizzes with other forms of assessment and learning activities to ensure a comprehensive educational experience.

Here are some challenges or drawbacks to implementing a mastery learning strategy in a course[20].

Time and Effort in Implementation

Mastery learning can take up a lot of time. Teachers have to allow students multiple attempts to master a topic, which slows down the pace of the class. Setting up the grading system for mastery learning is also hard work. Although it saves time in the long run, it's a lot of effort initially.[21] Students might also struggle to find time to retake quizzes when needed. Teachers may also feel that quizzes take too much time, leaving less time to teach new content. Additionally, estimating a student's final grade using mastery learning can be difficult until the end of the course.

Student Resistance and Engagement

Some students don't like redoing assignments or quizzes, preferring to move on, even if it means accepting a lower grade. Many students and even teachers don't always see the benefits of quizzing.[22] As a result, students prefer passive study methods like rereading notes instead of quizzing, yet, quizzing is more effective for learning.[23] Also, when students perform poorly on quizzes, it can discourage them and make them feel less confident.

Learning Effectiveness and Engagement

Many quizzes use multiple-choice questions, often testing short-term memory rather than deep understanding.[24] This reliance on short-term memory can lead to students quickly forgetting the information after the quiz, limiting their ability to apply the knowledge in different contexts or retain it for an extended duration.

Summative exams (the extensive tests at the end of a unit or course) can also be problematic. If used alone, they may come too late to help students improve their understanding of the material.[25] Without regular quizzes and feedback, these exams don't help students improve throughout the course. They also encourage cramming, which leads to short-term learning rather than long-term understanding.[26] Furthermore, the availability of online test prep resources makes it easier for students to memorize answers rather than truly understand the material.[27]

Motivation and Stress

Quizzing can add pressure and stress for students, though some stress can sometimes push them to work harder. Some students find formative quizzes (used to help students learn rather than as a final grade) more stressful than just reviewing their notes.[28]

Another issue is that students who do well on quizzes might feel overconfident, preventing them from studying more deeply.[29] This overconfidence may prevent them from recognizing areas where their understanding is still superficial or incomplete. As a result, they might not dedicate enough time to review or study further, which could negatively impact their performance on more comprehensive assessments.

If students do poorly on quizzes, it can lead to a negative cycle of feeling discouraged and less motivated to participate in class. Educators must balance identifying knowledge gaps with providing support and encouragement to help students overcome these challenges.

Challenges Summary

While quizzes can engage students and provide quick feedback, they have downsides, such as being time-consuming and potentially discouraging. Quizzes often focus on short-term memory, which might lead students to forget material quickly. Students may need more confidence in understanding the material. Additionally, the effort required to implement a mastery learning system and the resistance from some students who prefer to avoid retaking quizzes can complicate their use. Balancing quizzes with other teaching methods and providing appropriate support can mitigate these issues, making quizzes more effective as learning tools.

Conclusion

Quizzing is a powerful learning tool that goes beyond just assessing students—it helps them engage with the material, strengthen their memory, and build confidence in their abilities. By regularly using quizzes, students can improve their performance, retain long-term knowledge, and stay motivated in their learning journey. Whether through mastery quizzes, daily assessments, or game-based learning, quizzing provides valuable opportunities for students to practice and refine their understanding.

However, effective quizzing requires careful implementation. While it offers many benefits, one must consider challenges like time constraints, student resistance, and potential overreliance on short-term memory. Educators should balance quizzing with other instructional strategies, ensuring that students receive meaningful feedback and have the opportunity to apply what they learn in different contexts.

Quizzing helps students take ownership of their progress, encourages active engagement, and supports long-term academic success. By addressing challenges and leveraging its strengths, quizzing can be essential to a practical and engaging learning experience.

Quick Quiz

Test your knowledge with a quick quiz to end this chapter.

3.1. Which of the following is a primary benefit of low-stakes quizzing?

a) Testing short-term memory only.

b) Increasing student stress levels.

c) Improving performance through active engagement with material.

d) Reducing the amount of material covered in a course.

3.2. How do mastery quizzes help students succeed in summative exams?

a) By testing their ability to cram effectively.

b) By aligning questions with learning objectives and encouraging repeated practice.

c) By replacing summative exams entirely.

d) By providing questions that are unrelated to course content.

3.3. What is one major challenge of implementing a mastery learning strategy?

a) Students perform poorly in high-stakes exams.

b) It discourages formative assessments.

c) Teachers must dedicate significant time to setup and administration.

d) It reduces opportunities for students to apply knowledge in real-world contexts.

3.4. Why are formative quizzes particularly useful for instructors?

a) They ensure students memorize correct answers.

b) They provide immediate data to identify misconceptions and adapt teaching strategies.

c) They eliminate the need for summative exams.

d) They focus on testing short-term memory alone.

3.5. Which statement best describes the relationship between quizzing and student motivation?

a) Quizzing always increases student stress and reduces engagement.

b) Quizzing motivates students to prepare, engage actively, and improve study habits.

c) Students prefer quizzes over all other types of assessment.

d) Quizzing has no significant effect on student motivation or learning habits.

1. Chunliang Yang et al., "Frequent Quizzing Accelerates Classroom Learning," *In Their Own Words: What Scholars and Teachers Want You to Know about Why and How to Apply the Science of Learning in Your Academic Setting*, 2023, 190–99.

2. Ibid., 253.

3. Nicolas Garzone, Tracey Howell, and Daniela Tirnovan, "Mastering Anxiety: The Effect of Mastery-Based Testing on Quantitative Literacy College Students' Anxiety Levels and Mindsets," *International Journal for Mathematics Teaching and Learning* 24, no. 1 (2023): 62–73.

4. Justin J. Donato and Thomas C. Marsh, "Specifications Grading Is an Effective Approach to Teaching Biochemistry," *Journal of Microbiology & Biology Education* 24, no. 2 (2023): 1–9, https://doi.org/10.1128/jmbe.00236-22.

5. Ibid., 5.

6. Ibid.

7. Matthew T. Johnson et al., "Improving Student Preparation and Pass Rates in Flipped Multivariable Calculus with Low-Stakes, Daily Quizzes," *PRIMUS* 33, no. 7 (2023): 714–28, https://doi.org/10.1080/10511970.2022.2163329.

8. Ester Aflalo, "Students Generating Questions as a Way of Learning," *Active Learning in Higher Education* 22, no. 1 (2021): 63–75, https://doi.org/10.1177/1469787418769120.

9. Yang et al., "Frequent Quizzing Accelerates Classroom Learning."

10. Chunliang Yang et al., "Do Practice Tests (Quizzes) Reduce or Provoke Test Anxiety? A Meta-Analytic Review," *Educational Psychology Review* 35, no. 3 (2023): 1–26, https://doi.org/10.1007/s10648-023-09801-w.

11. Svitlana Mykytiuk et al., "Seamless Learning Model with Enhanced Web-Quizzing in the Higher Education Setting," *International Journal of Interactive Mobile Technologies* 16, no. 3 (2022): 4–19, https://doi.org/10.3991/IJIM.V16I03.27257.

12. Johnson et al., "Improving Student Preparation and Pass Rates in Flipped Multivariable Calculus with Low-Stakes, Daily Quizzes"; Yang et al., "Do Practice Tests (Quizzes) Reduce or Provoke Test Anxiety? A Meta-Analytic Review"; Jeffrey S. Nevid and Casey E. Armata, "Paying Attention in Class: Using In-Class Quizzes to Incentivize Student Attention," *Teaching of Psychology*, 2023, 1–6, https://doi.org/10.1177/00986283231185136.

13. Johnson et al., "Improving Student Preparation and Pass Rates in Flipped Multivariable Calculus with Low-Stakes, Daily Quizzes"; Yang et al., "Frequent Quizzing Accelerates Classroom Learning."

14. Jeffrey S. Nevid, Luke H. Keating, and Shari Lieblich, "Effects of In-Class Engagement Activities in Online Synchronous Classes," *Scholarship of Teaching and Learning in Psychology* 8, no. 4 (2022): 304, https://doi.org/10.1037/stl0000312.

15. Nese Sevim-Cirak and Omer Faruk Islim, "Paper versus Online Quizzes: Which Is More Effective?," *Active Learning in Higher Education*, 2022, 1–18, https://doi.org/10.1177/14697874221079737.

16. Lukas K. Sotola and Marcus Crede, "Regarding Class Quizzes: A Meta-Analytic Synthesis of Studies on the Relationship between Frequent Low-Stakes Testing and Class Performance," *Educational Psychology Review* 33, no. 2 (2021): 407–26, https://doi.org/10.1007/s10648-020-09563-9.

17. Joshua K. Strakos et al., "A Learning Management System-Based Approach to Assess Learning Outcomes in Operations Management Courses," *The International Journal of Management Education* 21, no. 2 (2023): 1–9, https://doi.org/10.1016/j.ijme.2023.100802.

18. Johnson et al., "Improving Student Preparation and Pass Rates in Flipped Multivariable Calculus with Low-Stakes, Daily Quizzes."

19. Yang et al., "Frequent Quizzing Accelerates Classroom Learning."

20. Garzone, Howell, and Tirnovan, "Mastering Anxiety"; Carlos Perez and Dina Verdin, "Mastery Learning in Undergraduate Engineering Courses: A Systematic Review," in *2022 ASEE Annual Conference & Exposition*, 2022.

21. Yang et al., "Frequent Quizzing Accelerates Classroom Learning."

22. Ibid., 254.

23. Lou Ann Griswold, "The Value of Quizzing Students to Support Transfer of Learning," in *In Their Own Words: What Scholars and Teachers Want You to Know about Why and How to Apply the Science of Learning in Your Academic Setting* (Society for the Teaching of Psychology, 2023), 481–87.

24. Sotola and Crede, "Regarding Class Quizzes."

25. Dimple Martin, "Are Your Assessments Fair and Balanced?," *Faculty Focus | Higher Ed Teaching & Learning* (blog), September 20, 2023, https://www.facultyfocus.com/articles/educational-assessment/are-your-assessments-fair-and-balanced/.

26. Donato and Marsh, "Specifications Grading Is an Effective Approach to Teaching Biochemistry."

27. Ibid., 1.

28. Yang et al., "Do Practice Tests (Quizzes) Reduce or Provoke Test Anxiety? A Meta-Analytic Review."

29. Sotola and Crede, "Regarding Class Quizzes."

Chapter Four

Technology

Imagine a classroom where every student receives personalized feedback seconds after completing a quiz, teachers can identify struggling learners in real-time, and lessons are so engaging that even the most reluctant students eagerly participate. This isn't a vision of the distant future—it's happening now, thanks to technology.

Classrooms leveraging digital quizzing platforms experienced increased student engagement and improved retention rates compared to traditional methods. For educators, these tools are no longer optional; they are essential to meeting the diverse needs of today's learners.

As we explore the role of technology in mastery quizzing, you'll discover how these tools can streamline your workload, enhance student learning, and transform your teaching practice. The future of education is here—are you ready to embrace it?

Objectives

- Describe how technology enhances mastery quizzing.

- Identify features of digital quizzing platforms.

- Compare technology tools for educational assessments.

Advantages of Digital Quizzing Platforms

Here are some general things to consider when exploring the use of technology to support your mastery quizzing program.

Digital quizzing platforms have become a popular tool in modern education. They offer many benefits that make learning and teaching more effective and enjoyable. Here are some key advantages and considerations:

Instant Feedback. Professor Kim teaches an introductory psychology course with over 100 students. She recently implemented a digital quizzing platform for weekly mastery quizzes. One evening, Lisa, a struggling student, completed her quiz and immediately saw which concepts she misunderstood. Motivated by the instant feedback, Lisa reviewed the course material that night and joined office hours the next day to ask targeted questions. Professor Kim noticed a marked improvement in Lisa's subsequent performance, highlighting the power of immediate feedback.

One of the most significant benefits of digital quizzing platforms is that they provide instant feedback. When students complete a quiz, they can see their scores and understand which questions they answered incorrectly. This helps them learn from their mistakes quickly and strive to better understand the material.

Easy to use. Digital quizzing platforms for delivering quizzes and questions must have a practical design and be user-friendly.[1] Navigation must be easy to use. Can students control their pace through a quiz/product? The platform must work error-free. Can students take quizzes on their computers, tablets, or smartphones? Can teachers easily create, distribute, and grade quizzes without the hassle of paper and pencil? Fortunately, most platforms I have encountered are easy to use.

Engaging and interactive. Professor Alvarez used Kahoot! in a history class to review key events before a midterm. Students, divided into teams, competed to answer questions on their smartphones. Laughter and cheers filled the room as they raced to answer correctly. Even students who rarely participated seemed energized. "I never thought I'd enjoy reviewing history this much," one student remarked. Professor Alvarez noted improved quiz scores and attendance in subsequent classes.

These platforms must be visually attractive, up-to-date, and feature high-quality multimedia.[2] Consider the entertainment factor when evaluating questions, quizzes, and quizzing platforms. These platforms often include interactive elements like videos, images, and animations, making quizzes more engaging for students. Do elements, e.g., multimedia, provide a fun factor?[3] Students are more likely to stay interested and motivated to learn when the material is presented as fun and interactive.

Accessible anytime, anywhere. Professor Nguyen teaches a hybrid algebra course. To ensure accessibility, she integrates a mobile-friendly quizzing app into her course. One weekend, her student Marcus, traveling for a basketball tournament, completed his quiz from the team bus. "Knowing I can stay on track, even on the road, helps me manage my academics," he said. Professor Nguyen appreciated the flexibility the platform offered her students.

Digital quizzes can be accessed from anywhere with an internet connection. Students can take quizzes at home, school, or even on the go. Creating digital quizzes also makes it easier for teachers to assign them as homework or for remote learning.

Customizable and versatile. Teachers can easily customize quizzes to fit their students' needs. They can create multiple-choice, true or false, or short answer questions. They can also adjust the difficulty level and the time students complete the quiz.

Data and analytics. A sociology professor, Dr. Bennett, used analytics from a digital platform to analyze quiz performance trends. She discovered that most students struggled with questions on social stratification. Adjusting her lecture and providing supplemental resources, she addressed these gaps. By the end of the term, students' understanding of the topic had significantly improved, thus reinforcing the value of data-informed teaching strategies.

Digital quizzing platforms provide valuable data and analytics. A lot of data can be collected from quiz attempts, such as time on task, number of attempts, time between attempts, questions missed, and much more.[4] Reports are easy to use. Teachers can see how well their students perform, identify areas where they struggle, and adjust their teaching strategies accordingly. This data-driven approach helps improve student learning outcomes.

Cost-effective. Using digital quizzing platforms can save money. Schools can spend less on paper, printing, and storage. Many digital platforms offer free or affordable options, making them accessible to various educational institutions.

Magnify effort. Professor Lopez teaches an introductory economics course with 300 students. Managing assessments was daunting until he started using a mastery quizzing platform. Even at this scale, he could implement a mastery learning approach by automating question generation and grading. Students appreciated the tailored feedback, and he found time to focus on individual consultations.

Quizzing platforms allow instructors to administer mastery grading strategies in large classes.[5] Mastery quizzing at scale includes creating questions based on learning objectives, uploading questions, and grading them.

Environmentally friendly. Digital quizzing reduces the need for paper, which helps save trees and reduce waste. This makes it a more environmentally friendly option compared to traditional paper-based quizzes.

Enhance learning. Educational effectiveness is focused on whether the questions and quiz align with learning objectives.[6] Do all elements support learning, e.g., multimedia? Do questions cause students to think? Are questions inclusive? Is the technology used transparent?

Digital quizzing platforms offer numerous advantages that benefit students and teachers. They make learning more interactive, accessible, and effective while providing valuable data to help improve educational outcomes.

Let's examine the three major platforms that can help you deliver a mastery quizzing strategy: learning management systems, student response systems, and mobile and game-based applications.

Learning Management System

Learning management systems are powerful digital tools for building, maintaining, delivering, and grading quizzes. Take time to learn as much as you can about the system you are using, particularly what is possible.

Here are some things to consider while you get to know your system.[7]

Question types. What types of questions can be created? Possibilities include multiple-choice, fill-in-the-blanks, multiple-selection, true or false, matching, short answer, essay, numerical or formula, ordering or sequencing, dropdown, hotspot, drag and drop, labeling, audio or video response, among others. Create different kinds of questions to make quizzes interesting and challenging.

Randomized questions and answers. Can instructors present questions and answers to students randomly, enhancing fairness? Your quiz tool should be able to mix the order of questions and answers to keep things fair and unpredictable. This means every student might get questions in a different order.

Test banks. Can instructors create, preview, and update questions in a database, selecting all or only some to include in quizzes? This enables instructors to create dynamic, scalable assessments aligned with course objectives and learning outcomes. Organized question categories and randomized sets ensure unique, fair quizzes while reducing answer-sharing.

Category. Can questions be organized into different categories based on specific topics, aiding efficient use of the question bank? This is demonstrated in the test bank chapter.

Layout. Can you customize how questions appear in a quiz? Can instructors display one question per page or multiple questions per page?

Quiz attempts. Can instructors specify how many times a student can attempt a quiz? Multiple quiz attempts are a hallmark of mastery quizzing.

Time limit. Can instructors control when a quiz or exam starts and stops, along with the time available to take the quiz? Can instructors adjust times for students needing accommodations or set periods for students who need to take the exam at a different time?

Question feedback. Can instructors add feedback to individual questions and answer possibilities? Can instructors control when this feedback is available to students? Can students get feedback after taking a quiz? This helps them understand what they got right and where to improve.

Import and export files. Can instructors import and export questions from various sources to different file types, facilitating sharing and reusability? Create questions once and use across different tools. For example, Moodle uses "GIFT" text files to simplify creating quizzes. Canvas uses a "QTI" format. You can prepare these files with all your questions and then upload them to your learning management system (LMS). See chapter 7 for more details.

Authentication. Are mechanisms in place to ensure exam security, such as authentication?

Grade report. Can instructors generate statistical reports of test results? Can students view their test and total grades to determine pass or fail status? Grade reports provide instructors with valuable statistical insights into test performance, enabling them to assess question validity, identify trends, and refine their teaching strategies. For students, access to grade reports offers clarity on their progress, helping them understand their pass/fail status and make informed decisions about their learning paths.

Feedback. Can instructors identify students' strengths and weaknesses in specific topics based on test results, with the ability to generate individual reports? Can students see feedback on incorrectly answered questions?

Course outcome. Can questions be linked to course outcomes outlined in the curriculum? Linking quiz questions to course outcomes ensures assessments align with course goals, helping instructors measure learning objectives, identify gaps, and adjust teaching strategies. It also demonstrates accountability by showing stakeholders that assessments support the course's educational mission.

Ensuring these features are available and implemented enhances the effectiveness and fairness of assessments within the learning environment.

Student Response System/Clickers

Student response systems (SRS) or clickers offer an innovative method for conducting quizzes in classrooms. These systems are user-friendly for students and teachers and support various teaching methods, including traditional and flipped classrooms.[8]

Teachers display a question on a screen or through a projector in a typical setup. Students then use electronic devices, like clickers or polling apps, to submit their answers.[9] This approach allows for immediate display and discussion of results. Electronic devices facilitate data collection from each device or application, linking responses directly to individual students. SRS takes many forms, such as electronic devices and online or manual polling systems.

Instructors can integrate SRS into traditional classrooms in more interactive settings, such as during Q&A sessions or lectures.[10] They offer flexibility, allowing teachers to incorporate them as part of a game or in other creative ways. Their primary use, however, is to conduct quizzes promoting active learning.[11]

Electronic devices. Clickers are single-purpose devices; only used to conduct in-class polling. What they can do, they do well. The supporting software can keep accurate records that can be used with a learning management system. Unfortunately, the cost of the devices is often passed onto the students. I prefer implementing learning technologies at no cost to the students.

Online polling systems. Tools like Poll Everywhere offer easy setup and user-friendly features, making them convenient for instructors and students.[12] Students can load these applications on their smartphones, iPads, or computers, and do not have to spend additional money on a single-purpose device. Instructors can tabulate quiz results through their instructor dashboard.

Manual polling. Polling the class can be as simple as asking students to participate by raising their hands or showing colored cards to answer multiple-choice questions. Colored cards can represent different choices (e.g., A, B, C, D) and provide a quick way to assess understanding. This technique helps instructors gauge students' progress effectively.

Plickers. Plickers are a hybrid of online and manual polling. Students orientate and raise their Plicker cards, and the instructor scans them by waving their smartphone across the room. Plickers are an inexpensive polling system similar to QR codes. They are printed on paper, and each student receives a unique code. Instructors can assign individual Plicker cards to students for a personalized learning experience. The orientation of the paper determines one of four correct answers (A, B, C, or D). Instructors use smartphones to scan students' responses. The Plicker's app automatically grades and records the cards. The instructor can then ask another question and capture another set of responses.

Benefits of Student Response Systems

There are several advantages to using SRS in the classroom, which align with quizzing in general.[13]

- **Increased engagement**. Students become more involved in the learning process.

- **Better attendance**. The interactive nature of SRS can encourage students to attend classes more regularly.

- **Improved academic performance**. Immediate feedback and interactive learning can enhance understanding and retention of material.

- **Facilitates discussion**. Instructors can quickly gauge student comprehension and initiate discussions based on their responses.

- **Reduced anxiety**. Studies have shown that students experience less anxiety with quizzes when familiar with the format and environment, as provided by SRS.[14]

Challenges With Student Response Systems

Despite their benefits, there are some hurdles in implementing student response systems.[15]

- **Time consumption**. Using SRS for quizzes can take up valuable class time.

- **Setup and resources**. They require initial setup and ongoing resources.

- **Cost and logistics**. Depending on the system, SRS can be expensive and challenging to deploy.[16] You must experiment with different systems to find the one that fits your style and needs. Your instructional technologist can help. More affordable options may be available.

Strategies for Using Student Response Systems

Clickers and polling questions can be seamlessly integrated into your class to enhance engagement and learning. Steven Pan demonstrated this by using clickers to administer a 10-question multiple-choice vocabulary quiz.[17] Half of the questions presented vocabulary words, while the other half provided definitions.

Before the quiz, Pan informed students about the upcoming clicker quizzes and specified which vocabulary words they should study. During the first 10 minutes of class, the instructor projected each question onto a screen.[18] Students used their clickers to submit their answers, and once everyone had responded, the instructor revealed the correct answer, creating an interactive and dynamic learning experience.

It is important to note that grading is flexible. You can simply give credit for participating in a clicker quiz, but you do not have to grade the response. Nonetheless, you can capture the results to improve instruction.[19]

While SRS brings various educational benefits and can transform the classroom experience, its implementation requires careful consideration of factors like time, cost, and resource availability.

Game-based Quizzing Applications

Game-based quizzing is a transformative approach in education. It combines the effectiveness of assessment with the enjoyment of gaming. Its ability to provide immediate feedback, encourage self-assessment, and reduce test anxiety while maintaining a positive learning environment makes it a valuable tool in the educational landscape.

Game-based quizzing represents a dynamic and engaging approach to learning. This method incorporates fun and interactive elements into the educational process, making it a preferred choice among students.[20] Unlike traditional "drill and kill" methods, game-based quizzing offers a more enjoyable experience that actively involves learners in their educational journey.

Game-based learning fits neatly within Piaget's Game-Based Learning Theory, which emphasizes the importance of meaningful, interactive, impactful, and entertaining learning experiences.[21] Quizzing becomes educational and engaging when incorporated with gaming elements.

I have found Duolingo to be an enjoyable tool for practicing language skills. Its game-based approach makes learning a new language enjoyable and effective. Well-implemented game-based elements help to make learning addictive. I have checked into Duolingo daily for over two years. The app sends daily reminders, and completing quests boosts points, encouraging continued engagement. There are also collaborative quests that you can participate in with friends.

Hundreds of applications, such as Quizlet, Kahoot!, Nearpod, and Quizizz, have emerged as practical tools for game-based quizzing. These platforms make learning more enjoyable and serve as active formative assessment tools.[22] They provide a unique blend of testing and playing, ensuring students learn while engaged in a game-like environment.

When integrating game-based elements, it's crucial to balance entertainment with education. Elements like music, visuals, and competitive point systems should enhance, not distract, the learning process.[23] The primary focus should always be on the content and cognitive aspects of learning.

Web-based gamified quizzing systems offer a budget-friendly alternative to expensive student response systems.[24] They are also device-independent, meaning they can be accessed on phones, tablets, or computers without complex setups. However, some systems require a campus-wide license and single sign-on setup.

Benefits and Features of Game-based Quizzing

Game-based quizzing using apps like Quizizz and Kahoot! has also improved performance from pre to posttest.[25] The level of improvement varies according to the application used.

Game-based quizzing tools also empower students with self-assessment opportunities.[26] This aspect is crucial in helping learners understand their progress and areas needing improvement. Another advantage of these tools is their reusability. Educators can quickly adapt and use these applications across different classes, making them a versatile resource.

Game-based systems capture students' attention through various engaging features:[27]

- **Entertaining elements**. Including gaming elements like points and timers adds fun.

- **Visual and auditory appeal**. Different colors and sounds make the experience more captivating.

- **Competitive edge**. Leaderboards allow students to compare their performance with peers. Leaderboards can be a motivating factor for some students to improve their ranking.[28] I am a fan of leaderboards and will often note my standings.

- **Instant gratification**. The ability to earn points and receive immediate feedback keeps students motivated.

- **Challenging aspects**. Incorporating countdown timers increases engagement by introducing an element of challenge to quizzes.

Despite its benefits, game-based quizzing also faces certain challenges:

- **Limited feedback**. While it provides immediate right or wrong feedback, deeper, more elaborate feedback is often needed.[29]

- **Question depth**. Relying on multiple-choice questions may only sometimes promote deep learning.[30]

- **Higher-order thinking skills**. Game-based quizzing apps may be less effective with higher-order levels of Bloom's Taxonomy.[31]

Game-based Quizzing Applications

Many game-based quizzing apps are available, each with unique features and focus. Quizizz and Kahoot! are two of the more commonly used applications. While game-based learning offers a range of benefits in keeping students engaged and motivated, it's essential to use these tools thoughtfully to ensure that the core educational objectives are met.

Quizizz

Quizizz is an innovative online platform that transforms assessments into engaging games.[32] It's accessible on any internet-connected device, making it a versatile tool for learning. Quizizz incorporates multimedia elements like text, images, animations, videos, and audio to make education more fun. This variety ensures the quizzes are informative, visually appealing, and engaging.

Teachers can create an interactive and enjoyable learning environment, although they should be mindful of its limitations, especially concerning higher-order thinking skills. Quizizz can contribute to a more engaging and effective learning experience as part of a diverse educational toolkit.

Kahoot!

Kahoot! is a fun, interactive, game-based learning tool used in classrooms. It combines multimedia elements like images and sounds. Educators can create a game-show atmosphere that students love.[33] With Kahoot!, students can compete with each other and see their scores on a leaderboard. The teacher can control the timing of each question. Here are other benefits:

- **Engagement**. Kahoot! makes learning fun and keeps students engaged.

- **Improved performance**. Studies have shown that students who use Kahoot! tend to do better on exams compared to those who don't use such tools.[34]

- **Immediate feedback**. Unlike paper-based methods, Kahoot! provides instant feedback, letting students know immediately if they got an answer right or wrong. This helps in furthering classroom discussions.

- **Attention and motivation**. Kahoot! increases student attentiveness and motivation, leading to better classroom and academic performance.[35]

Using Kahoot! is quite simple. Teachers present Kahoot! on a screen, and students participate using an app on any device – a computer, tablet, or phone.[36] This versatility means schools don't need to buy extra equipment like clickers.

Kahoot! is an exciting and effective tool for classroom learning, especially for keeping students engaged and motivated. While it offers immediate feedback and a dynamic learning environment, it's important to balance its use with traditional methods depending on the learning objectives and outcomes desired. Additional concerns include:

- **Paper-based learning**. Some studies suggest that traditional paper-based learning can be more effective in certain areas, like midterm retention tests.[37]

- **One-try questions**. In Kahoot!, students get only one chance per question, whereas paper-based quizzes often allow students to review and change their answers.[38]

- **Similar learning outcomes**. Research indicates that learning outcomes with Kahoot! are comparable to traditional student response systems and paper-based assessments but not significantly better.[39]

Conclusion

Technology is not just a tool—it's a catalyst for transforming education. You can create a dynamic, engaging, and effective learning environment by embracing digital quizzing platforms, student response systems, and game-based applications. Imagine your students mastering the material while developing confidence and enthusiasm for learning.

Now is the time to take action. Start small. Experiment with one tool or platform and integrate it into your next quiz or class activity. As you see the results, you'll realize the profound impact these technologies can have. Your dedication to innovation has the power to inspire lifelong learning and success for your students. Don't wait for the future of education to arrive—begin shaping it today.

Quick Quiz

Test your understanding with a brief quiz on using technology for mastery quizzing.

4.1. What is one primary advantage of using digital quizzing platforms?

a) They are labor-intensive.

b) They provide instant feedback.

c) They eliminate the need for learning objectives.

d) They are only accessible in physical classrooms.

4.2. Which of the following is NOT a benefit of learning management systems (LMS)?

a) Randomized question order.

b) Detailed grade reporting.

c) Limited scalability.

d) Customizable quiz layouts.

4.3. What feature is common in student response systems (SRS)?

a) Paper-based grading.

b) Ability to link quiz questions to course outcomes.

c) Use of electronic clickers or polling apps for real-time interaction.

d) Lack of immediate feedback for students.

4.4. Which game-based quizzing tool is known for its leaderboard feature to promote competition?

a) Quizlet.

b) Kahoot!

c) Plickers.

d) Google Forms.

4.5. How do game-based quizzing applications like Quizizz improve student engagement?

a) By focusing solely on traditional question-and-answer formats.

b) By incorporating multimedia elements and competitive features.

c) By requiring additional hardware for each student.

d) By removing the need for teacher involvement.

1. Billy Hermanto, Sudarsono Sudarsono, and Yanti Sri Rezeki, "Designing Quizizz as Media to Assess the Mastery of Simple Past Tense," *Journal of English Education Program* 4, no. 1 (2023): 1–10, https://doi.org/10.26418/jeep.v4i1.54976

2. Ibid., 7.

3. Ibid., 7.

4. Joshua K. Strakos et al., "A Learning Management System-Based Approach to Assess Learning Outcomes in Operations Management Courses," *The International Journal of Management Education* 21, no. 2 (2023): 1–9, https://doi.org/10.1016/j.ijme.2023.100802.

5. Darryl Chamberlain Jr, "How One Instructor Can Teach a Large-Scale, Mastery-Based College Algebra Course Online," *PRIMUS*, 2023, 1–22.

6. Hermanto, Sudarsono, and Rezeki, "Designing Quizizz as Media to Assess the Mastery of Simple Past Tense."

7. Randa Obeidallah and Aayat Shdaifat, "An Evaluation and Examination of Quiz Tool within Open-Source Learning Management Systems," *International Journal of Emerging Technologies in Learning (iJET)* 15, no. 10 (2020): 191–201, https://doi.org/10.3991/ijet.v15i10.11638.

8. Nese Sevim-Cirak and Omer Faruk Islim, "Paper versus Online Quizzes: Which Is More Effective?," *Active Learning in Higher Education*, 2022, 1–18, https://doi.org/10.1177/14697874221079737.

9. Sevim-Cirak and Islim, "Paper versus Online Quizzes."

10. Ibid., 3.

11. Abderrahim Mimouni, "Using Mobile Gamified Quizzing for Active Learning: The Effect of Reflective Class Feedback on Undergraduates' Achievement," *Education and Information Technologies*, no. Journal Article (2022), https://doi.org/10.1007/s10639-022-11097-2.

12. Robin Boyle-Laisure, "Didn't Cover That in Class? Low-Stakes Technique of Quizzing to the Rescue," *The Journal of the Legal Writing Institute* 27 (2023): 299–307.

13. Sevim-Cirak and Islim, "Paper versus Online Quizzes."

14. Chunliang Yang et al., "Do Practice Tests (Quizzes) Reduce or Provoke Test Anxiety? A Meta-Analytic Review," *Educational Psychology Review* 35, no. 3 (2023): 1–26, https://doi.org/10.1007/s10648-023-09801-w.

15. Sevim-Cirak and Islim, "Paper versus Online Quizzes."

16. Mimouni, "Using Mobile Gamified Quizzing for Active Learning."

17. Steven C. Pan et al., "Using Online and Clicker Quizzes to Learn Scientific and Technical Jargon," in *In Their Own Words: What Scholars and Teachers Want You to Know about Why and How to Apply the Science of Learning in Your Academic Setting* (Society for the Teaching of Psychology, 2023), 473–480.

18. Ibid., 475.

19. Ibid., 475.

20. Vilogini Chandra Segaran and Harwati Hashim, "'More Online Quizzes, Please!'The Effectiveness of Online Quiz Tools in Enhancing the Learning of Grammar among ESL Learners," *International Journal of Academic Research in Business and Social Sciences* 12, no. 1 (January 29, 2022): 1756–70, https://doi.org/10.6007/IJARBSS/v12-i1/12064.

21. Ibid., 1760.

22. Ibid., 1761.

23. Mimouni, "Using Mobile Gamified Quizzing for Active Learning."

24. Ibid., 2.

25. Segaran and Hashim, "'More Online Quizzes, Please!'The Effectiveness of Online Quiz Tools in Enhancing the Learning of Grammar among ESL Learners."

26. Ibid., 1768.

27. Mimouni, "Using Mobile Gamified Quizzing for Active Learning."

28. Baidowi Baidowi, Defi Kamilia, and Ilhami Sukmaningsih, "The Effectiveness of Online Learning Using Quizizz toward Students' Mathematics Concept Mastery," in *AIP Conference Proceedings*, vol. 2619 (The 1st International Conference on Science Education and Sciences, AIP Publishing, 2023), 1–5, https://doi.org/10.1063/5.0122828.

29. Mimouni, "Using Mobile Gamified Quizzing for Active Learning."

30. Ibid.

31. Baidowi, Kamilia, and Sukmaningsih, "The Effectiveness of Online Learning Using Quizizz toward Students' Mathematics Concept Mastery."

32. Hermanto, Sudarsono, and Rezeki, "Designing Quizizz as Media to Assess the Mastery of Simple Past Tense."

33. Sevim-Cirak and Islim, "Paper versus Online Quizzes."

34. Sevim-Cirak and Islim, "Paper versus Online Quizzes"; Segaran and Hashim, "'More Online Quizzes, Please!'The Effectiveness of Online Quiz Tools in Enhancing the Learning of Grammar among ESL Learners."

35. Sevim-Cirak and Islim, "Paper versus Online Quizzes"; Segaran and Hashim, "'More Online Quizzes, Please!'The Effectiveness of Online Quiz Tools in Enhancing the Learning of Grammar among ESL Learners."

36. Sevim-Cirak and Islim, "Paper versus Online Quizzes."

37. Ibid., 11.

38. Ibid., 13.

39. Ibid., 13.

Chapter Five

Question Design

Are you looking to refine your questioning techniques to better assess and engage your students? This chapter delves into the art and science of designing effective questions for mastery quizzing.

Effective question design involves more than asking students to recall information; it involves crafting questions that stimulate critical thinking, creativity, and deeper understanding. This chapter guides you through setting clear learning objectives and aligning them with quiz design, crafting high-quality questions, selecting appropriate question types, structuring quizzes effectively, and considering accessibility and inclusivity in quiz design.

I'll also introduce you to the principles of crafting straightforward, concise, and compelling questions aligning with educational goals. This chapter will use examples to guide you through designing questions that test knowledge and encourage students to connect ideas and apply their learning in new contexts.

By the end of this chapter, you will have a solid foundation for creating questions that enhance the mastery learning process. Let's begin with the learning objective.

Objectives

- **Design effective learning objectives** using the performance, condition, and criterion framework to align with instructional goals.

- **Develop high-quality multiple-choice questions** that align with Bloom's Taxonomy and facilitate mastery learning.

- **Evaluate the suitability of different question types** (e.g., closed-ended vs. open-ended) for assessing various levels of cognitive skills in students.

Learning Objectives

Many students struggle because learning objectives aren't clear. As an educator, your goal is to help students learn. But if they do not understand your instructions, your objectives might not be well defined. Let's learn how to write practical learning objectives to improve instruction.

What Are Learning Objectives?

Learning objectives describe what learners should be able to know or do after completing a lesson or course. They consist of three main parts: performance, condition, and criterion.

Performance. Performance describes the observable behavior that indicates learning has occurred. It clearly states what the learner should be able to know or do. Use action verbs to describe measurable behavior. For example (in italics):

- *Analyze* the impact of social media on modern political campaigns.

- *Design* a mobile application that addresses a specific community need.

- *Evaluate* the effectiveness of different leadership styles in organizational change management.

Condition. Condition describes the environment or resources involved in the assessment. It sets the context for the performance. Be clear about what resources or conditions are available to the learner during assessment. The condition may also describe what is denied. For example, you may indicate that students may not use a calculator. Here are examples of condition statements (**bolded**):

- **Given access to a digital library of scholarly articles and databases, as well as analytical software to organize and present data**, analyze the impact of social media on modern political campaigns.

- **Provided with a standard software development kit, access to a computer lab equipped with necessary programming tools, and a user requirement**

document to guide the design, develop a mobile application addressing a specific community need.

- **Using a collection of case studies available through the university's online portal and access to video lectures and textbooks on leadership theories**, evaluate the effectiveness of different leadership styles in organizational change management.

Criterion. The learning objective criterion sets the standard for acceptable performance. It defines how well the learner must perform to meet the objective. Criteria can include speed, accuracy, or quality factors. For example, here are learning objectives with criteria *italicized*:

- **Given access to a digital library of scholarly articles and databases, as well as analytical software to organize and present data**, analyze the impact of social media on modern political campaigns. *The analysis must correctly apply at least three analytical frameworks and include a comprehensive report with citations, achieving a minimum of 90% accuracy in data interpretation as evaluated by the instructor.*

- **Provided with a standard software development kit, access to a computer lab equipped with necessary programming tools, and a user requirement document to guide the design**, design a mobile application that addresses a specific community need. *The application must meet all specified user requirements, function correctly on multiple devices, and pass a usability test with at least an 85% approval rating from a sample group of users.*

- **Using a collection of case studies available through the university's online portal and access to video lectures and textbooks on leadership theories**, evaluate the effectiveness of different leadership styles in organizational change management. *The evaluation must include a detailed comparative analysis of at least three leadership styles, with conclusions supported by evidence from the case studies, and the final report must be coherent, well-structured, and free of critical errors.*

Why Are Learning Objectives Important?

Clear objectives serve several purposes:

- They guide instruction planning.

- They help in designing assessment methods.

- They ensure that instruction focuses on important content.

- They help students understand what is expected of them and how to prepare for assessments.

Crafting Learning Objectives

The best place to start when crafting learning objectives is with the performance part of the objective. Bloom's Taxonomy can help you ensure it is actionable.

Benjamin Bloom developed Bloom's Taxonomy in 1968. This system classifies levels of learning. It comprises six categories that help us understand how learning progresses. These categories, in order, are:[1]

- **Remember**. This is the basic level of recalling facts, terms, and concepts.

- **Understand**. At this stage, one starts to grasp what is remembered.

- **Apply**. Using the information in new ways.

- **Analyze**. This involves breaking down information into parts to explore understandings and relationships.

- **Evaluate**. You start making judgments based on criteria and standards at this level.

- **Create**. This is the highest level of combining information to form something new.

Bloom's Taxonomy is often divided into "lower levels" and "higher levels."[2] The lower levels (Remember and Understand) focus on memorizing and understanding the content, including learning key terms and basic processes. The higher levels (Apply, Analyze, Evaluate, Create) involve deeper comprehension and the application of knowledge.

Education strives to help students move from the lower to higher levels of Bloom's Taxonomy. This means guiding them from simply remembering facts to using knowledge creatively and critically.

Generative AI tools like ChatGPT are powerful tools to help you develop goals and objectives. You can guide ChatGPT and other generative AI tools in creating applicable learning objectives by including references to Bloom's Taxonomy in your prompt. You can find some examples in appendix B that you can tailor to your needs. The more detail you provide, the more specific the results will be.

Begin with the performance statement. Once you have a performance statement you like, you can then add the condition and criterion.

Common Errors to Avoid

When writing learning objectives, watch out for these common mistakes:

- Using vague verbs like "know," "appreciate," or "understand."

- Mixing learning outcomes with learning processes. For example, "complete a group project" is a learning process, whereas "analyze and apply the principles of social psychology" is the preferred learning outcome.

- Including unnecessary details in conditions: For example, 'Given a 300-page manual, a set of color-coded highlighters, and access to a quiet study room, students will identify the main themes of the text.' Instead, streamline the condition to focus on what's essential: 'Given the text, students will identify the main themes.'

- Failing to provide clear standards for assessment. For instance, stating 'Students will write an essay on climate change' without specifying the criteria for success—such as clarity of argument, use of evidence, organization, and adherence to formatting guidelines—can lead to confusion and inconsistency in grading.

By crafting clear and specific learning objectives, you can enhance your instruction and help students achieve their learning goals effectively. Learning objectives also help you develop appropriate quiz questions. Let's look at different question types, how to frame them, and how to use learning objectives to write impactful questions. First, we will explore different question types in more detail.

***

Question Types

Understanding the differences between closed- and open-ended questions is key when developing written questions.

Closed-ended questions. These questions are more straightforward and often used to assess students' knowledge of specific facts, definitions, or concepts. They are well-suited for assessing recall and comprehension of material. Closed-ended questions in academic quizzes typically have a single correct answer, making them easier to grade and providing immediate feedback to students. They help test students' mastery of basic concepts and terminology.

Examples of closed-ended questions include:

- "What is the capital of France?"

- "Who wrote 'Romeo and Juliet'?"

- "Which organelle is responsible for protein synthesis in a cell?"

Multiple-choice, multiple-selection, true or false, matching, and fill-in-the-blank questions are generally considered closed-ended. These types of questions are optimal for automated grading quizzes. Building randomly generated self-graded quizzes can be effectively used for mastery quizzing.

Answering a closed-ended question takes less time than open-ended questions. Instructors can include more selection items in a limited time frame, allowing for comprehensive testing of course material. These types of questions are also easier and quicker to grade.

Answers to closed-ended questions are cut and dry, making statistical analysis more manageable.

Open-ended questions. These questions are beneficial for assessing higher-order thinking skills such as analysis, synthesis, and evaluation. They require students to demonstrate a deeper understanding of the material by providing detailed, thoughtful responses. Open-ended questions allow students to express their ideas in their own words, encouraging critical thinking and creativity. Open-ended questions ask students to explain concepts, analyze data, solve problems, or express opinions. For example:

- Explain the process of photosynthesis.

- Discuss the impact of globalization on cultural diversity.

- Solve the following calculus problem and justify your solution.

Short answer and essay questions are considered open-ended questions. These questions are effective for deeper levels of thinking and learning; however, they are more time-intensive to answer and grade because they often require human involvement.

Suggestions for Writing Quiz Items

Maintaining a record of past questions and include options frequently marked incorrect will be beneficial when creating new questions.[3] This approach encourages students to think critically.

When you're creating test questions, it's essential to follow these general guidelines:[4]

- **Keep it simple**. Use clear and straightforward language. Refrain from impressing with fancy words. Ensure the question uses language students understand. The language necessary for lower-level cognitive questions is more constrained.[5] If questions are too wordy or complex due to unnecessary information, it may affect cognitive load and overload working memory.

- **Avoid tricks**. Avoid tripping up students with tricky or leading questions. Everyone should have a fair chance to answer correctly.

- **Avoid negative-worded questions**. Avoid negative-worded questions; even if they are emphasized, some people might miss them. For example, "Which of the following is NOT a key feature of mastery quizzing?" Negative-worded questions can increase confusion and reduce performance on exams and quizzes.[6]

- **Independence**. Each question should stand alone. One question shouldn't give away the answer to another, and students shouldn't need to rely on answers from previous questions.

- **Highlight key points**. To make important words or phrases stand out, underline, capitalize, italicize, or highlight them.

- **Use visual aids**. Sometimes, pictures or diagrams can explain things better than words alone. Include them when they'll help students understand the question better.

- **Be fair and clear**. Your questions should be fair to all students and easy to understand and answer. Good questions will help identify who understands the material and needs more help.

- **Naming questions**. Correctly naming questions will help develop modular quizzes based on topic and difficulty.[7] (See chapter 7).

- **Frame questions**. Be consistent in question framing to avoid confusion and enhance clarity. Use self-referential language to foster a personal connection with the material.[8] Framing questions is discussed in more detail towards the end of this chapter.

Question Development Formula

We will explore specific strategies for crafting different question types. To start, here is a generalized question development formula that you can use when developing questions:[9]

- **Define learning objectives**. Clearly define what you want students to learn. As discussed in the beginning of this chapter, this serves as the foundation for your questions.

- **Identify concepts**. Once you have your learning objectives, identify the key concepts or skills students need to master to achieve those objectives.

- **Question development**. Develop questions that directly assess the identified concepts. Ensure questions vary in format (e.g., multiple-choice, short answer) and align with the expected mastery level.

- **Incorporate context and formulas**. When appropriate, integrate relevant real-world contexts or formulas into your questions to provide context and relevance to students' learning.

- **Provide feedback**. Construct feedback for each question to help students understand why their answer was correct or incorrect. Feedback is crucial for reinforcing learning and promoting improvement.

- **Classify questions**. Categorize questions based on their format, difficulty level, or the specific concept they assess to organize and select questions for different assessments.

- **Test bank integration**. Add the developed questions to an appropriate test bank within your learning management system. This allows for easy access and reuse of questions in various assessments, ensuring consistency and efficiency in evaluating student mastery.

***

Closed-Ended Questions

Let's take a closer look at closed-ended questions. These questions require students to remember specific information.[10] Examples include multiple-choice, true or false, matching, and "select all that apply." These are easier to grade because they have clear, concise answers. Another example is fill-in-the-blank, which falls under this category.

We will focus on four question types: multiple-choice and multiple-selection, true or false, matching, and fill-in-the-blank.

For the rest of the chapter, I will provide sample questions focusing on introductory biology, drawing from the OpenStax: *Biology -2e* open textbook.

Multiple-Choice and Multiple-Selection Questions

Let's begin with the multiple-choice question (MCQ). It is one of the most commonly used questions for automated quizzes.

Multiple-choice questions are frequently used in both practice assessments and high-stakes exams, such as certification tests.[11] They can assess a range of cognitive functions, from basic memory and recognition to higher levels of thinking.

A multiple-choice question consists of the stem (the question itself) and the alternatives (choices provided).[12] The alternatives include a keyed response (correct answer) and several distractors (incorrect answers).

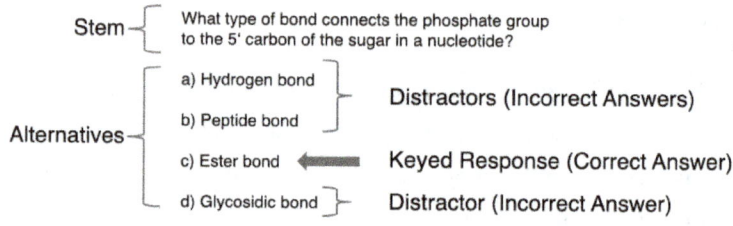

Figure 1. Question nomenclature

The only difference between an MCQ and a multiple-selection question is the number of keyed responses. Additionally, you should provide feedback for each option. This feedback will enhance learning.

It's crucial to align MCQs with specific learning objectives in educational settings.[13] This alignment helps in creating more effective exams. Questions should be written to closely match these objectives, facilitating the construction of meaningful assessments.

Using Bloom's Taxonomy will enable you to develop MCQs varying in difficulty and understanding.[14] Bloom's taxonomy outlines different levels of cognitive skills, ranging from basic knowledge recall to complex analysis and evaluation. Well-constructed MCQs can measure all levels, for example:

- **Confirmation questions**. These are useful for beginners or when dealing with unfamiliar material.[15] They focus on clarifying, defining, and explaining concepts, laying the foundation for deeper understanding.

- **Transformation questions**. Aimed at learners with advanced knowledge, these questions involve reconstructing and reorganizing understanding.[16] They delve into relationships, synthesis, and analysis, representing higher-order thinking per Bloom's Taxonomy.

The multiple-choice question is more challenging to construct than all other test items. Extreme care must be taken when writing stems and distractors.

Writing Stems

Stems can take several different forms. Here are some examples:[17]

- **Questions**. This is a natural way to create stems, as this is what learners expect. Example: "What are the complementary base pairs in DNA?"

- **Incomplete statement**. Incomplete sentences are sentence fragments in which learners add the missing segment. Avoid providing clues or unrelated alternatives. Example: "_____ bonds hold together the base pairing in DNA."

- **Multiple response**. This option instructs learners to select all appropriate keyed responses. Example: "Which of the following statements about DNA base pairing are true?"

- **Definition**. There are two basic options for this stem: a) a definition forms the stem, and learners choose from the terms, or b) the stem is the term, and the alternatives are possible definitions. Example a: "The bond that holds together complementary base pairs is a _____ bond." Example b: "_____ is the term used to describe the specific pairing of adenine with thymine and cytosine with guanine in DNA."

- **Illustration**. An image serves as part of the stem with identifiers or instructions related to the image.

Writing Alternatives

Writing effective alternatives, specifically distractors, is as essential as writing the stem and the keyed response.[18] Here are different strategies you can use to craft alternatives:

- **Generate plausible alternatives**. Write plausible alternatives to challenge a student who has not mastered the material. They should be answers that sound plausible but are incorrect.

- **Common misconceptions**. Include responses that learners provide but are incorrect.

- **Accurate but not complete statements**. Provide alternatives that partially satisfy the requirements of the stem.

- **Too broad or narrow**. Include alternatives that are too wide or narrow for the question.

The purpose of the alternative, specifically the distractors, is to make the content appear correct to a learner who has not mastered it.

The following guidelines help educators create more effective and challenging MCQs catering to different learner expertise and cognitive skill levels.

- **Avoid giveaway answers**. Avoid using words in the stem and options to prevent unintentional clues.[19] For instance, if the question stem asks, 'Which theory explains human motivation based on a hierarchy of needs?' and one of the answer options is 'Maslow's hierarchy of needs,' the repeated use of 'hierarchy' provides an unintended clue to the correct answer.

- **Randomize options**. When using a learning management system, randomize options to prevent pattern recognition.[20] Remember, you are trying to avoid one question supplying the answer to another question.

- **Distinguish definite and indefinite answers**. Definite answers often start with words like "all," "never," or "none," while indefinite answers use words like "usually," "sometimes," or "often."[21] Mixing these can lead to confusion. For instance, consider the question: 'Which of the following statements is true about photosynthesis?' If one option states 'Photosynthesis always requires sunlight,' while another says 'Photosynthesis sometimes occurs in the absence of direct sunlight,' the mix of 'always' (definite) and 'sometimes' (indefinite) can confuse students and lead to misinterpretation of the intended answer.

- **Ensure grammatical consistency**. Ensure grammatical consistency between the stem and the options. This includes matching singular and plural forms and maintaining option balance.[22] For instance, if the stem asks, 'Which of the following is a primary benefit of group projects?' the options should also maintain grammatical consistency:

  - Encourages collaboration

  - Improves communication skills

  - Develops problem-solving abilities

- **Consider option length**. Longer options are often the correct response. Be mindful of this tendency to avoid bias.[23]

- **Disguise numeric options**. Students can use brute force to solve MCQs by plugging in possible solutions.[24] Disguising numeric options helps prevent blind testing. For example, avoid including numbers unrelated to the problem's context, include "distractor" options resembling correct answers but are based on common misconceptions or minor calculation errors, and ensure the options are not in a pattern making guessing easier (e.g., evenly spaced or forming a simple sequence like 2, 4, 6, 8). Also, list numbers in ascending or descending order of magnitude.[25]

- **Avoid "All of the Above" or "None of the Above"**. Don't use "all of the above" or "none of the above" too often. If you do use them, be very careful. "All of the above" can make it easy to guess right or wrong by looking at other options. "None of the above" might only test if you can spot what's wrong, not if you know what's right. Additionally, this can look strange when randomizing the alternatives.

When designing multiple-choice quizzes, it's essential to create adaptable assessments, set high expectations, offer constructive feedback, and guide students toward a deeper understanding and improvement of their skills.

Multiple-Choice Question Examples

Questions. Traditional multiple-choice questions where the learner selects the best answer from a list of options.

What type of bond connects the phosphate group to the 5' carbon of the sugar in a nucleotide?

a) Hydrogen bond

b) Peptide bond

c) Ester bond

d) Glycosidic bond

Incomplete statement. A sentence with a missing part that the learner completes by choosing the correct option.

In a polynucleotide, one end of the chain has a free 5' phosphate, and the other end has a free _____.

a) 2' OH

b) 3' OH

c) Nitrogenous base

d) 5' phosphate

Multiple response. Questions that allow learners to select multiple correct answers from the given choices.

Which of the following statements about the structure of DNA are TRUE?

a) The two strands of DNA are anti-parallel.

b) The diameter of the DNA double helix is uniform throughout its length.

c) Base pairing takes place between two purines or two pyrimidines.

d) The sugar and phosphate groups form the backbone of the structure.

Definition. A question where learners choose the term or concept that matches the provided definition.

A _____ comprises one, two, or three phosphate groups attached to a nucleoside.

a) Nucleoside

b) Purine

c) Nucleotide

d) Pyrimidine

Histones are _____.

a) Enzymes that help maintain the supercoiled structure of DNA.

b) Proteins that are involved in the supercoiling of DNA.

c) Evolutionarily conserved proteins rich in basic amino acids and DNA wrap around them to form nucleosomes.

d) Scaffolding proteins that help condense metaphase chromosomes.

True or False Questions

True or false questions are primarily for lower levels of Bloom's Taxonomy and are relatively easy to construct. True or false questions are handy for testing facts when it's clear if a statement is right or wrong. They can also reveal common misunderstandings without giving away the correct answer too quickly. However, the downside is that guessing correctly is easier for true or false questions than for other types.

It's common to see poorly constructed true or false questions. Some instructors pick statements from the text, make half of them false, and expect students to remember where they found the answer. Designing questions in this manner mainly checks if someone can remember details, not if they understand.

Writing True or False Questions

To write good true or false questions, you should consider these guidelines.[26]

- Stick to one idea per question.

- Do not mix true and false parts in a statement.

- Avoid using negative words, as they can confuse readers.

- Keep statements simple; avoid complicated wording and structure.

- Use terms with the same meaning for all students to ensure clarity and fairness.

- Try not to use absolute terms like "all," "every," or "never," as they're rarely true; likewise, avoid terms like "some" or "generally," which are usually true.

- Avoid creating patterns in the sequence of responses to prevent students from guessing based on the pattern.

- Ensure statements are consistently brief; don't unintentionally make true statements longer than false ones.

True or False Question Examples

You can use various models when writing a true or false question.

Declarative statement. The most common types of true or false statements are statements a learner must determine to be true or false.

True or False: The nitrogenous base is attached to the 3ʻ carbon of the sugar in a nucleotide.

Answer: False. The nitrogenous base is attached to the **1'** carbon of the sugar in a nucleotide.

Include illustration. You may elect to support a declarative statement with an illustration. This may be useful to identify a relationship between items.

Examine the image and determine if the statement is TRUE or FALSE:

Statement: The image depicts a pyrimidine.

Answer: False. The image depicts guanine, which is a **purine**. Purines have a double-ring structure, while pyrimidines have a single-ring structure.

Double true or **false**. This true or false question closely resembles an MCQ. The stem contains a declarative statement and a reason. There are also four alternatives:

- True, and the reason for the statement is correct.

- False, and the reason is incorrect.

- True, and the reason is incorrect.

- False, and the reason is correct.

Statement: DNA polymerase is used in the dideoxy chain termination method of DNA sequencing because it can add dideoxynucleotides to a growing DNA strand.

Reason: Dideoxynucleotides have a free 3' OH group allowing the DNA strand to continue extending.

Choose from the following:

a) True, and the reason for the statement is correct.

b) False, and the reason is incorrect.

c) True, and the reason is incorrect.

d) False, and the reason is correct.

Answer: c) True, and the reason is incorrect. DNA polymerase is used in the dideoxy chain termination method because it can add dideoxynucleotides to a growing DNA strand. However, dideoxynucleotides **lack** a free 3' OH group, which is what **prevents** further extension of the DNA strand.

Matching Questions

With typical matching questions, learners will pair a response from an item in a left-hand column with one on the right. However, these questions have variations, making them more challenging and interesting.

The matching item offers numerous benefits compared to other test questions, especially the multiple-choice item. It's convenient for testing how well you understand closely connected topics or recall facts. Think of the matching item as related multiple-choice questions bundled together. This format facilitates a more concise and efficient measurement of learning, helping save time during testing.

Writing Matching Questions

Matching test items offer flexibility in assessing student understanding. Here are different formats instructors can employ:[27]

Equal columns. In this format, both the columns (options to match) have an equal number of items. To prevent students from guessing by elimination, either plan to use items in the response column more than once or not at all.

Match the vocabulary term with its definition.

Column A: Column B:

1. Photosynthesis   A. Cellular division resulting in two identical daughter cells.

2. Mitosis   B. Gradual wearing away of land by natural forces.

3. Erosion   C. Process by which plants convert sunlight into energy.

Figure 2. Example of Equal Columns

Unequal Columns. This format is preferable when the number of items in each column differs. It helps maintain fairness in assessment, mainly when alternatives may not be used more than once.

Match the country with its capital.

Column A: Column B:

1. Brazil   A. Brasília

2. France   B. London

3. Japan   C. Paris

                             D. Tokyo

Figure 3. Example of Unequal Columns

Inference Matching. This type of matching item is designed to gauge comprehension-level learning. Students are required to infer relationships between concepts, demonstrating their understanding.

Instructions: Match the situations on the left with the most likely economic outcomes on the right. Draw a line from each situation to the most likely economic outcome.

Situations:

1. A significant decrease in global oil production

2. A major technological breakthrough in renewable energy

3. Introduction of high tariffs on imported goods

4. A rise in the national minimum wage

Possible Outcomes:

A. Decrease in unemployment and increase in consumer spending

B. Increase in the cost of imported goods and potential trade wars

C. Reduction in the reliance on fossil fuels and lower carbon emissions

D. Increase in the price of gasoline and heating oil

E. Increase in overall production costs leading to inflation

F. Improvement in trade balance due to increased local production

Figure 4. Example of an Inference Matching Question

Cause-and-effect matching. This format prompts students to match cause-and-effect relationships and assesses comprehension-level learning. It helps instructors evaluate how well students grasp the cause-and-effect dynamics within a topic.

Example of a Cause-and-Effect Matching Question:

Directions: Listed below are specific facts followed by several statements. Select the letter (a, b, or c) representing the best statement of the relationship between each statement and the fact preceding it.

- a. The statement is the cause of the fact.

- b. The statement indicates a result of the fact.

- c. The statement is not related to the fact.

Fact: Water levels in the reservoir have significantly decreased.

Statements:

1. A prolonged drought has been affecting the region.

2. Many residents have reported issues with water supply in their homes.

Fact: There has been a noticeable increase in asthma cases in the city.
Statements:

1. Air quality has deteriorated due to increased industrial emissions.

2. The local team won the national sports championship.

Coded alternatives for scientific reasoning. These matching items are beneficial for differentiating achievement levels among students who are exceptionally high-achieving. They typically measure comprehension-level understanding or higher and are coded to challenge students' scientific reasoning abilities.

Example of Coded Alternatives for Scientific Reasoning
Directions: Below are some hypotheses and methods for testing them. On your answer sheet, fill in the space corresponding to the following conditions:
a. The item directly helps to prove the hypothesis true.
b. The item indirectly helps to prove the hypothesis true.
c. The item directly helps to prove the hypothesis false.
d. The item indirectly helps to prove the hypothesis false.
e. The item is unrelated to proof or disproof of the hypothesis.

Hypothesis: Plants grow taller in direct sunlight.
1. Observations show that plants in a sunny window grow taller than those in a shaded area.

2. Plants in a greenhouse, receiving consistent sunlight, exhibit increased growth compared to those in a darkened room.

Hypothesis: Adding fertilizer to soil increases plant growth.
1. A controlled experiment demonstrates that plants given fertilizer exhibit more significant growth than those without fertilizer.

2. Plants in nutrient-depleted soil show stunted growth regardless of fertilizer application.

Take into consideration these guidelines to enhance your matching questions.[28]

- **Provide clear instructions**. Give students specific and complete instructions, and make sure they understand what is expected of them.

- **Focus on essential information**. Test only the most critical information. Avoid testing trivial details, focus on the learning objectives.

- **Use related materials**. Ensure the options in each matching item are closely related. If the options can be easily grouped into distinct categories, it becomes more like a multiple-choice question, increasing the likelihood of guessing.

- **Make alternatives plausible**. To reduce guessing by elimination, ensure all options are plausible. Students should not be able to eliminate incorrect possibilities easily.

- **Arrange alternatives logically**. Arrange the options logically to make it easier for students to match them. Alphabetical order is a standard arrangement method.

- **Provide extra alternatives**. If options are not intended to be used more than once, include three or four extra options. This helps reduce guessing and ensures students focus on making meaningful matches.

Fill-in-the-Blank Questions

Fill-in-the-blank questions are a type of completion question in which participants enter the missing word or words in a sentence or sentences to complete it. These question types can be considered open or closed. The key characteristic of fill-in-the-blank questions is that they typically have only one correct answer or a small set of acceptable answers making them straightforward to grade but also challenging for the participant, as they require precise knowledge or recall of information.

In an automated environment, these questions can be challenging to grade because exact answers are necessary. Many LMSs allow multiple answer options, but students must still enter their answers exactly to receive credit. Instructors may have to spend additional time verifying answers. This is not optimal for mastery quizzing, where students repeatedly take quizzes on their schedule. If a quiz is mismarked because of a typo, it may confuse or frustrate them.

Benefits of fill-in-the-blank questions

Fill-in-the-blank questions offer several benefits, particularly in educational and assessment contexts:

- **Enhanced recall**. These questions require respondents to retrieve information from memory rather than recognizing it from a list of options, as in multiple-choice questions. This can help reinforce learning and improve memory retention.

- **Precision testing**. Fill-in-the-blank questions can test precise knowledge of terminology, facts, or processes, making them useful for subjects where exact answers are essential, such as language learning, science, and mathematics.

- **Reduced guessing**. Without multiple-choice options, the likelihood of guessing the correct answer is minimized, leading to a more accurate assessment of a student's knowledge or understanding.

- **Flexibility**. They can be used to test a wide range of subjects and can be adjusted in difficulty by altering the context clues provided in the questions.

- **Time efficiency**. These questions can be quick to answer, allowing for more content to be covered in the same amount of time as other types of questions.

- **Ease of grading**. When the answers are specific words or short phrases, fill-in-the-blank questions can be relatively straightforward and quick to grade, especially with digital tools that can automate the process.

Challenges of fill-in-the-blank questions

While fill-in-the-blank questions offer several benefits, they also come with some challenges and limitations:

- **Limited assessment scope**. These questions typically focus on specific facts or terms, so they may not effectively measure higher-order thinking skills such as analysis, synthesis, or evaluation. They are less suitable for assessing complex understanding or the ability to apply knowledge in new contexts.

- **Ambiguity in responses**. Sometimes, multiple correct answers or variations in spelling, phrasing, or terminology that are technically correct but the person who designed the test did not anticipate can lead to unfairly marked responses unless the grading criteria are clearly defined.

- **Language sensitivity**. Fill-in-the-blank questions can be particularly challenging for students who struggle with spelling or grammar, especially in language learning contexts. This can disadvantage non-native speakers or younger students who have yet to fully develop their language skills.

- **Overemphasis on memorization**. These questions may encourage rote learning rather than understanding, as students might focus on memorizing specific terms or data points without grasping the underlying concepts.

- **Stress and anxiety**. Some students may find fill-in-the-blank questions more stressful than others because they require exact answers. The lack of cues or options can increase anxiety, which might affect performance.

- **Difficulty in construction**. Creating effective fill-in-the-blank questions can be challenging. They need to be precisely formulated to ensure that only one or a few specific answers are correct, which requires careful consideration and crafting by educators or test designers.

Considerations for writing fill-in-the-blank questions

When crafting fill-in-the-blank questions, teachers can enhance both the reliability and effectiveness of these questions by adhering to the following consolidated set of guidelines:[29]

- **Use only one blank per sentence**. This avoids confusion and increases the clarity and reliability of the question.

- **Place the blank at the end**. Positioning the blank at or near the end of the sentence helps students understand what they need to fill in without rereading the text.

- **Ensure a single correct answer**. Limit each blank to one correct or best answer to maintain fairness and clarity in grading.

- **Vary the language**. Avoid using the exact phrases from teaching materials. Using varied phrasing in questions can evaluate understanding more effectively than rote memorization.

- **Uniform blank length**. Keep all blanks the same size to prevent inadvertently giving clues about the answer. Specify whether the blank may require a word or a phrase.

- **Separate answer blanks**. Use a separate blank space for each answer to simplify and improve grading accuracy.

- **Use simple and clear language**. Clear questions allow students to focus on providing the correct answer rather than deciphering the question.

- **Provide adequate context**. Give enough information in the question to guide the student, but avoid making the answer obvious.

- **Focus on key concepts**. Choose content that tests understanding of main ideas or critical facts, avoiding minor details unless they are essential.

- **Accept synonyms and variants**. Prepare to accept various correct answers, particularly in subjects like literature or social studies, and clarify if you require specific terms.

- **Specify expected answer types**. Indicate the type of answer expected (e.g., date, name, concept), which helps students prepare and reduces confusion.

- **Provide practice opportunities**. Offer practice questions to help students understand the format and expectations before testing.

- **Avoid leading auestions.** Write questions that test knowledge or recall without giving away answers through the phrasing.

- **Provide feedback**. Explain why answers are correct or incorrect, aiding learning and understanding.

- **Mix question types**. Combine fill-in-the-blank questions with other questions to assess student knowledge and skills comprehensively.

- **Consider accessibility**. Adjust questions to accommodate all students, including those with disabilities or language barriers, ensuring fairness in assessment.

By integrating these practices, educators can create more effective and fair fill-in-the-blank questions that accurately assess student learning and comprehension.

Examples of Fill-in-the-Blank Questions

Incomplete statement. This refers to a sentence with blank spaces where students must provide the missing word or words to complete the sentence accurately. This type of question is designed to test a student's knowledge or recall of specific information. The key aspect of an incomplete statement is it presents part of the information, requiring the student to fill in the missing piece based on their understanding or memory.

For instance, a fill-in-the-blank question might say, "The capital of France is ___." The student would then need to know and write "Paris" in the blank to complete the statement correctly. Incomplete statements must be crafted carefully to ensure they are clear and have a specific, correct answer, minimizing ambiguity and confusion.

- The sugar in DNA is _____.

- The method used for the human genome sequencing project is known as the _____ method.

- The tightly packaged region of a eukaryotic chromosome is known as _____.

Sentence or paragraph completion. When you make fill-in-the-blank questions, only leave out the most important words or phrases in a sentence or paragraph. Don't mindlessly copy the words straight from the textbooks. Instead, use your own words or change the sentences a bit. This way, you're testing if students understand the material and not simply if they can remember exactly what the book says.

- In a DNA molecule, adenine always forms _____ hydrogen bonds with thymine, while guanine forms _____ hydrogen bonds with cytosine.

- The DNA molecule is a right-handed helix. The backbone is composed of _____ and _____ groups, while the _____ bases are stacked inside.

Formula questions. Formula questions in LMSs like Canvas are a powerful way to generate dynamic, randomized math or science questions. These questions use variables that can change each time they are presented, allowing for a virtually unlimited number of unique problems.[30] Students are provided with random questions from this set.

A **formula question** involves a template-based setup where:

- You define a formula with variables (e.g., $A \times B + C$).

- Each variable is assigned a range of possible values (e.g., $A = 1$ to 10, $B = 5$ to 15).

- The LMS calculates the correct answer automatically based on the formula and the randomly selected values for each variable.

Benefits of Formula Questions

- **Personalized learning**: Each student sees a slightly different question, which reduces cheating and ensures individualized assessment.

- **Efficient practice**: You can set up one question but generate hundreds of variations automatically.

- **Automatic grading**: The LMS grades the responses based on the defined formula, saving instructors time.

Formula Question Examples

Formula Question 1: Calculating the number of base pairs per turn of the DNA Helix

Question: A DNA molecule has [x] turns. How many base pairs are present in this DNA molecule?

Formula: x * 10

Explanation: The source states that "each turn of the helix measures 3.4 nm. Therefore, 10 base pairs are present per turn of the helix." This formula multiplies the number of turns by 10 to calculate the number of base pairs.

Formula Question 2: Calculating the Length of a DNA Molecule

Question: A DNA molecule has [y] base pairs. What is the length of this DNA molecule in nanometers?

Formula: y * 0.34

Explanation: The source explains, "Each base pair is separated from the next base pair by a distance of 0.34 nm." This formula multiplies the number of base pairs by 0.34 nm to calculate the total length of the DNA molecule.

***

Open-ended Questions

Next, the focus shifts to open-ended questions, which include fill-in-the-blank, short answer, and essay questions. Since fill-in-the-blank questions are closed- and open-ended, they will not be revisited here. This section will concentrate on short answer and essay questions. Open questions require more detailed and comprehensive responses.

Open questions pose a more significant challenge on many levels. Grading open-ended questions is more time-consuming and complex, often requiring manual evaluation.[31] An essay, for instance, might involve several steps that need to be meticulously checked. While artificial intelligence is making strides in this area, grading these questions requires human discernment and understanding.

Open questions are generally more challenging for students than closed ones because they need to remember more information and make connections beyond simple recall.[32] Answering open questions, which allow for a longer response, is harder than answering multiple-choice questions.[33] Students need to remember the information independently, without any hints. As a result, students often miss more of these questions, which can lead to lower test scores.[34]

Short Answer

A short answer question requires a brief response, typically a few words to a sentence or two, rather than a detailed explanation or essay. These questions are common in quizzes and exams. They assess understanding of specific facts or concepts.

Short answer questions are often more effective than multiple-choice questions.[35] This is because they require students to have a solid understanding of the material. Students might see a familiar word in multiple-choice questions and guess the answer. But with short answers, they must know the terms well. Other benefits include:

- **Focused assessment**. They allow educators to test specific knowledge and understanding of a topic, ensuring students grasp essential facts or concepts.

- **Quick to answer**. Because they require only a brief response, short answer questions can cover a wide range of topics in a limited amount of time, making them efficient for teaching and testing.

- **Development of writing skills**. They help students develop the ability to express themselves concisely and directly, improving their writing and communication skills.

- **Encourages recall**. These questions require students to recall information from memory, reinforcing learning and aiding in material retention.

- **Versatility**. They can assess various levels of learning, from basic recall of facts to more complex understanding involving the application of knowledge to new situations.

It's important to note these types of questions also present challenges. For instance, they can be more time-consuming for teachers to prepare and grade.[36] The length of the answer is another factor to consider. These questions can be graded automatically if the answer is only one word (as in fill-in-the-blank questions). However, elements like spelling, punctuation, and capitalization are crucial. Short answer questions can pose a grading challenge if the answer is longer. Other challenges or limitations include:

- **Subjectivity in grading**. Short answers can be more subjective to grade than multiple-choice questions, especially if the responses vary significantly. This can lead to scoring inconsistencies unless one uses clear rubrics or answer keys. Students will negotiate for points if there are ambiguities.

- **Limited depth**. These questions typically do not allow an in-depth demonstration of a student's understanding or critical thinking skills. They are more suited for assessing factual knowledge rather than complex reasoning.

- **Time-consuming to grade.** Although they are quick for students to answer, short answer questions can be time-consuming for educators to grade, especially with large class sizes.

- **Potential for ambiguity**. Poorly worded questions can lead to ambiguity, causing students to misinterpret what is being asked and potentially answer incorrectly despite understanding the material.

- **Restricted response**. They limit the student's response to a narrow field, preventing students from demonstrating additional knowledge or connections they might see between concepts.

- **Preparation bias**. These questions favor students who are better at memorization and quick recall over those who excel in critical thinking and problem-solving but might need more time to articulate their thoughts.

Creating Short Answer Questions

When writing short answer questions, follow these tips:[37]

- **Be clear**. Ensure the question tells students exactly what they need to do. If the question isn't straightforward, the answers you get might not show what students know. Here are two examples:

  ○ **Clear question - What is the main function of the mitochondria in a cell? (Answer in one sentence.)** This question is straightforward and tells students exactly what to focus on (the primary function of mitochondria) and how detailed their answer should be (one sentence).

- ○ **Unclear question - Explain mitochondria.** This question needs to be more specific and specify what aspect of mitochondria to focus on (e.g., structure, function, or role in energy production). It also does not indicate the level of detail or format expected in the response.

- **Keep it simple**. Each answer should be about one simple idea or fact. This makes it easier to see if the students understand your material.

- **Explain how much to write**. Let students know how detailed their answers should be. You can often do this by wording the question. Sometimes, the space you give for an answer shows how long the answer should be. But remember, the space is to help guide how much they write, not to give hints about the correct answer.

Examples of Short Answer Questions

Short answer questions can take different forms: direct questions, associations, short explanations, pictures or diagrams, and lists.[38]

Direct questions. These are the most basic of short answer questions. You ask a question, which results in a brief but specific answer.

Example of a Direct Question

- What are the building blocks of DNA?

- What type of bond links nucleotides together?

Associations. Associations are similar to matching, except the short answer response is written in.

Example of an Association Question

Match the following concepts related to DNA with the scientists who contributed to our understanding. Write the name of the scientist next to each discovery. (Rosalind Franklin, Francis Crick, James Watson, Frederick Sanger)

1. Structure of DNA _____

2. DNA Sequencing _____

3. X-Ray Diffraction Images of DNA _____

Short explanations. A short explanation question asks for a quick response, usually just a few sentences, with a simple explanation or reason. These questions check if students understand a topic by asking them to explain or clarify their answers briefly. For example, "Explain why adenine and thymine are considered complementary base pairs." A good response would be: "Adenine and thymine are two of the four nitrogenous bases found in DNA. The structure of DNA is a double helix, resembling a twisted ladder. The 'rungs' of this ladder are formed by pairs of nitrogenous bases. Adenine (A) always pairs with thymine (T), and guanine (G) always pairs with cytosine (C). This specific pairing is referred to as complementary base pairing."

Example of a Short Explanation Question

In one sentence, explain a significant contribution each of the following individuals made to understanding DNA.

1. Rosalind Franklin _____

2. Francis Crick _____

3. James Watson _____

4. Frederick Sanger _____

Picture or diagram. A short answer picture or diagram question shows a picture or a diagram and asks the student to answer a question about what they see. Their answer should be brief, maybe only a few words or sentences. These questions check if one can understand and discuss information shown in pictures or diagrams. For instance, if there's a water cycle diagram, the question might ask the student to point out where rain comes from or explain how the cycle works.

Example of a Picture or Diagram Question

Based on the Voronoi diagram below, answer the following questions:

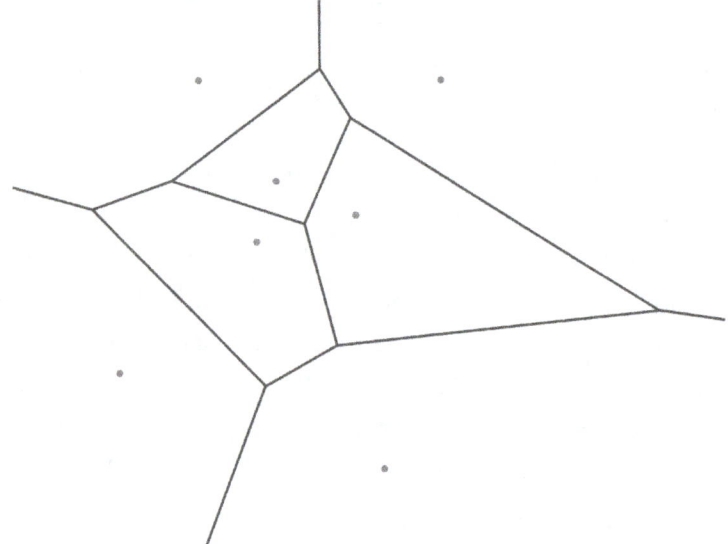

Figure 5. Voronoi Diagram

How many regions are formed in this Voronoi diagram? _____

How many generating points (sites) are shown in this Voronoi diagram?

_____

Choose one cell from the Voronoi diagram and describe its properties in relation to the generating point and its neighboring cells.

Explain how Voronoi diagrams can be used in real-life applications. Provide at least one specific example based on the structure seen in the diagram.

Lists. A short answer list question is a question where you need to give several short answers in a list. This type of question is often used in exams or quizzes where you don't have to give lengthy explanations—list things briefly. For example, the question might be, "Name three renewable energy sources." You would answer by listing "solar, wind, hydro" without adding more details.

Example of a List Question

List three differences between purines and pyrimidines.

a. _____

b. _____

c. _____

Essay

Educators use essay questions to evaluate students' ability to understand and articulate complex ideas. The questions ask students to respond in essay form, allowing them to explore a topic in depth. This format requires more than just recalling facts; it demands critical thinking, organization of thoughts, and an ability to argue or explain ideas effectively.

For instance, an essay question might be: "Discuss the structure of DNA, including its components, the arrangement of those components, and the significance of its double helix shape for its function." Students are expected to not only list the causes but also explain their impacts and connect them to broader historical contexts.

Essay questions are valuable in the classroom because they assess various skills, including analytical thinking, information synthesis, and written communication. They also encourage students to engage with learning material more deeply and personally, promoting a more comprehensive understanding of the subject.

As part of my doctoral program, I had to complete my general exams. My program chair gave me seven essay questions, and I chose four to answer. He gave me five days to craft my scholarly answers to these questions. My committee expected each answer to be 10-12 pages long. I had to research and cite each answer fully. I spent approximately 16 hours on each question. This exercise was rewarding but exhausting.

Your questions may not need to go to the same lengths to achieve your purpose. However, essay questions allow you to assess student knowledge in a way other question types don't.

Benefits of Using Essay Questions

Using essay questions for quizzes has several benefits for students and teachers. Here are some of the key advantages:

- **Improves writing skills**. Writing essays help students better organize their thoughts and put them into words. This is an essential skill students will use throughout their lives.

- **Encourages critical thinking**. Essay questions make students think deeply about a topic. They must analyze information, draw connections, and develop their ideas, which helps hone their critical thinking skills.

- **Shows understanding**. Essays allow students to demonstrate what they know and how they understand and interpret information. This is great for complex topics or having multiple viewpoints.

- **Supports creativity**. When students write an essay, they often have the chance to present their ideas creatively. This can make learning and writing more interesting and personal.

- **Helps memory and learning**. Writing about a topic can help students remember it better. Organizing and explaining their thoughts in their own words makes them more likely to remember what they've learned.

- **Prepares for the future**. Many high school, college, and job application exams include essay writing. Getting practice now is good preparation for those challenges.

Challenges of Using Essay Questions

While essay questions offer many educational benefits, they also come with several challenges and limitations that educators should consider:

- **Time-consuming to grade**. Essay questions can take a lot of time to read and evaluate properly, especially if there are many students. This can be demanding for teachers who have tight schedules and multiple classes.

- **Subjectivity in scoring**. Grading essays can sometimes be subjective. Different teachers might have different opinions on the quality of the same essay, which can lead to inconsistent grades. Creating clear rubrics and scoring checklists can help, but some level of subjectivity often remains.

- **Requires strong writing skills**. Students struggling with writing or still learning English might find essay questions particularly challenging. This can make it hard for them to express their understanding of a topic fully.

- **Potential for ambiguity**. Sometimes, essay questions can be unclear or too broad, confusing students about what is expected of them. Teachers need to be very clear and specific in their wording.

- **Time-intensive for students**. Writing a good essay can take a lot of time, which might be stressful for students, especially if they have multiple essays for different classes.

- **Not always the best for all types of learning**. Essays mainly assess writing and analytical skills. Other types of assessments might be more effective for topics involving problem-solving or practical skills.

Guidelines for Writing Essay Questions

Creating essay questions might seem simple at first, but making good ones that are fair and have clear scoring rules is quite challenging. Here's what teachers need to keep in mind:[39]

- **Understand the objectives**. Know what learning objectives you want to assess with the essay question. This ensures the question aligns with what you've been teaching.

- **Clear instructions**. Tell students exactly what you expect in their answers, including how long their essays should be. This helps students understand what they must do and allows the instructor to grade more fairly.

- **Clarity and precision**. State the questions clearly so all students understand what's required. Avoid vague or double-meaning questions that might confuse them.

- **Manageable length and detail**. Consider having more questions with shorter answers to cover more material and simplify grading.

- **Time limits and length guidelines**. To manage the test duration effectively, suggest how much time to spend on each question and guide the length of responses.

- **Explain scoring**. Tell students how each question affects their overall score and how partial credit works. Everyone should know how they are being evaluated.

- **Avoid dependent questions**. Don't make the answer to one question necessary to answer the next. This can unfairly penalize students who get the first one wrong, affecting their performance on subsequent questions.

Examples of Essay Questions

Essay questions can be classified into seven major categories: comparison, decision, causes or effects, explanation, summary, illustration, and guided essay.[40] Here is an explanation of each type.

- **Comparison essay**. In a comparison essay, students examine two or more items (such as characters, stories, articles, or processes) to highlight their similarities and differences. The goal is to show an understanding of each item's features and how they relate or contrast. For example, "Compare the structure and function of eukaryotic and prokaryotic DNA. How do these differences impact DNA replication and gene expression?"

- **Decision essay**. This type of essay requires students to decide between options and justify their choice. For example, they might decide which of two characters is more heroic or which solution is best for a problem. Students should provide reasons and evidence to support their decision. For example, "Should modern genome sequencing techniques entirely replace older methods like Sanger sequencing, or should both be retained for different applications? Justify your answer."

- **Causes or effects essay**. In these essays, students explore either the causes of a particular event or situation or its effects. For example, they might write about the causes of pollution or the impact of a new school policy. They must link their ideas clearly to show the cause-effect relationship. For example, "What were the causes leading to the development of Sanger's chain termination method, and how has it affected modern biology?"

- **Explanation essay**. Students explain how something works or describe a process in detail. For instance, they could explain photosynthesis or how a bill becomes a law. The focus should be on clarity and a thorough understanding of the process. For example, "Explain the process of DNA sequencing using the Sanger method, including the role of dideoxynucleotides."

- **Summary essay**. In a summary essay, students are asked to read a text and then condense it into a shorter form, capturing only the main points and key details. This type of essay teaches students to focus on the most important information and to express it in their own words. For example, "Summarize the key steps involved in the Sanger DNA sequencing method."

- **Illustration essay**. This essay type asks students to illustrate a statement with clear examples and detailed descriptions. For instance, if the essay is about "Hard work leads to success," students would provide real-life examples or hypothetical scenarios demonstrating this theme. For example, "Illustrate how the structure of DNA facilitates its replication and stability using examples from its chemical composition."

- **Guided essay**. A guided essay is structured by specific questions or prompts that lead the student through the writing process. The prompts help direct the student's thoughts and ensure they cover different aspects of the topic. This type of essay helps students coherently organize their ideas and arguments. For example, "What is the basic structure of a nucleotide, and how do these structures form the DNA double helix?"

Framing Quiz Questions

The wording of questions significantly impacts student performance, engagement, and understanding.[41] Studies suggest three effective approaches for framing a question: using real scientists' or experts' names for authenticity, referencing classmates' names, and employing self-referential language (using "you").[42] Each method has its merits and drawbacks, affecting student motivation and comprehension differently.

- **Authentic framing**. Using real scientists' or experts' names can enhance diversity and realism but might create a perceived distance between students and the subject matter.[43]

- **Classmate referential questions**. While least preferred, this approach can help some students visualize themselves and their classmates conducting experiments, thus boosting their confidence.[44] This framing has resulted in lower stress, increased familiarity with the subject (comfort), higher motivation, and lower cognitive load.

- **Self-referential questions**. Students generally prefer these questions because they help them visualize themselves in the scenario. This leads to better organization of material, problem-solving, and reduced need for clarification.[45]

Using real-world scenario-based questions adds variety in framing questions and increases wording variations. It is important to note there is no difference in performance when using the different referential variants.[46] Students prefer a particular style if they see it more than others. According to a study, the style predominately used in prior assessments may influence student preference for a specifically worded referential style.[47] They tend to gravitate to the style they are most familiar with.

When framing questions, consider these tips:[48]

- Survey students for their question referential framing preference.

- Be consistent with class and homework examples and assessment questions.

Using ChatGPT to Help Write Questions

Recognizing the effort and time required to create written questions is essential. Technology makes this task significantly more manageable, so it is wise to invest in it.[49] Generative AI tools like ChatGPT and NotebookLM can accelerate the creation of questions. Creating prompts based on learning objectives and instructional content will result in rapid test bank development.

Using Learning Objectives to Write Quiz Questions

Learning objectives lie at the heart of building robust assessments. I will briefly share an example of how you can use ChatGPT to help write learning objectives and associated quiz questions. In this example, I am going to use the Marketing Mix (4Ps) as my point of focus.

First, I will ask ChatGPT to draft a set of learning objectives (see appendix B for more prompts).

ChatGPT Prompt: Write learning objectives focusing on Marketing Mix (4Ps) at the remembering level of Bloom's Taxonomy using verbs like Cite, Define, Describe, Draw, Enumerate, Identify, Index, Indicate, Label, List, Match, Meet, Name, Outline, Point, Quote, Read, Recall, Recite, Recognize, Record, Repeat, Reproduce, Review, Select, State, Study, Tabulate, Trace, Write

Result: Here are learning objectives focusing on the Marketing Mix (4Ps) at the remembering level of Bloom's Taxonomy:

- **Define** the Marketing Mix (4Ps) and **cite** its components.

- **List** the four elements of the Marketing Mix (4Ps).

- **Identify** the component of the Marketing Mix (4Ps) that deals with product development and branding.

- **Recall** the aspect of the Marketing Mix (4Ps) that involves pricing strategies.

- **Recognize** the element of the Marketing Mix (4Ps) related to distribution channels and logistics.

- **Describe** the promotional activities included in the Marketing Mix (4Ps).

- **State** the importance of each element in the Marketing Mix (4Ps) for developing a comprehensive marketing strategy.

- **Outline** the role of each component of the Marketing Mix (4Ps) in influencing consumer behavior.

- **Recite** the four Ps of the Marketing Mix and briefly explain each.

- **Point** out how the Marketing Mix (4Ps) can be adjusted to meet the needs of different target markets.

Naturally, it is important to vet each learning objective to see if it meets your needs. If necessary, reword the learning objectives before proceeding to the next step. Additionally, you could provide your instructional content to ChatGPT to help build the learning objectives.

Once you have learning objectives you like, you can use them as part of the ChatGPT prompt. In the example below, I am asking ChatGPT to create five multiple-choice questions based on the learning objective "Define the Marketing Mix (4Ps) and cite its components."

ChatGPT Prompt: Write three multiple-choice questions based on this learning objective:

Persona = First-year college student just being introduced to the content
***

Learning Objective: Define the Marketing Mix (4Ps) and cite its components.

Note: I learned to use (***) to delineate between the task I want completed and the content I am providing for the prompt.

Result:

1. What is the Marketing Mix (4Ps)?

a) A blend of marketing strategies aimed at product differentiation

b) A framework for analyzing consumer behavior

c) A comprehensive approach to marketing planning and execution

d) A set of variables used to define marketing objectives

Correct answer: c) A comprehensive approach to marketing planning and execution

2. Which components are included in the Marketing Mix (4Ps)?

a) Product, Place, Profit, Promotion

b) Price, Product, Place, People

c) Price, Product, Promotion, Process

d) Product, Place, Promotion, Packaging

Correct answer: b) Price, Product, Place, People

3. What is the role of the Marketing Mix (4Ps) in marketing strategy?

a) To identify target markets

b) To analyze competitor behavior

c) To develop pricing strategies

d) To create a comprehensive marketing plan

Correct answer: d) To create a comprehensive marketing plan

Now, it is up to you to determine if the questions and answers are correct and which questions you want to add to your test bank. See chapter 7 to learn more about building test banks.

You can make your question creation even easier if you know your LMS's format for importing questions. You can then let ChatGPT see the structure of this format, and it will format your questions accordingly. For example, I use the New York Institute of Technology's Canvas Exam Converter to create QTI files. They provide instructions for formatting questions. (https://tubarksblog.com/MQQTIConverter) Using the prompt above and the New York Institute of Technology's formatting instructions, the prompt would look like this:[50]

ChatGPT Prompt: Write five multiple-choice questions based on this learning objective:

Persona = First-year college student just being introduced to the content

Question Format Example =

Multiple-Choice: Each choice must start with a lowercase alphabet, a, b, c, d, etc. with a close parenthesis. The correct choice is designated with an asterisk.

1. What is 2+3?

a) 6

b) 1*

c) 5

d) 10

***

Learning Objective: Define the Marketing Mix (4Ps) and cite its components.

Conclusion

Designing effective quiz questions goes beyond testing memory—it fosters critical thinking and deeper understanding. By aligning questions with clear learning objectives, educators can create assessments that accurately measure student progress. A balanced mix of closed-ended and open-ended questions ensures both efficiency and depth, helping students recall key concepts while also demonstrating their reasoning and application skills.

Well-crafted questions should be clear, fair, and aligned with instructional goals. Avoiding ambiguity, unnecessary complexity, and trick questions helps create assessments that genuinely reflect student understanding. Precise wording and logical structure ensures that quizzes enhance learning rather than just measure retention.

Leveraging technology, including generative AI tools like ChatGPT, can streamline question creation while maintaining quality and relevance. Quizzes can become more than just assessments. They become valuable tools for learning, reinforcing concepts, and guiding students toward mastery.

Quick Quiz

Test your understanding with a brief quiz.

5.1. Which of the following best describes the purpose of a learning objective?

a) To provide detailed lesson plans for instructors.

b) To describe observable behaviors that indicate learning has occurred.

c) To outline assessment strategies for educators.

d) To evaluate the effectiveness of a curriculum.

5.2. What are the three main components of a well-written learning objective?

a) Condition, Performance, Assessment.

b) Performance, Condition, Criterion.

c) Condition, Assessment, Feedback.

d) Assessment, Performance, Feedback.

5.3. Which question type is best suited for assessing higher-order thinking skills according to Bloom's Taxonomy?

a) Multiple-choice questions.

b) True or False questions.

c) Short answer or essay questions.

d) Fill-in-the-blank questions.

5.4. What is the primary goal of mastery quizzing?

a) To assess memorization of key facts.

b) To encourage students to retake quizzes for full understanding.

c) To identify students who need additional help.

d) To grade students based on their first attempt.

5.5. Why should instructors avoid negative-worded questions in quizzes?

a) They make grading more difficult.

b) They often increase student confusion and reduce performance.

c) They are harder to align with learning objectives.

d) They require more time for students to answer.

1. "Bloom's Taxonomy," Vanderbilt University, January 20, 2025, https://cft.vanderbilt.edu/guides-sub-pages/blooms-taxonomy/.

2. Jeffrey S. Nevid and Casey E. Armata, "Paying Attention in Class: Using In-Class Quizzes to Incentivize Student Attention," *Teaching of Psychology*, 2023, 1–6, https://doi.org/10.1177/00986283231185136.

3. Tamara Swenson and Brad Visgatis, "Providing Feedback in Moodle Question Bank Items," *Osaka Jogakuin University*, 2022, 203–24.

4. *Guidebook for Air Force Instructors*, AFMAN 36-2236 (U.S. Air Force, 2003), https://www.angtec.ang.af.mil/Portals/10/Courses%20resources/afman36-2236.pdf?ver=2018-10-02-084122-173.

5. Jeremy L. Hsu et al., "Investigating the Influence of Assessment Question Framing on Undergraduate Biology Student Preference and Affect," *CBE—Life Sciences Education* 22, no. 4 (December 2023): ar45, https://doi.org/10.1187/cbe.22-12-0249.

6. Ibid., 2.

7. Joshua K. Strakos et al., "A Learning Management System-Based Approach to Assess Learning Outcomes in Operations Management Courses," *The International Journal of Management Education* 21, no. 2 (2023): 1–9, https://doi.org/10.1016/j.ijme.2023.100802.

8. Beckie Supiano, "What's the Best Way to Frame Test Questions?," The Chronicle of Higher Education, October 26, 2023, https://www.chronicle.com/newsletter/teaching/2023-10-26.

9. Strakos et al., "A Learning Management System-Based Approach to Assess Learning Outcomes in Operations Management Courses."

10. Gena C. Sbeglia and Ross H. Nehm, "Measuring Evolution Learning: Impacts of Student Participation Incentives and Test Timing," *Evolution: Education and Outreach* 15, no. 1 (2022): 1–15, https://doi.org/10.1186/s12052-022-00166-2.

11. David Ray Velez, Stefan Walter Johnson, and Robert Peter Sticca, "How to Prepare for the American Board of Surgery In-Training Examination (ABSITE): A Systematic Review," *Journal of Surgical Education* 79, no. 1 (2022): 216–28, https://doi.org/10.1016/j.jsurg.2021.08.004.

12. R. K. Prasad, "How Not to Write Effective Assessment Questions: 8 Pitfalls," *Rapid eLearning Blogs – CommLab India* (blog), September 27, 2022, https://blog.commlabindia.com/elearning-design/online-assessments-pitfalls-avoid.

13. Nevid and Armata, "Paying Attention in Class."

14. Ester Aflalo, "Students Generating Questions as a Way of Learning," *Active Learning in Higher Education* 22, no. 1 (2021): 63–75, https://doi.org/10.1177/1469787418769120.

15. Ibid., 64.

16. Ibid., 64.

17. *Guidebook for Air Force Instructors*.

18. Ibid., 242.

19. Prasad, "How Not to Write Effective Assessment Questions: 8 Pitfalls."

20. Ibid.

21. Ibid.

22. Ibid.

23. Ibid.

24. Darryl Chamberlain Jr, "How One Instructor Can Teach a Large-Scale, Mastery-Based College Algebra Course Online," *PRIMUS*, 2023, 1–22.

25. *Guidebook for Air Force Instructors*.

26. Ibid., 254.

27. Ibid., 248.

28. Ibid., 252.

29. Ibid., 257-258.

30. Strakos et al., "A Learning Management System-Based Approach to Assess Learning Outcomes in Operations Management Courses."

31. Sbeglia and Nehm, "Measuring Evolution Learning."

32. Sbeglia and Nehm, "Measuring Evolution Learning"; Lukas K. Sotola and Marcus Crede, "Regarding Class Quizzes: A Meta-Analytic Synthesis of Studies on the Relationship between Frequent Low-Stakes Testing and Class Performance," *Educational Psychology Review* 33, no. 2 (2021): 407–26, https://doi.org/10.1007/s10648-020-09563-9.

33. John P. Marinelli et al., "Harnessing the Power of Spaced Repetition Learning and Active Recall for Trainee Education in Otolaryngology," *American Journal of Otolaryngology* 43, no. 5 (2022): 1–2, https://doi.org/10.1016/j.amjoto.2022.103495.

34. Chunliang Yang et al., "Do Practice Tests (Quizzes) Reduce or Provoke Test Anxiety? A Meta-Analytic Review," *Educational Psychology Review* 35, no. 3 (2023): 1–26, https://doi.org/10.1007/s10648-023-09801-w.

35. Velez, Johnson, and Sticca, "How to Prepare for the American Board of Surgery In-Training Examination (ABSITE)."

36. Ibid., 227.

37. *Guidebook for Air Force Instructors*.

38. Ibid., 260.

39. Ibid., 263.

40. Ibid., 263-264.

41. Hsu et al., "Investigating the Influence of Assessment Question Framing on Undergraduate Biology Student Preference and Affect."

42. Supiano, "What's the Best Way to Frame Test Questions?"; Hsu et al., "Investigating the Influence of Assessment Question Framing on Undergraduate Biology Student Preference and Affect."

43. Hsu et al., "Investigating the Influence of Assessment Question Framing on Undergraduate Biology Student Preference and Affect."

44. Ibid., 14.

45. Ibid., 12.

46. Ibid., 9.

47. Ibid., 14.

48. Ibid., 15.

49. Nese Sevim-Cirak and Omer Faruk Islim, "Paper versus Online Quizzes: Which Is More Effective?," *Active Learning in Higher Education*, 2022, 1–18, https://doi.org/10.1177/14697874221079737.

50. "Canvas Exam Converter," *New York Tech* (blog), accessed November 29, 2024, https://www.nyit.edu/its/canvas_exam_converter.

Chapter Six

Feedback

Sophia, a first-year biology student, struggled with the complexities of photosynthesis. Her quiz results consistently showed errors in understanding key processes. Her instructor implemented a mastery quizzing system with detailed feedback for each question. After each quiz, Sophia received explanations for incorrect answers, including diagrams and analogies to simplify concepts. Over six weeks, her quiz scores improved significantly, culminating in a perfect score on the summative exam. Sophia later shared that the personalized feedback made the subject matter more accessible and boosted her confidence in tackling complex material.

Objectives

- Explain the role of feedback in the mastery quizzing process and its impact on learning outcomes.

- Evaluate the effectiveness of different feedback methods (e.g., automated, reflective class feedback) in addressing student misconceptions and promoting long-term retention.

- Design and implement feedback strategies for quizzes, balancing immediate response with the opportunity for deeper reflection and understanding.

Feedback

Feedback is a crucial element in mastery quizzing. Feedback should be part of low-stakes quizzing and include correct answers.[1] To be most effective, feedback for questions within quizzes should be immediate.[2]

The primary purpose of providing feedback is to help test-takers understand their mistakes or reinforce what they got right.[3] Feedback is vital in quizzing because it guides learners in correcting their errors. Good feedback indicates right or wrong answers and connects back to the learning objectives and the specific criteria for those objectives.

In a mastery quizzing environment, feedback aids students in closing knowledge gaps.[4] Researchers recommend adding feedback during practice quizzes since formative quizzes are designed to build knowledge and address those gaps.[5] Instructors should include feedback for distractors or incorrect answers because it accelerates learning.[6] Feedback helps students make necessary adjustments or improvements in their learning.

Feedback becomes even more impactful when the feedback explanation goes beyond a simple right or wrong indication.[7] Explaining why an answer was incorrect is valuable, even though it may require extra effort. The concept of feedback is essential for learning because it bridges the gap between a student's current knowledge and their desired level of understanding.[8] It helps learners connect with learning objectives and assess their current knowledge.[9]

Students must be able to make sense of the feedback and use it to improve their work. Effective feedback encourages students to apply what they have learned to enhance their future performance. Do not despair if students miss questions during quizzes. Students will do better during summative exams even if they miss questions during a formative quiz.[10]

I previously emphasized the importance of timely feedback; however, other research findings suggest immediate feedback might not always be the optimal approach.

Mr. Carter, a high school history teacher, experimented with immediate versus delayed feedback during a unit on the American Revolution. For half the class, he provided instant feedback after each quiz question. For the other half, he delayed feedback until the following class, summarizing common errors. While both groups performed better in the summative assessment than prior units, the group with delayed feedback exhibited stronger retention of key dates and events. Mr. Carter concluded that while immediate feedback benefited engagement, delayed feedback allowed students time to reflect and internalize corrections.

You will have to experiment. There's a balance to strike regarding the timing of feedback. Providing hints and answers too quickly may offer short-term benefits, but it can lead to dependency in the long run.[11] Striking the right balance is challenging because students also need challenges and opportunities to struggle instead of receiving answers immediately. LMSs provide options for controlling when to release feedback.

Improving Feedback

Your goal in designing quiz questions is to provide feedback for each question, correct answer, and distractor.[12] Multiple-choice and true or false quiz questions are well suited for immediate feedback.

When creating feedback for MCQs, it is important to provide detailed feedback that will work for most students.[13] Thorough feedback can help students narrow down solutions for resolving problems. Highlight key misconceptions and strategies for overcoming knowledge gaps.

It is important to review missed questions and improve the question feedback frequently.[14] Students might miss a quiz question due to unclear wording, poor alignment with instruction, or overly complex content exceeding their preparedness. Knowledge gaps, misinterpretation of the question, or confusing distractors in multiple-choice options can also contribute to widespread errors. Analyzing missed questions helps identify these issues, ensuring assessments better support learning and accurately reflect instructional goals. Make changes to questions in the test bank to generate subsequent corrected quizzes.

Feedback Forms

Feedback can take various forms.[15]

Use automated feedback whenever possible. This feedback is built into digital quizzes and exams. You can provide it immediately after students complete a quiz or delay the release of feedback.

Question   Points 5

> What type of bond connects the phosphate group to the 5' carbon of
> the sugar in a nucleotide?

Answers:

Possible Answer   a) Hydrogen bond

> **Feedback:** Sorry, this is incorrect - Hydrogen bonds occur between
> complementary nitrogenous bases in DNA (e.g., A-T, G-C) but do not
> form the linkage between the phosphate group and sugar.

Possible Answer   b) Peptide bond

> **Feedback:** Sorry, this is incorrect - Peptide bonds link amino acids
> together in proteins, not nucleotides.

Possible Answer   c) Ester bond

> **Feedback:** Correct - In a nucleotide, the phosphate group is connected
> to the **5' carbon** of the sugar (ribose or deoxyribose) via a
> **phosphoester bond**. Specifically, this is a type of **ester bond** that forms
> when a phosphate group reacts with a hydroxyl group (-OH) of the sugar,
> resulting in the loss of a water molecule (condensation reaction).

Possible Answer   d) Glycosidic bond

> **Feedback:** Sorry, this is incorrect - Glycosidic bonds connect the sugar
> and nitrogenous base in a nucleotide but not the phosphate group.

Overall Feedback for a Correct Answer:

> **Great job!** The phosphate group is connected to the 5' carbon of the
> sugar via an **ester bond**. This bond forms through a condensation
> reaction, linking the phosphate and sugar in the nucleotide structure.

Overall Feedback for a Wrong Answer:

> Not quite. The bond that connects the phosphate group to the 5' carbon of
> the sugar in a nucleotide is an **ester bond**. Consider reviewing how
> nucleotides are structured, particularly how the phosphate, sugar, and
> nitrogenous base are connected.

Figure 6. Example of question and answer feedback

I recommend you provide feedback as soon as possible. Automated feedback saves instructors time and energy while helping students understand concepts.[16]

If you use questions in a classroom setting, peers, instructors, or even tutors can provide feedback, depending on how the test is administered. For example, during my time at the Air Force Academy Prep School, we would present our answers and work on the blackboard. Classmates or the instructor would step in if we answered incorrectly.

One effective strategy for providing feedback in a classroom setting is **reflective class feedback**. This method involves a real-time class review of questions projected on the screen.[17] The review could be in conjunction with clickers or game-based applications. This integration allows for a more comprehensive and effective learning experience, ensuring the entertainment aspect of gaming is consistent with the educational goals.

Here is how this method works: Students respond to the questions. The instructor then engages them in a conversation about why they answered a certain way, especially if their response is incorrect. This method encourages students to respond verbally or in writing and can lead to the instructor clarifying questions and concept reteaching.[18] Reflective class feedback should be brief, lasting only a few minutes at a time.[19]

The reflective component of this feedback method helps students actively engage with the questions, receive immediate answers, and participate in discussions about the feedback.[20] When using this approach in a classroom, you don't have to cover many questions. The goal is to use a handful of questions effectively. Learners benefit most when actively participating and engaging in dialogue during the feedback process.

An essential aspect of reflective class feedback is providing **elaborate feedback**, which involves offering detailed explanations, reflective questions, or more examples to help students grasp the concepts better.[21] This approach fosters social construction, where students learn from one another. Research demonstrates that students who receive reflective class feedback during gamified quizzes perform better on subsequent exams than those who do not.[22] Reflective class feedback slows the learning process, allowing students time to reflect and create meaningful connections between concepts.[23] Slowing the pace helps students better make sense of the content.

This method offers formative feedback as students actively recall information while answering questions.[24] It helps clarify misconceptions and strengthens long-term memory. Reflective class feedback also empowers students to self-evaluate their performance, request additional feedback, and make necessary adjustments.[25] When an instructor and qualified peers provide guidance, it aids students in progressing through the Zone of Proximal Development (ZPD) toward mastery. The **Zone of Proximal Development (ZPD)** is the range of tasks or skills a person can do with help but cannot yet do independently. The goal is to move them from dependence on the instructor to independence. For example, a high school chemistry teacher, Ms. Elkins, designed quizzes with scaffolded feedback to guide students through the Zone of Proximal Development (ZPD). During a quiz on chemical bonding, students first received automated hints for minor errors. Ms. Elkins provided detailed feedback and examples during class discussions if they struggled. Over time, students became less reliant on hints, independently mastering complex problems such as molecular geometry.

Feedback Challenges

One significant challenge in providing feedback is you can't guarantee students will use it effectively.[26] Some students struggle to understand detailed or high-information feedback.[27] Nevertheless, it's crucial to encourage students to use feedback to improve their quiz performance.[28]

Jacob, a sophomore struggling with literary analysis, often misunderstood automated feedback. For instance, his quizzes flagged vague thesis statements, but he didn't understand how to improve them. His English teacher, Ms. Roberts, scheduled a one-on-one session to review his answers. She broke down the feedback into simpler terms and demonstrated how to craft stronger arguments. With additional opportunities to revise his work, Jacob's skills improved, leading to higher quiz scores and a newfound appreciation for the writing process. Ms. Roberts used what she learned and tried in the one-on-one session to improve the question feedback.

Instructors must teach students how to use automated feedback in quizzes and assignments.[29] This instruction should occur early in the term so students can maximize the benefits. Instructors should provide do-over opportunities so students can benefit from the feedback. For homework, students can work on fixing identified issues and resubmit their work. For quizzes, they can take a new quiz on the same topic. This is made possible by creating robust test banks where you can randomly draw questions.

Instructor Follow Up

When possible, provide automated feedback. This will ultimately reduce your workload and allow you to focus on serious deficits.

As automated feedback improves, more students will have their misconceptions effectively addressed. Instructors can use this feedback as a reference during review sessions with students, identifying areas for improvement and refining the feedback accordingly.[30] Instructors can guide students toward mastering the concepts by reviewing attempts, providing targeted feedback, and iterating this process.[31]

It can be challenging for students to know where they stand in a mastery grading scheme driven by mastery quizzing. In a study, students could not see their final grades, but instructors gave them weekly feedback and reported progress.[32] I used this strategy to keep my graduate students informed. I provided weekly email messages indicating the class average and where they should be at that point in the class schedule.

Conclusion

Effective feedback is a cornerstone of mastery quizzing, helping students bridge knowledge gaps and build confidence in their learning. Whether provided immediately or with a delay, feedback enhances understanding and retention, allowing students to correct misconceptions and refine their knowledge. Instructors must consider the balance between immediate responses and opportunities for deeper reflection, ensuring feedback remains meaningful and actionable.

The method of delivering feedback also plays a critical role. Automated feedback can save time and provide instant clarification, while reflective class discussions engage students in active learning. Personalized feedback, whether from instructors or peers, further strengthens comprehension by guiding students through complex concepts at their own pace. Encouraging students to actively use feedback is key to their success.

Ultimately, feedback should not be seen as merely a response to quiz answers but as an ongoing conversation that supports student growth. By continuously refining their feedback strategies and teaching students how to use it effectively, educators can create a learning environment that fosters curiosity, mastery, and long-term retention of knowledge.

Quick Quiz

Here is a quick quiz to pull together your knowledge about providing quiz feedback.

6.1. What is the primary purpose of feedback in mastery quizzing?

a) To reinforce correct answers.

b) To encourage competition among students.

c) To help students understand their mistakes and improve their performance.

d) To prepare students for summative assessments.

6.2. Why is it important to include explanations for incorrect answers in feedback?

a) It saves instructors time and effort.

b) It bridges the gap between current knowledge and desired understanding.

c) It reduces the need for formative quizzes.

d) It discourages students from making the same mistake again.

6.3. What is a potential drawback of providing immediate feedback during quizzes?

a) It creates a dependency on the feedback.

b) It slows down the learning process.

c) It decreases student motivation.

d) It leads to incomplete learning objectives.

6.4. Which of the following is a benefit of reflective class feedback?

a) It allows instructors to avoid reteaching concepts.

b) It provides students with detailed explanations through group discussions.

c) It replaces the need for formative feedback.

d) It ensures that all students answer questions correctly.

6.5. How can instructors encourage students to use automated feedback effectively?

a) By assigning grades based solely on automated feedback.

b) By teaching students how to interpret and apply feedback early in the term.

c) By limiting the availability of feedback to specific quizzes.

d) By removing the option for feedback revisions.

1. Steven C. Pan et al., "Using Online and Clicker Quizzes to Learn Scientific and Technical Jargon," in *In Their Own Words: What Scholars and Teachers Want You to Know about Why and How to Apply the Science of Learning in Your Academic Setting* (Society for the Teaching of Psychology, 2023), 473–80.

2. Lukas K. Sotola and Marcus Crede, "Regarding Class Quizzes: A Meta-Analytic Synthesis of Studies on the Relationship between Frequent Low-Stakes Testing and Class Performance," *Educational Psychology Review* 33, no. 2 (2021): 407–26, https://doi.org/10.1007/s10648-020-09563-9.

3. David Ray Velez, Stefan Walter Johnson, and Robert Peter Sticca, "How to Prepare for the American Board of Surgery In-Training Examination (ABSITE): A Systematic Review," *Journal of Surgical Education* 79, no. 1 (2022): 216–28, https://doi.org/10.1016/j.jsurg.2021.08.004.

4. Dimple Martin, "Are Your Assessments Fair and Balanced?," *Faculty Focus | Higher Ed Teaching & Learning* (blog), September 20, 2023, https://www.facultyfocus.com/articles/educational-assessment/are-your-assessments-fair-and-balanced/.

5. Chunliang Yang et al., "Do Practice Tests (Quizzes) Reduce or Provoke Test Anxiety? A Meta-Analytic Review," *Educational Psychology Review* 35, no. 3 (2023): 1–26, https://doi.org/10.1007/s10648-023-09801-w.

6. Tamara Swenson and Brad Visgatis, "Providing Feedback in Moodle Question Bank Items," *Osaka Jogakuin University*, 2022, 203–24; Nese Sevim-Cirak and Omer Faruk Islim, "Paper versus Online Quizzes: Which Is More Effective?," *Active Learning in Higher Education*, 2022, 1–18, https://doi.org/10.1177/14697874221079737.

7. Chunliang Yang et al., "Frequent Quizzing Accelerates Classroom Learning," *In Their Own Words: What Scholars and Teachers Want You to Know about Why and How to Apply the Science of Learning in Your Academic Setting*, 2023, 190–99.

8. Swenson and Visgatis, "Providing Feedback in Moodle Question Bank Items."

9. Sevim-Cirak and Islim, "Paper versus Online Quizzes."

10. Danney Rasco, "Throw Them in the Deep End? Quizzing With Factual Versus Application Items," in *In Their Own Words: What Scholars and Teachers Want You to Know about Why and How to Apply the Science of Learning in Your Academic Setting* (Society for the Teaching of Psychology, 2023), 499–504.

11. David J. Epstein, *Range: Why Generalists Triumph in a Specialized World* (New York: Riverhead Books, 2019).

12. Darryl Chamberlain Jr, "How One Instructor Can Teach a Large-Scale, Mastery-Based College Algebra Course Online," *PRIMUS*, 2023, 1–22.

13. Ibid., 877.

14. Ibid., 885.

15. Swenson and Visgatis, "Providing Feedback in Moodle Question Bank Items."

16. Chamberlain Jr, "How One Instructor Can Teach a Large-Scale, Mastery-Based College Algebra Course Online."

17. Abderrahim Mimouni, "Using Mobile Gamified Quizzing for Active Learning: The Effect of Reflective Class Feedback on Undergraduates' Achievement," *Education and Information Technologies*, no. Journal Article (2022), https://doi.org/10.1007/s10639-022-11097-2.

18. Mimouni, "Using Mobile Gamified Quizzing for Active Learning"; Baidowi Baidowi, Defi Kamilia, and Ilhami Sukmaningsih, "The Effectiveness of Online Learning Using Quizizz toward Students' Mathematics Concept Mastery," in *AIP Conference Proceedings*, vol. 2619 (The 1st International Conference on Science Education and Sciences, AIP Publishing, 2023), 1–5, https://doi.org/10.1063/5.0122828.

19. Abderrahim Mimouni, "Using Mobile Gamified Quizzing for Active Learning: The Effect of Reflective Class Feedback on Undergraduates' Achievement," *Education and Information Technologies*, no. Journal Article (2022), https://doi.org/10.1007/s10639-022-11097-2 .

20. Mimouni, "Using Mobile Gamified Quizzing for Active Learning."

21. Ibid.

22. Ibid.

23. Ibid.

24. Ibid.

25. Ibid.

26. Mark Lubrick and Bill Wellington, "Formative Learning Assessment with Online Quizzing: Comparing Target Performance Grade and Best Performance Grade Approaches," *Journal of Learning and Teaching in Digital Age* 7, no. 2 (2022): 297–306, https://doi.org/10.53850/joltida.1036295.

27. Chamberlain Jr, "How One Instructor Can Teach a Large-Scale, Mastery-Based College Algebra Course Online."

28. Carlos Rojas and Gina M. Quan, "Mastery Grading in a Software Engineering Course," in *2023 ASEE Annual Conference & Exposition* (Baltimore Convention Center, MD, 2023).

29. Chamberlain Jr, "How One Instructor Can Teach a Large-Scale, Mastery-Based College Algebra Course Online."

30. Ibid., 885.

31. Carlos Perez and Dina Verdin, "Mastery Learning in Undergraduate Engineering Courses: A Systematic Review," in *2022 ASEE Annual Conference & Exposition*, 2022.

32. Chamberlain Jr, "How One Instructor Can Teach a Large-Scale, Mastery-Based College Algebra Course Online."

Chapter Seven

Test Banks

Professor Smith, overwhelmed by the complexity of teaching 100 students in her introductory biology course, found that assessments needed to be more consistent. This caused student frustration. Determined to improve, she developed a structured test bank. Each question was carefully categorized by topic, Bloom's Taxonomy level, and difficulty. Using her LMS, she created randomized quizzes mirroring her learning objectives. Her efforts paid off: students reported feeling better prepared for exams, and Smith saved hours previously spent on assessment design.

Test banks are a powerful tool in the world of mastery quizzing. Test banks are collections of quiz questions organized based on learning objectives and categories. They offer various question types and difficulty levels, aligning with Bloom's Taxonomy. You can curate these questions and later use them in tailored quizzes. Question banks are a valuable resource for educators. They help educators give students extra practice by enabling them to generate random quizzes. Retaking quizzes enables students to improve their performance and demonstrate their ability to succeed on exams.[1] Let's explore creating and using test banks effectively to enhance learning.

Objectives

- Explain the role of test banks in enhancing learning and preparing students for assessments.

- Identify effective methods for creating and maintaining test banks.

- Evaluate the benefits of organizing test banks based on Bloom's Taxonomy and difficulty levels.

Maximizing the Benefits

Test banks provide many benefits for both students and instructors.

Test banks play a vital role in preparing students for exams, such as those preparing for medical assessments using the American Board of Surgery's training examination.[2] Colleges often invest in extensive test banks, containing over a thousand questions, to boost student success.[3] Research indicates that for every additional 100 questions a learner takes beyond 1,000 in a test bank, there's a 2-3% increase in performance.[4] Having a robust test bank can significantly enhance learning outcomes.

Storing questions in an LMS test bank helps maintain and share questions.[5] Updating questions in a test bank reduces the subsequent workload if instructors keep them current in a test bank. Updating test banks means correcting poorly performing questions and layering in helpful feedback. Test item analysis is a way to check how well quiz questions work. It looks at how hard each question is, how well it separates students who know the material from those who don't, and how good the wrong answers (distractors) are at testing understanding. Good questions are neither too easy nor hard and help tell the difference between high and low performers. This process allows teachers to improve quizzes by fixing weak questions and ensuring the test measures what it should. Quizzes drawn from a test bank will then use the most current version.

Instructors can easily share test banks among themselves.[6] Question and test interoperability (QTI) allows for sharing questions between platforms. This helps standardize the curriculum, reduce the burden on one instructor, and increase the size of the test banks, which can help mitigate cheating. One instructor told me some of his students retained the questions he recycled and passed them on to friends in subsequent classes. The instructor can use this to his advantage by utilizing the knowledge of the questions' results as an extensive student study guide and steadily increasing the size of his test banks to cover his full curriculum.

Test Bank Creation

Several effective methods exist for creating test bank questions. This section explores different approaches, including writing questions from scratch, using textbooks and open education resources, employing artificial intelligence, and having students generate questions.

Writing Questions From Scratch

Adding questions to a test bank can be time-consuming. Developing questions from scratch can take the most time but provides the most control.

The best place to start when creating questions is with your learning objectives. Learning objectives state what you want a student to know or be able to do. A well-written learning objective can serve as the stem of your question.

In the question design section of this book (chapter 5), I provide more details on how to write questions that will assess a student's knowledge level.

When starting, write enough questions to create a single quiz. You can then build upon this each time you teach the course. Aim to build a test bank robust enough to randomly draw questions for future quizzes and exams.

Using Vendor Textbook Resources

At a small liberal arts college, the sociology department adopted a new textbook with a test bank. Faculty members initially had concerns about its relevance to their courses. Instead of working individually, the instructors took a collaborative approach, reviewing and refining the test bank. They customized the questions to fit their courses, tagged them by learning objectives, and shared the improved version across all course sections. This collaborative effort standardized assessments, ensuring the questions were meaningful for students, and significantly reduced the workload for everyone involved.

Instructors often adopt traditional textbooks and use associated resources like presentations and question banks to support their courses. While these resources can save time, the instructor's role in reviewing and adapting them is crucial to ensuring alignment with course goals.

If you decide to use a publisher test bank, remember it is more than a ready-made solution. Although the questions are organized by book chapter and easy to upload into an LMS, it is up to you to determine their relevance and make necessary adjustments. By reviewing, adapting, or even relocating questions to your customized test bank, you gain complete control over the assessment process—ensuring it reflects your course's specific needs and objectives.

Using a publisher test bank provides a quick foundation to build randomized quizzes and exams. However, taking the extra time to tailor these questions can make assessments more effective, ultimately enhancing student learning.

Using Open Textbooks and Open Educational Resources

In his economics course, Professor Green frequently received complaints from students about the cost of textbooks. To address this, he switched to open educational resources (OER) and built a test bank based on them. He also wrote additional questions to ensure they aligned with his course goals. The result? His students saved money and praised the quizzes for being highly relevant to the class material.

OER and open test banks are other sources for quiz questions. Self-developed or in-house test banks significantly benefit students because they remove the cost burden from students.[7] Students rated self-developed test banks positively in terms of effectiveness.[8]

Another benefit of OER is that you can adapt the materials to better align with your learning objectives.

Using Generative AI

Dr. Kim juggled a packed schedule while teaching an advanced computer science course. She needed a way to expand her test bank without spending weeks writing questions. Turning to ChatGPT, she inputted OER and generated various well-structured questions. After tweaking them to meet her course's learning objectives, she had a robust test bank ready to use. Her students appreciated the challenge and variety, while she appreciated the time saved.

Open textbooks, OER, and generative AI are a match made in heaven. You can create test banks using tools like ChatGPT and NotebookLM.

Artificial intelligence, particularly tools like ChatGPT, has emerged as a powerful aid for instructors in improving assessments. ChatGPT can assist in crafting all types of questions and developing rubrics.[9]

You can input content from OER into ChatGPT and have it generate various questions. I recommend doing this one section at a time rather than uploading an entire open textbook.

Apply Bloom's Taxonomy to refine your questions to target different cognitive levels. Here are examples of ChatGPT prompts you can use:

Remembering (Knowledge).

Prompt: Generate multiple-choice questions focusing on recall of factual information from the provided chapter. Ensure questions ask about specific details, dates, names, or definitions mentioned in the text.

Understanding (Comprehension).

Prompt: Generate multiple-choice questions assessing understanding of the chapter's main ideas, themes, and relationships. Ensure questions require comprehension of the text's meaning and implications rather than merely factual recall.

Applying.

Prompt: Generate multiple-choice questions requiring the application of concepts, principles, or procedures discussed in the chapter. Ensure questions present scenarios or problems where learners must use the knowledge gained to solve a new situation.

Analyzing.

Prompt: Generate multiple-choice questions focusing on analyzing the chapter's content. Ensure questions ask about relationships between ideas, identification of patterns or trends, or evaluation of different perspectives presented in the text.

Evaluating.

Prompt: Generate multiple-choice questions requiring learners to evaluate the validity, credibility, or effectiveness of arguments, claims, or solutions proposed in the chapter. Ensure questions prompt critical thinking and the application of criteria to make judgments.

Creating (Synthesis).

Prompt: Generate multiple-choice questions that challenge learners to generate new ideas, solutions, or interpretations based on the chapter's content. Ensure that the questions encourage creativity, innovation, and the synthesis of multiple concepts or perspectives.

You can change the question type to fit your needs.

This method is a rapid way to build a robust test bank. You must vet each question and move it into the appropriate test bank. (See appendix C for more examples).

Having Students Generate Questions

In her history course, Professor Jones noticed her students were disengaged during review sessions. She shook things up by having students create test questions based on class discussions. After peer review, she added the best questions to her course's test bank. The students loved seeing their work used in class, and their exam scores reflected their newfound engagement and deeper understanding.

Using your students to generate questions can quickly expand your test banks if you have multiple class sections. This is an underused strategy in higher education.[10] This approach has several benefits:

- **Engagement and difficulty**. Students often create more challenging questions, which can lead to higher engagement. Including their questions in a test bank motivates them further.

- **Understanding student interests**. When students formulate questions, they focus on topics that intrigue them, providing insights into their interests.

- **Assessing knowledge gaps**. The nature of the questions students create can reveal their understanding of the subject and areas where they may need more guidance.

- **Academic benefits**. Research shows that students who generate questions improve their questioning skills and perform better academically. Activities like creating, exchanging, and evaluating questions among peers can lead to enhanced exam performance, increased confidence, better critical thinking, and refined cognitive strategies.

- **Diverse perspectives**. Working in groups, students bring different viewpoints to question creation, offering a variety of perspectives and enhancing the learning experience.

Using student-generated questions for clickers, polling, quizzes, etc., helps to focus attention.[11]

Students need guidance on crafting practical questions for successful implementation.[12] They should understand the principles of good question writing and be familiar with different levels of Bloom's Taxonomy. Mastery of the course content is essential, especially for creating higher-level questions.

- **Sample questions and peer review**. Students can practice creating sample questions at different Bloom's Taxonomy levels and reviewing their peers' questions for clarity and level appropriateness.

- **Group exercises**. In groups, students can select topics and develop a set of questions, including several at higher cognitive levels. These sessions can be timed and collaborative, and instructors can review and add the resulting questions to the test bank.

- **Integration into quizzes and discussions**. The generated questions can be used in quizzes and classroom discussions, practically applying their work and reinforcing their learning.

By adopting these methods, instructors can build a comprehensive and engaging test bank while actively involving students in learning. This approach enhances the quality of the assessments and contributes significantly to the student's overall educational experience.

Here is one specific exercise that is fun and quick to implement. I learned it at a conference from Sivasailam (Thiagi) Thiagiarajan. It is called "21." In short, give each student an index card and have them write a question on it. Once the students are done, have them stand up, find a partner, and exchange cards. Students must then agree to a score for each card by splitting 7. They are scoring based on the quality of the question. The appropriate division would be 0 and 7, 1 and 6, 2 and 5, and 3 and 4. Once the first scoring round is done, they find a new partner, exchange cards, and score the cards. After a total of three rounds, the scores on the cards are tallied. The highest possible number is 21. The instructor now asks the class for anyone holding a card with 21 and reads the card to the class. Discuss the question as necessary and collect it for possible use in the test bank. Next, move to 20, then 19, etc. Review, vet, and modify the questions for addition to the test bank.

Adding and Importing Questions

A couple of strategies exist for adding new questions to your test banks. You could add one question at a time by typing in the questions and answers or copying and pasting them. This is time-consuming and only useful for adding one or two questions at a time.

Tools like spreadsheets can streamline the process by organizing questions into different parts, making it easier to format for your learning management system.[13] I prefer to batch my work to increase efficiency. By batching your work, you can save a significant amount of time. To do this, you can build a document of all the questions you want to add. Tools like Respondus and the Canvas Exam Converter [https://www.nyit.edu/its/canvas_exam_converter] can then convert these questions into a file you can upload into a learning management system.

Each tool requires a specific format for building questions. Fortunately, the format is easy to learn, and you can incorporate it into your AI prompts. Batching your questions will save you a lot of time.

Building a Comprehensive test bank

Test banks are repositories from which you will draw questions. You should take time to make your test banks as specific as possible to gain the maximum benefit when you create quizzes and exams. This means identifying test banks based on topic or learning objective, Bloom's Taxonomy, and knowledge level. This ensures variety and depth in your quizzes.

Dividing questions into individual test banks separates their maintenance from the actual assessment building.[14] When a question is updated in the test bank, it is correct for subsequent quizzes.

Dividing questions into test banks by topic and difficulty allows instructors the flexibility to create quizzes in multiple configurations.[15] Instructors can develop multiple sets of quiz questions that align with the topic and scaffold using Bloom's Taxonomy from basic to complex knowledge levels. For example, creating quizzes for a specific difficulty or Bloom's Taxonomy level means controlling for deadlines, availability dates, and the points per question.

Topic/learning objective. The first place to begin when organizing questions is learning objectives and topics.[16] I recommend creating a master spreadsheet of your course's learning objectives. Number your learning objectives to quickly reference them as you make test banks. Also, indicate when you are using the learning objective in your course, e.g., week 2 or module 4. This will help you know when to include a specific test bank in your quiz development.

Bloom's Taxonomy level. The next meaningful delineator is to align questions with Bloom's Taxonomy stages, such as remembering, understanding, applying, analyzing, evaluating, and creating.[17] Consider varying the types of questions in your test banks. Include entry-level questions focusing on remembering and basic understanding and higher-order questions challenging students to demonstrate comprehension, analysis, and synthesis. This diversity will enrich your quizzes and offer a broader assessment of students' knowledge.

Difficulty level. When developing questions, arrange them in a test bank by topic and difficulty level.[18]

When adding questions to a test bank, it is essential to include feedback linking to LMS-based content and objectives.[19]

To create a test bank, you can focus on a specific learning objective or encompass an entire chapter, depending on your needs. Specify the sources of questions as you build your bank. You can choose the number of questions to draw from each objective or chapter, allowing flexibility in quiz creation.

Question Naming Convention

Here's a suggested naming convention for your test banks that considers the topic, Bloom's Taxonomy level, and level of difficulty while keeping it short and concise:[20]

1. **Topic identifier.** Use a short abbreviation or keyword to represent the topic of the test bank. For example:

- Math: MTH

- Science: SCI

- Literature: LIT

- Learning Objective 1: LO1

2. **Bloom's Taxonomy level**. Assign a number or letter to represent the Bloom's Taxonomy level of the questions. For instance:

- Remembering (Knowledge): R

- Understanding (Comprehension): U

- Applying: A

- Analyzing: AN

- Evaluating: E

- Creating: C

3. **Difficulty level**. Use a numerical scale to indicate the difficulty level of the questions. For example:

- Easy: 1

- Moderate: 2

- Difficult: 3

Putting it all together, your test bank names could look like this:

- MTH-R1: Math, Remembering (Knowledge) level, Easy

- SCI-A2: Science, Applying level, Moderate

- LIT-AN3: Literature, Analyzing level, Difficult

- LO43-U2: Learning objective #43, Understanding level, Moderate

This naming convention quickly identifies each test bank's content, cognitive level, and difficulty while keeping the names short and intuitive.

Tailoring Questions to Your Needs

The time required to prepare assessments decreases as your test bank grows.[21] You can quickly assemble quizzes in your LMS. An extensive test bank offers variety and reduces the effort needed to create multiple quiz versions, essential for allowing students to retake exams.[22]

The flexibility of test banks allows instructors to mimic summative exams closely.[23] This alignment helps students perform better on the actual assessments.

Conclusion

Test banks are a powerful resource for educators, enabling them to provide students with effective practice and enhance learning outcomes. Building and maintaining a comprehensive test bank is an investment that pays off in improved student performance and streamlined assessment preparation.

Quick Quiz

Wrap up this chapter about test banks by taking a quick quiz.

7.1. What is the primary purpose of a test bank?

a) To store academic textbooks.

b) To collect and organize quiz questions for educational assessments.

c) To replace traditional exams with quizzes.

d) To track student attendance.

7.2. How can instructors use Bloom's Taxonomy in test banks?

a) To classify students by their grades.

b) To create questions tailored to different cognitive levels.

c) To reduce the number of questions in a test bank.

d) To calculate the average difficulty of questions.

7.3. What is a key benefit of using generative AI in test bank creation?

a) It eliminates the need for student evaluations.

b) It provides instant and automated grading for exams.

c) It helps generate a variety of questions quickly and efficiently.

d) It replaces the role of the instructor entirely.

7.4. Which strategy helps reduce the workload when updating test banks?

a) Randomly removing outdated questions.

b) Sharing test banks among instructors.

c) Avoiding feedback on quiz questions.

d) Using a single type of question throughout.

7.5. Why is organizing test banks by difficulty levels important?

a) To make assessments easier for all students.

b) To allow for flexibility in creating quizzes that scaffold from basic to complex knowledge.

c) To eliminate the need for Bloom's Taxonomy.

d) To ensure all questions have the same level of challenge.

1. Tamara Swenson and Brad Visgatis, "Providing Feedback in Moodle Question Bank Items," *Osaka Jogakuin University*, 2022, 203–24; David Ray Velez, Stefan Walter Johnson, and Robert Peter Sticca, "How to Prepare for the American Board of Surgery In-Training Examination (ABSITE): A Systematic Review," *Journal of Surgical Education* 79, no. 1 (2022): 216–28, https://doi.org/10.1016/j.jsurg.2021.08.004.

2. Velez, Johnson, and Sticca, "How to Prepare for the American Board of Surgery In-Training Examination (ABSITE)."

3. Ibid., 226.

4. Ibid., 226.

5. Joshua K. Strakos et al., "A Learning Management System-Based Approach to Assess Learning Outcomes in Operations Management Courses," *The International Journal of Management Education* 21, no. 2 (2023): 1–9, https://doi.org/10.1016/j.ijme.2023.100802.

6. Ibid., 7.

7. Ibid., 7.

8. Ibid., 7.

9. Shellon Samuels-White, "Level Up Higher Education Assessments with ChatGPT," *Faculty Focus | Higher Ed Teaching & Learning* (blog), May 3, 2023, https://www.facultyfocus.com/articles/educational-assessment/level-up-higher-education-assessments-with-chatgpt/.

10. Ester Aflalo, "Students Generating Questions as a Way of Learning," *Active Learning in Higher Education* 22, no. 1 (2021): 63–75, https://doi.org/10.1177/1469787418769120.

11. Jeffrey S. Nevid and Casey E. Armata, "Paying Attention in Class: Using In-Class Quizzes to Incentivize Student Attention," *Teaching of Psychology*, 2023, 1–6, https://doi.org/10.1177/00986283231185136.

12. Aflalo, "Students Generating Questions as a Way of Learning."

13. Swenson and Visgatis, "Providing Feedback in Moodle Question Bank Items."

14. Strakos et al., "A Learning Management System-Based Approach to Assess Learning Outcomes in Operations Management Courses."

15. Ibid., 7.

16. Swenson and Visgatis, "Providing Feedback in Moodle Question Bank Items."

17. Strakos et al., "A Learning Management System-Based Approach to Assess Learning Outcomes in Operations Management Courses."

18. Ibid., 7.

19. Ibid., 6.

20. Ibid., 4.

21. Carlos Rojas and Gina M. Quan, "Mastery Grading in a Software Engineering Course," in *2023 ASEE Annual Conference & Exposition* (Baltimore Convention Center, MD, 2023).

22. Sydney L. Noell et al., "A Bridge to Specifications Grading in Second Semester General Chemistry," *Journal of Chemical Education* 100, no. 6 (2023): 2159–65, https://doi.org/10.1021/acs.jchemed.2c00731.

23. Hillary Parcell et al., "Evaluating the Effect of Pre-Exam Adaptive Quizzing on Nursing Student Exam Scores," *Nursing Education Perspectives* 43, no. 6 (December 2022): 100–102, https://doi.org/10.1097/01.NEP.0000000000000988.

Chapter Eight

Quiz Design

Quizzes are often seen as simple checkpoints for assessing student knowledge, but they are much more than that. When thoughtfully designed, quizzes can transform from mere evaluation tools into powerful instruments for promoting active, ongoing learning. In this chapter, we'll explore the different types of quizzes, their role in education, and how to craft them to foster deeper understanding and mastery of concepts.

Quizzes, especially in support of mastery learning, provide opportunities for students to practice, fail, and try again, effectively lowering anxiety while improving confidence. Leveraging the **backward testing effect** and **forward testing effect**, quizzes can significantly boost memory and readiness for future learning.

This chapter aims to guide educators in designing quizzes that challenge students while remaining accessible, allowing them to focus on learning rather than just the grade. We'll also cover best practices, including quiz frequency, design considerations, and how naming conventions can impact student perception. Through these insights, you will be equipped to create quizzes supporting a classroom culture of learning and mastery.

Objectives

- Identify and differentiate between formative and summative assessments, including their roles and benefits in education.

- Explain the principles of effective quiz design, including transparency, feedback, and alignment with learning objectives.

- Evaluate the impact of mastery quizzing on student engagement, anxiety reduction, and long-term retention.

Understanding Quiz Types

Assessments in education fall into two main categories: formative and summative.[1] While summative assessments evaluate the overall learning at the end of an instructional period, formative assessments are designed to build and refine knowledge throughout the learning journey. Formative assessments, such as quizzes, are often misunderstood as mere tools for evaluation, yet their true power lies in enhancing learning through targeted feedback and practice. By providing timely insights, these assessments help students adjust their learning strategies, ultimately improving retention and reducing anxiety.

Mastery quizzing, which I classify primarily under the formative assessment category, is particularly effective for fostering deep learning.

Formative Quizzes

Formative quizzing enhances long-term retention through the backward testing effect and primes the brain for new material, known as the forward testing effect.[2] These effects help students retain information for a more extended period. Additional benefits include:

- **Improving learning**. Formative quizzes help students understand where they stand, what they must work on, and how to improve.[3]

- **Reducing anxiety**. Regular practice tests have been shown to lower test anxiety, especially when they include a mix of question types.[4]

- **Enhancing knowledge retention**. Because these quizzes are given often, they help students remember information better.[5]

- **Boosting preparedness**. Students will be more engaged in classes, take better notes, and perform better on exams.

When conducting formative assessment learning, one can employ various methods tailored to different aspects of comprehension and engagement.[6] Quizzes stand out as a central focus, offering a robust means of evaluating understanding and retention. Quizzes serve as checkpoints throughout the learning process, providing valuable feedback on individual progress.

In addition to quizzes, both in-person and virtual discussions serve as dynamic platforms for gaining insights and fostering deeper understanding. These interactive sessions encourage active participation and facilitate collaborative learning experiences. Furthermore, **one-minute papers** (essay questions) offer a concise yet effective way to measure immediate comprehension.

We also leverage electronic tools to enhance engagement and interactivity. Platforms like Kahoot or Quizlet inject an element of gamification into the learning process, making it more enjoyable and accessible. Similarly, polls and surveys, whether conducted online or in class, provide rapid insights into student comprehension and can inform instructional adjustments in real-time.

Creative assessment methods cater to diverse learning preferences. Techniques such as "Muddiest Point," "Jigsaw," or summary writing offer alternative approaches to evaluate understanding and promote critical thinking skills. We can cultivate a dynamic learning environment supporting holistic growth and comprehension by incorporating these multifaceted assessment strategies.

Formative assessments are a dynamic part of the learning process. They help students identify areas for improvement and reduce anxiety through regular practice. Although there are different formative assessment methods, our focus is on quizzing.

Summative Exams

Summative exams are crucial in the educational process. They offer a comprehensive measure of student learning and instructional effectiveness. They should be used in conjunction with regular formative assessments to ensure continuous learning and understanding for the best educational outcomes.

Summative exams are comprehensive tests designed to evaluate students' understanding of complex concepts and high-order skills. Instructors typically administer summative assessments at the end of a course or at significant milestones, such as midterm exams.[7]

Summative assessments offer multifaceted advantages in education. They provide a standardized basis for comparing student performance across different course sections while catalyzing long-term improvements in teaching methodologies and course content.[8] These assessments not only evaluate student learning comprehensively but also serve as a valuable tool for measuring the quality of instruction. Summative assessments are pivotal in fostering continuous improvement within the educational landscape by offering insights into student progress and instructional effectiveness.

As educators, you play a crucial role in designing these exams. You can combine fundamental tasks or objectives, typically learned through competency-based instruction, into more complex questions. You can build exams from the questions you used for your formative quizzes effectively stacking learning objectives to create a comprehensive exam covering the previous instructional phase.

Common examples of summative assessments include midterm and final exams, which cover material taught earlier in the course, but they may take other forms, including:[9]

- Oral Presentations

- Research Papers

- Projects (Group or Individual)

- Portfolios

- Lab Reports

- Development of Multimedia Projects

- Creation of Concept Maps

Key traits of a summative include:[10]

- **Timing**. These assessments typically occur at the end of a course or at key intervals like midterms.

- **Focus**. They concentrate on how well students have absorbed and retained the taught material.

- **Scope**. Summative exams usually cover a broad instruction unit, unlike quizzes which focus on smaller sections.

- **Nature of results**. These exams' results can be qualitative and quantitative, offering detailed insights into student learning.

Design Considerations

Effective quiz development requires a balance of well-considered question design, test format, frequency of administration, spacing of questions, appropriate grading methods, thoughtful delivery strategies, and feedback mechanisms.[11] By understanding and applying these principles, educators can create quizzes that assess student knowledge, stimulate learning and engagement, and optimize learning outcomes.

Assessment Distribution

A sociology professor, Dr. Simmons scheduled quizzes only before midterms and finals. She noticed her students often crammed before these quizzes, leaving gaps in their understanding. This approach resulted in inconsistent performance, with some students excelling while others struggled to keep up.

Determined to improve, Dr. Simmons revised her syllabus to include short weekly quizzes aligned with the week's learning objectives. Each quiz focused on key concepts covered in lectures and readings, providing students with regular checkpoints for understanding.

Midway through the semester, she saw a shift. "The weekly quizzes help me stay on track," one student said. "I don't feel as overwhelmed by the material anymore." By the end of the term, class discussions were livelier, and students performed better on cumulative exams. Dr. Simmons realized that evenly spaced assessments kept her students engaged and gave them continuous opportunities to demonstrate and deepen their understanding.

Distributing assessments evenly throughout the weeks and aligning with learning objectives promotes a balanced approach to gauging progress.[12] This approach ensures learners are consistently engaged and have ample opportunity to demonstrate their understanding.

Transparent Assignment Design

Dr. Patel's first-year psychology students were often confused about her quizzes. Some thought they were meant to be major exams, while others didn't understand how the quizzes aligned with course goals. Frustrated, she redesigned her quizzes with clear instructions, outlined their purpose in the syllabus, and included a sample question to show the expected level of detail.

Her students' performance improved by the second quiz, and they asked fewer clarification questions. One student remarked, "It's easier to prepare now that I know exactly what the quiz is testing." Dr. Patel realized how transparency transformed what once felt like a "gotcha" into a meaningful learning opportunity.

Transparency in assignment design is crucial. Clearly outlining assessments' purpose, requirements, and evaluation criteria fosters understanding and mitigates confusion.[13] Learners who know what instructors expect of them can focus their efforts more effectively and feel confident in their approach.

Comprehensive Feedback

In her biology course, Dr. Alvarez realized students weren't learning from their mistakes on quizzes. They would skim over their grades and move on. To address this, she started providing detailed feedback for each question, explaining why the correct answers were right and offering improvement tips.

One student emailed, writing, "The feedback on my quiz helped me understand photosynthesis better than the textbook did!" Over time, Dr. Alvarez noticed that students who engaged with the feedback made fewer repeated errors, turning quizzes into a springboard for deeper understanding.

Providing clear and detailed feedback is paramount. Feedback should highlight areas for improvement and offer actionable insights to facilitate learning from mistakes.[14] This clarity empowers learners to address weaknesses effectively and reinforces their understanding of the material. Timely feedback is essential for ongoing improvement. Swift responses enable learners to promptly adjust their learning strategies and address any misconceptions or gaps in understanding. This iterative process fosters continuous growth and development. Ensuring feedback is comprehensible and constructive enhances its effectiveness.[15] Feedback should be easily understandable and offer practical guidance for improvement. Learners can more readily apply feedback to improve their learning journey by prioritizing accessibility and relevance.

Elaboration Theory

Professor Ramirez taught a challenging chemistry course and noticed many students dropped out early, overwhelmed by the material's difficulty. Determined to help, she redesigned her quizzes to follow a structured progression. Each module began with a basic-level quiz covering foundational concepts, followed by intermediate quizzes applying these concepts and advanced quizzes requiring critical thinking and synthesis.

One student, Alex, who had struggled in previous science courses, found the new system transformative. "The first quiz was easy, which gave me the confidence to keep going," Alex said. "By the time I got to the harder quizzes, I felt ready because I had already built a solid base."

By the end of the semester, Professor Ramirez saw significant improvement in student engagement and performance. Her students no longer viewed chemistry as an insurmountable subject but a challenge they could tackle step by step. The progressive quiz structure kept them engaged and supported their understanding at every level.

Educational content should progress from simple to complex to facilitate learning.[16] This is known as the **Elaboration Theory**. It is an effective tactic for structuring quizzes in levels. For instance, students start with easier quizzes and, upon mastering them, move on to intermediate and advanced levels. This progressive difficulty maintains engagement and ensures a thorough understanding of the material.

Focus repeated quizzes on key concepts students must remember rather than fleeting information.[17] Follow the **ESIL strategy**: E (information exists), S (performs under supervision), I (performs independently), and L (lifelong concepts).[18] Most of your quiz questions should focus on the I and L elements.

Desirable Difficulties

Dr. Moreno wanted her history students to move beyond rote memorization of dates and names. Inspired by the concept of **desirable difficulty**, she began crafting quizzes with challenging application questions. Instead of asking students to recall a battle date, she would ask them to analyze the political and cultural consequences of the event, requiring deeper reflection and critical thinking.

At first, students resisted. "These quizzes are so much harder than just memorizing facts!" one student complained. But as the semester progressed, they began to see the benefits. During a class discussion, Emily, a sophomore, remarked, "I hated these quizzes at first, but now I realize they make the final exam easier. I don't just memorize—I actually understand."

When final exam results came in, Dr. Moreno saw an average score increase of 15% compared to previous semesters. The challenging quizzes initially frustrated students and forced them to engage deeply with the material, making long-term recall easier and elevating their understanding of history.

Quizzes are of desirable difficulty.[19] This means they present a challenge to students, but the reward for overcoming them is positive. By engaging with quizzes, students can elevate their learning and progress to higher levels of understanding.

Difficult test questions require more effort, leading to stronger long-term memory.[20] This is the **retrieval effort theory**. The greater the difficulties of levels-of-processing (LOP), the better for memory.[21] Harder retrieval in practice leads to easier retrieval in exams.

A LOP approach, incorporating strategies such as connecting material to personal experiences, creating visual imagery, or explaining concepts in your own words, leads to improved performance on future exams.[22] Ways of deep processing include:

- Open-ended questions

- Encourage reflection

- Provide contextual information

- Promote active learning

- Concept mapping

- Varying questions.

Giving students more difficult quizzes, such as application questions, will yield better performance on subsequent exams with factual and application questions than preparing with only factual question quizzes.[23]

Repeatable Quizzes

Professor Lang used to assign lengthy quizzes in his business course, thinking the more questions, the better. However, students often complained about feeling drained and overwhelmed, and the quizzes could have done more to improve long-term retention.

Determined to make a change, Professor Lang reduced his quizzes to 20 questions, carefully curated from a large test bank aligned with learning objectives. He allowed students unlimited retakes, with questions randomized each time. "The goal isn't just to grade you," he told his students, "but to help you truly learn the material."

One student, Priya, took full advantage of the retakes. "I kept going until I felt confident," she said. "Each quiz attempt reinforced the material, and I didn't even need to cram for the midterm."

By the end of the semester, Professor Lang noticed a marked improvement in overall performance and engagement. His concise, repeatable quizzes reduced stress and became a powerful tool for helping students build long-term memory and mastery of the subject.

When it comes to quizzes, less is often more. It's essential to keep your quizzes concise. Deliver only a limited number of questions at a time.[24] Quizzes should only contain 15-25 questions. Students can make multiple attempts to improve their scores if the quizzes are drawn from large test banks. The primary purpose of such quizzes is to strengthen long-term memory. Encourage students to retake quizzes as much as possible.

Transfer-Appropriate Processing

Dr. Collins noticed her students struggled with the multiple-choice final exam despite doing well in short answer quizzes. Realizing the disconnect, she redesigned her quizzes to match the exam format.

"I want you to practice how you'll be tested," she explained. By the end of the semester, students reported feeling more prepared. "The quizzes felt like mini versions of the exam," one student said, "so there were no surprises."

Final scores improved significantly, showing that aligning quiz and exam formats helped students succeed by reinforcing their retrieval and recall skills under similar conditions.

Transfer-appropriate processing is effective when the assessment format used to acquire knowledge matches the one used for evaluating students.[25] For instance, if multiple-choice questions are employed for the exam, it is also advisable to use them for quizzes. The goal is to make the quizzing experience closely resemble the test conditions to achieve optimal results.[26] Individuals should employ tools that assess retrieval and recall skills to maximize students' success, mirroring the actual exam format.[27]

The Power of Naming

Professor Lee noticed her students grew anxious whenever she mentioned the word "test." To ease their nerves, she started calling her assessments "mastery quizzes."

Skeptical at first, students soon felt the difference. "It doesn't feel as intimidating," one student said. "It's like a chance to improve instead of being judged."

By the end of the semester, Professor Lee saw more confident participation and improved scores. A simple name change transformed the classroom culture, reducing anxiety and fostering a focus on learning.

One significant aspect of mastery quizzing is the terminology used. A study found students reacted more positively to the term "mastery quiz" compared to "test," "exam," or "final exam."[28] The way assignments are named can impact students' anxiety levels.

Creating a Quiz

When creating a test for your students, paying close attention to its structure is essential. These recommendations apply whether you are making an online or paper-based quiz.[29]

Quiz Identity

Provide clear identification. Ensure all necessary information to identify the test is on the first or cover page. This includes the course name and section number, quiz title, a place for the date, and a place for the student's name. Provide a clear title to the quiz if you are building an online quiz. The other identifying information will already be captured for online quizzes.

Give clear instructions. Include complete instructions, either written, oral, or visually presented. These instructions should specify what materials, texts, or tools students can use during the assessment and how much time they have for each part or the whole quiz or exam. It's helpful to provide a sample item with the correct response. Students should know whether to proceed individually through the assessment or wait for further instructions. Also, explain what to do when they finish it. Consistency in testing instructions across classes is essential for gathering reliable data.

Quiz Questions

Format test items. Arrange test items on the page so each stands out clearly. For example, true or false items should be single-spaced with two spaces between them. Multiple-choice items should have the stem separated from the alternatives, presented in a single column beneath the stem, and indented. A single question should not span multiple pages.

Consider machine scoring. For machine-scored paper-based tests, ensure items can be quickly processed. Special answer sheets may be necessary for specific test objectives, while stock answer sheets can often be used for specific items.

Use test banks. Ideally, you built extensive test banks to help with online quiz design. Pull one or two questions from each test bank based on the learning objective and difficulty level. You can also use question type to group questions.

General Quiz Considerations

Arrange items by difficulty. Arrange test items in ascending order of difficulty within groups. Students tend to feel more comfortable when they encounter easier items at the beginning of the test.

Ensure manageability. Design the test so most students can complete it within time. If too many students struggle to finish, the test's effectiveness is compromised, and student morale may suffer. However, it's also important not to rush students excessively. Allowing students to leave as they finish may distract those still working in a classroom environment.

Accessibility Considerations

Creating quizzes everyone can use is an integral part of teaching. Accessible quizzes aren't just about meeting legal requirements—they show students we care about their learning and want to remove barriers. By considering accessibility, we ensure every student has a fair chance to show what they know. With thoughtful design, we can create quizzes that empower all learners to succeed. You can find a handy checklist in appendix E that will assist you.

Use technology that works for everyone. Start by choosing a quiz platform that supports accessibility. This means the platform should work with tools like screen readers, magnifiers, and speech-to-text software. Students may need to navigate the quiz using a keyboard, mouse, or touch pad. And since many students use phones or tablets, ensure your quiz works well on any device.

Keep the content clear. Clear content is key. Use simple, easy-to-read fonts and make the text large enough (at least 12–14 points). Also, ensure enough contrast between the text and the background—black text on a white background usually works well. If your quiz includes images or diagrams, add descriptive text ("alt text") so students using screen readers understand what's shown.

Avoid making quizzes too rushed. If you need to set a time limit, be flexible and allow extra time for students who request it.

Design questions thoughtfully. Write questions in plain, simple language. Avoid using complicated words or long sentences that might confuse students. Keep the structure consistent so students know what to expect during the quiz. When students answer, give them meaningful feedback to help them understand what they got right or wrong and why.

Make the design inclusive. Visual design matters. For example, don't rely on color alone to explain things. If you ask students to "pick the red option," include a label or description. Strong color contrast is helpful for students who have trouble seeing. Avoid flashing or flickering images because they can cause seizures in students with epilepsy.

Offer different ways to participate. Not all students use a mouse. Make sure your quiz can be completed using a keyboard or touch screen. For open-ended questions, let students type or use voice-to-text tools. Checkboxes, dropdown menus, and other input types should be clearly labeled to work with screen readers.

Support sudio and video needs. If your quiz includes videos or audio, add captions or transcripts so students can read along. Let students adjust the volume or playback speed to match their needs.

Accommodate students' needs. Some students may need extra time to complete the quiz. Build in flexibility by offering extended or unlimited time for those who ask. Be ready to provide alternate formats, such as a printable version of the quiz, for students who need it.

Test and improve. The best way to know if your quiz is accessible is to test it with students who use different tools and approaches. Gather their feedback and use it to fix any problems they face.

Exam Blueprint

An exam blueprint is like a map that guides teachers in creating tests. It outlines what topics or skills you will test, how many questions there will be for each topic, and how much each part of the test counts toward the final grade. It's a plan that helps teachers ensure the test covers everything students need to know. Just as a blueprint for a house shows where each room will go, an exam blueprint helps teachers organize their tests to measure how well students understand the material. Exam blueprints enhance the process of creating quizzes by linking exam questions directly to student learning objectives.

You can create an exam blueprint for each exam or guide your exam development for the entire course.

Typically, an exam blueprint includes:

- **Content areas**. It outlines the topics or domains the exam will cover. These areas are often based on the learning objectives or standards for the subject.

- **Weighting or allocation.** It indicates the relative importance or weight assigned to each content area. This helps ensure the exam reflects the emphasis placed on different topics within the subject.

- **Format**. It describes the exam's questions or tasks, such as multiple-choice, short answer, essays, and practical demonstrations.

- **Cognitive level**. It specifies the cognitive levels or thinking skills the exam will assess as outlined in Bloom's Taxonomy.

- **Example items**. Sometimes, the blueprint may include sample questions or tasks to illustrate the items included in each content area.

This approach offers several benefits:[30]

- **Consistency**. It provides a more consistent experience for students.

- **Clear expectations**. Students understand precisely what they need to focus on.

- **Improved outcomes**. Linking questions to specific learning outcomes allows a more accurate measurement of student progress on each objective.

- **Increased fairness**. The approach ensures students receive consistent information and are well-prepared without surprises.

Exam blueprints, which outline all the objectives and topics that will be tested, are helpful but can also limit creativity.[31] When students know exactly what will be on the test, it may decrease their motivation to learn beyond the given material. These structured exams can also increase the risk of cheating since students can easily focus on only the material they know will appear on the exam. Additionally, the rigid nature of these exams may not allow for flexibility or creativity in testing students' complete understanding.

Overall, an exam blueprint guides educators and test developers to ensure the exam accurately assesses the desired learning outcomes and maintains fairness and validity. It helps ensure the exam adequately covers the material taught and aligns with instructional goals.

Exam Blueprint Development

Developing an exam blueprint involves several vital steps to ensure the assessment accurately reflects the intended learning outcomes and effectively measures student knowledge and skills. Here's a step-by-step guide to developing an exam blueprint:

1. **Define learning objectives or standards**. Define the objectives or standards the exam assesses. These objectives outline what students are expected to know and be able to do by the end of the course or instructional unit.

2. **Identify content areas**. Break down the learning objectives into specific content areas or topics. Consider the scope of the subject matter and the key concepts, principles, and skills students need to master.

3. **Determine weighting or allocation**. Assign relative weights to each content area based on its importance to the learning objectives. Consider factors such as instructional time spent on each topic, the significance of the content for future learning, and its relevance to real-world applications.

4. **Select assessment formats**. Decide on the types of questions or tasks included in the exam. Consider which assessment formats (e.g., multiple-choice, short answer, essays, performance tasks) best assess the desired learning outcomes and cognitive levels.

5. **Align with cognitive levels**. Align each content area with the appropriate cognitive level or thinking skill students are expected to demonstrate. Use Bloom's Taxonomy or similar frameworks to guide the alignment process, ensuring the exam assesses a range of cognitive abilities, from basic recall to higher-order thinking.

6. **Create example items**. Develop sample questions or tasks for each content area and assessment format. These examples serve as prototypes for the actual exam items and help clarify expectations for both educators and students.

7. **Review and refine**. Seek feedback from subject matter experts, colleagues, or instructional designers to review the exam blueprint. Ensure the content coverage, weighting, and cognitive alignment appropriately and accurately reflect the learning objectives.

8. **Finalize the blueprint**. Based on feedback, make any necessary revisions and finalize the exam blueprint. Document the blueprint in a clear and accessible format, such as a table or chart, that outlines the content areas, weighting, assessment formats, and cognitive levels.

9. **Use and adapt**. Implement the exam blueprint in the assessment development process, using it as a guide to create exam items and construct the exam. As you gain experience with assessment development, refine the blueprint based on insights from student performance and ongoing evaluation.

By following these steps, educators and instructional designers can develop a well-structured exam blueprint that guides the creation of assessments aligned with learning objectives and instructional goals.

Example: Science Test Blueprint with Learning Objectives Alignment (Also included in appendix F)

Exam Overview:

- Total Points: 100

- Duration: 90 minutes

Section 1: Biology (40 points)

- 10 Multiple-Choice Questions (2 points each)

  - Learning Objectives:

    - LO1: Describe the structure and function of cells.

    - LO2: Explain the process of photosynthesis.

    - LO3: Understand the basic principles of genetics.

- 5 Short Answer Questions (4 points each)

  - Learning Objectives:

    - LO4: Identify major human body systems and their functions.

    - LO5: Classify living organisms based on taxonomy principles.

Section 2: Chemistry (40 points)

- 5 Multiple-Choice Questions (3 points each)

  - Learning Objectives:

    - LO6: Define elements and compounds and differentiate between them.

    - LO7: Describe common chemical reactions and their applications.

- 5 Short Answer Questions (5 points each)

- Learning Objectives:

  - LO8: Explain the properties of acids and bases.

- LO9: Analyze periodic table trends and their significance.

Section 3: Physics (20 points)
  - 5 Multiple-Choice Questions (2 points each)

    - Learning Objectives:

      - LO10: Understand fundamental concepts of forces and motion.

      - LO11: Explain different forms of energy and their conversions.

  - 2 Essay Questions (5 points each)

    - Learning Objectives:

      - LO12: Apply principles of electricity and magnetism to everyday examples.

      - LO13: Describe the function and applications of simple machines.

Exam Grading:
  - Multiple-Choice: 45 points

  - Short Answer: 45 points

  - Essays: 10 points

  - Total: 100 points

In this blueprint, each exam section is directly aligned with specific learning objectives (LO1 to LO13). This alignment ensures the test comprehensively assesses students' understanding of key concepts and skills outlined in the curriculum. Teachers can use this blueprint to design the exam and ensure their teaching strategies effectively cover all the targeted learning objectives.

Implementation Strategies

To effectively implement exam blueprints, consider these strategies:[32]

- **Transparency**. Communicate with students about the purpose and process of the exam blueprints.

- **Feedback**. Obtain student feedback on how the exam blueprints impact their learning.

- **Combat cheating**. Use test banks and carefully select questions aligning with the learning objectives.

- **Align with Bloom's Taxonomy**. Ensure that questions correspond with learning objectives, considering different levels of knowledge, skills, and attitude (KSA).

Focusing on these strategies can help educators create a more effective and fair testing environment closely aligned with learning objectives.

Conclusion

Effective quiz design balances thoughtful question structure, clear instructions, and strategic assessment distribution. Using principles like mastery learning, transparent grading, and accessibility ensures quizzes support student growth rather than just measure performance. Spacing quizzes throughout a course and aligning them with learning objectives help reinforce knowledge and reduce anxiety.

Exam blueprints provide a structured approach to quiz creation, ensuring fairness and alignment with course goals. By mapping content areas, cognitive levels, and question types, educators can design assessments that accurately measure student understanding while promoting deeper learning and retention.

Quick Quiz

Test your knowledge with a quick quiz to end this chapter on quiz design.

8.1. Which of the following best defines formative assessments?

a) Evaluations conducted at the end of a course to assess overall learning.

b) Tools used primarily to grade students on their performance.

c) Assessments designed to provide feedback and enhance learning during the instructional process.

d) Exams focusing on a comprehensive understanding of high-order skills.

8.2. What is one benefit of the "backward testing effect?"

a) It enhances understanding of future learning materials.

b) It improves retention of previously studied material.

c) It increases students' focus during quizzes.

d) It simplifies complex concepts for exams.

8.3. Which principle is critical to effective quiz design?

a) Using only difficult questions to challenge students.

b) Providing timely and detailed feedback to learners.

c) Avoiding transparency to prevent over preparation.

d) Limiting the frequency of quizzes to maintain their impact.

8.4. What is the primary purpose of mastery quizzing?

a) To evaluate students' final knowledge of a topic.

b) To create a competitive learning environment.

c) To support ongoing learning through practice and feedback.

d) To reduce the importance of summative exams.

8.5. How can the naming of assessments influence student perceptions?

a) It reduces anxiety and makes assessments seem less intimidating.

b) It encourages competition among students.

c) It determines the difficulty level of the assessment.

d) It has no measurable impact on student performance.

---

1. Nese Sevim-Cirak and Omer Faruk Islim, "Paper versus Online Quizzes: Which Is More Effective?," *Active Learning in Higher Education*, 2022, 1–18, https://doi.org/10.1177/14697874221079737.

2. Chunliang Yang et al., "Frequent Quizzing Accelerates Classroom Learning," *In Their Own Words: What Scholars and Teachers Want You to Know about Why and How to Apply the Science of Learning in Your Academic Setting*, 2023, 190–99.

3. Mark Lubrick and Bill Wellington, "Formative Learning Assessment with Online Quizzing: Comparing Target Performance Grade and Best Performance Grade Approaches," *Journal of Learning and Teaching in Digital Age* 7, no. 2 (2022): 297–306, https://doi.org/10.53850/joltida.1036295.

4. Chunliang Yang et al., "Do Practice Tests (Quizzes) Reduce or Provoke Test Anxiety? A Meta-Analytic Review," *Educational Psychology Review* 35, no. 3 (2023): 1–26, https://doi.org/10.1007/s10648-023-09801-w.

5. Ibid., 87.

6. Dimple Martin, "Are Your Assessments Fair and Balanced?," *Faculty Focus | Higher Ed Teaching & Learning* (blog), September 20, 2023, https://www.facultyfocus.com/articles/educational-assessment/are-your-assessments-fair-and-balanced/.

7. Matthew Spencer, "Implementation of Competency-Based Learning in a Laboratory-Focused Analog Design Course," in *2022 ASEE Annual Conference & Exposition* (Minneapolis, MN, 2022), 17.

8. Martin, "Are Your Assessments Fair and Balanced?"; Lubrick and Wellington, "Formative Learning Assessment with Online Quizzing."

9. Martin, "Are Your Assessments Fair and Balanced?"

10. Ibid.

11. David Ray Velez, Stefan Walter Johnson, and Robert Peter Sticca, "How to Prepare for the American Board of Surgery In-Training Examination (ABSITE): A Systematic Review," *Journal of Surgical Education* 79, no. 1 (2022): 216–28, https://doi.org/10.1016/j.jsurg.2021.08.004.

12. Lubrick and Wellington, "Formative Learning Assessment with Online Quizzing."

13. Ibid., 298.

14. Ibid., 298.

15. Ibid., 298.

16. Monir M. Almotairy et al., "Comprehensive Licensure Review and Adaptive Quizzing Assignments for Enhancement of End-of-Programme Exit Examination Scores in Saudi Arabia: A Quasi-Experimental Study," *BMJ Open* 13, no. 7 (2023): 1–7, https://doi.org/10.1136/bmjopen-2023-074469.

17. Yang et al., "Frequent Quizzing Accelerates Classroom Learning."

18. Maria Andersen, "ESIL: A Learning Lens for the Digital Age," *Edge of Learning* (blog), December 6, 2018, https://edgeoflearning.com/esil-a-learning-lens-for-the-digital-age/.

19. Yang et al., "Do Practice Tests (Quizzes) Reduce or Provoke Test Anxiety? A Meta-Analytic Review."

20. Svitlana Mykytiuk et al., "Seamless Learning Model with Enhanced Web-Quizzing in the Higher Education Setting," *International Journal of Interactive Mobile Technologies* 16, no. 3 (2022): 4–19, https://doi.org/10.3991/IJIM.V16I03.27257.

21. Danney Rasco, "Throw Them in the Deep End? Quizzing With Factual Versus Application Items," in *In Their Own Words: What Scholars and Teachers Want You to Know about Why and How to Apply the Science of Learning in Your Academic Setting* (Society for the Teaching of Psychology, 2023), 499–504.

22. Ibid., 499.

23. Ibid., 501.

24. Robin Boyle-Laisure, "Didn't Cover That in Class? Low-Stakes Technique of Quizzing to the Rescue," *The Journal of the Legal Writing Institute* 27 (2023): 299–307.

25. Lukas K. Sotola and Marcus Crede, "Regarding Class Quizzes: A Meta-Analytic Synthesis of Studies on the Relationship between Frequent Low-Stakes Testing and Class Performance," *Educational Psychology Review* 33, no. 2 (2021): 407–26, https://doi.org/10.1007/s10648-020-09563-9; Rasco, "Throw Them in the Deep End? Quizzing With Factual Versus Application Items."

26. Mykytiuk et al., "Seamless Learning Model with Enhanced Web-Quizzing in the Higher Education Setting."

27. Velez, Johnson, and Sticca, "How to Prepare for the American Board of Surgery In-Training Examination (ABSITE)."

28. Nicolas Garzone, Tracey Howell, and Daniela Tirnovan, "Mastering Anxiety: The Effect of Mastery-Based Testing on Quantitative Literacy College Students' Anxiety Levels and Mindsets," *International Journal for Mathematics Teaching and Learning* 24, no. 1 (2023): 62–73.

29. *Guidebook for Air Force Instructors*, AFMAN 36-2236 (U.S. Air Force, 2003), https://www.angtec.ang.af.mil/Portals/10/Courses%20resources/afman36-2236.pdf?ver=2018-10-02-084122-173.

30. Pradeep Malreddy, "Exam Blueprints: A Student-Centric Approach to Assessment," *Faculty Focus | Higher Ed Teaching & Learning* (blog), October 9, 2023, https://www.facultyfocus.com/articles/educational-assessment/exam-blueprints-a-student-centric-approach-to-assessment/.

31. Ibid.

32. Ibid.

Chapter Nine

Quiz Delivery

Educators play a crucial role when it comes to giving tests. They decide when and where to administer tests, which can significantly impact students' performance. You have some decisions to make when deploying your quiz or exam. Will students take the quiz in class, or is it a take-home quiz?

Once you decide on the quiz format, the next step is to consider how to deliver it. Will it be online, paper and pencil, or interactive? Finally, is the quiz machine-graded or manually graded? These decisions empower you to choose the best method for your students.

Objectives

- Understand different quiz formats and delivery methods (e.g., in-class vs. take-home, online vs. paper-based).

- Evaluate the factors influencing effective quiz deployment (e.g., timing, environment, preparation).

- Differentiate between machine-graded and manually graded quizzes, and identify the advantages and disadvantages of each method.

General Considerations

As you are probably beginning to realize, there is much to consider when developing quizzes. Each element you take into consideration improves the learning opportunity for your students. Here are some general considerations to take into account when deploying your quiz:[1]

Timing matters. Professor Allen noticed a pattern during her morning and afternoon classes. Despite covering the same material, her morning students consistently scored higher on their quizzes than her afternoon students. After some experimentation, she started administering all quizzes in the morning, giving afternoon classes their quizzes online first thing on test days. The result? A noticeable improvement in performance and student confidence across the board.

Tests should ideally be scheduled in the morning when students are most alert. Afternoons, when fatigue sets in, may not be the best time for testing as students may not perform at their best.

Build confidence. Dr. Ramirez always began quiz days with a pep talk. "Remember, this is a learning tool, not a final judgment. You've got this!" She even added a light-hearted "fun fact" question at the end of each quiz, unrelated to the course, to ease students' tension. Her students reported feeling more at ease, and average scores improved.

Your approach as an educator matters. Create a supportive atmosphere that puts students at ease. Encourage them and show confidence in their abilities.

Provide clear directions. One semester, Professor Chen was swamped with questions mid-quiz, disrupting the flow for everyone. She revamped her quiz instructions, adding a step-by-step breakdown with examples. She also set aside five minutes before each quiz to answer procedural questions. The difference was immediate: fewer interruptions and more focused students.

Written directions should be part of the test, but it's also helpful to give oral instructions. Before starting the test, invite questions about procedures and clarify whether students can ask questions after the test begins. Any errors in the test should be identified and explained beforehand.

Time management. Professor Jacobs once underestimated how long a particularly tricky quiz would take. As the frustrated groans began to rise, she knew she'd miscalculated. She piloted the following quiz with her teaching assistant and adjusted the timing. Her students appreciated the fairness, and she made it a habit for all future quizzes.

Announce any time limits for tests and stick to them. Let students know if they can leave once they finish or if they need to stay until the end. Clear guidelines help students manage their time effectively.

Delivery Methods for Quizzes

You can deliver quizzes in several ways depending on your preferences and resources.[2] Students can respond to quiz questions in multiple ways, such as writing on paper, typing answers on a shared PowerPoint slide, or participating in digital or analog polling.[3] The response method should align with the learning environment, the quiz's format, and the learning objectives.

Online quizzes. Ms. Johnson was hesitant to shift her paper quizzes online, but after a colleague introduced her to an LMS, she tried it. She loved the ability to randomize questions and provide instant feedback. Her students appreciated the immediate grading, and she appreciated the saved time.

Use online platforms like LMSs, Quizlet, Kahoot!, or Quizizz to generate and administer quizzes efficiently. Automated quizzes offer several benefits, including quickly analyzing data for areas needing improvement, randomizing questions and shuffling the order in which answers appear to minimize cheating, and supporting multiple student attempts.[4] They also allow for flexibility in question design and can incorporate multimedia elements like images or videos. One key advantage of online quizzes is the instant feedback provided.[5] Students can immediately gauge their understanding of the material and identify areas needing more focus. Students often find online quizzes more engaging and enjoyable than traditional methods.[6] The interactive nature of these quizzes keeps students interested and motivated. Students report higher satisfaction levels when online quizzes are integrated into blended learning courses through LMSs.

Paper and pencil. Professor Scott ran into a technical glitch during a scheduled online quiz. Thinking quickly, he handed out blank sheets of paper and wrote questions on the board. The impromptu solution worked so well that he decided to mix in handwritten quizzes periodically to keep his students on their toes.

For many educators, the simplicity and accessibility of traditional paper-based quizzes make them a comfortable and viable option. They are easy to deploy and work when other options are not available. Paper-based quizzes can be prepared with multiple pages and questions or spontaneously, with students pulling out a blank piece of paper.

Research has shown students are more likely to attend classes when quizzes are involved, especially if these quizzes contribute to their final grades.[7] Regular attendance leads to better performance on quizzes. This creates a positive cycle where good quiz results encourage further attendance.

Interactive methods. In Dr. Nguyen's history class, quizzes were anything but ordinary. She used colored cards for polling quiz answers, creating an energetic and collaborative environment. Students loved the novelty, and class participation skyrocketed.

Use engaging and cost-effective interactive methods like analog polling to actively engage students. These methods can be as simple as raising hands, using colored cards, or something more advanced like Plickers. Ensure there are multiple ways to identify correct answers to accommodate accessibility needs.

Take-Home Quizzes vs. In-Class Quizzes

My experience with college quizzes has been primarily in the classroom, using paper and pencil. I took quizzes online only later in my academic career.

In-class quizzes. Instructors set aside time in class for students to complete a quiz. At the Air Force Academy Prep School, we took quizzes at the beginning of class. They were timed quizzes lasting 10-15 minutes. We received quizzes every other day. Some instructors administer quizzes toward the end of class and allow students to leave when they finish. Compared to take-home quizzes, in-class quizzes tend to yield higher learning gains.[8] In-class quizzes require immediate recall and application of knowledge, which can lead to better retention and understanding. One downside is they take away from class time. Here are some considerations specific to in-class quizzes:

- **Choose the right environment**.[9] Where you administer the test matters. An ideal room is quiet, well-lit, and well-ventilated, with a comfortable temperature. There should be enough space for students to work comfortably, especially if they need scratch paper for calculations. If students are uncomfortable or distracted, their scores may suffer, and the reliability of the test decreases.

- **Preparation is key**.[10] Prepare the examination room well in advance, ensuring all necessary materials are organized. Many instructors value having everything in place before students arrive. Stock up on extra test papers, answer sheets, and pencils. Provide students with clear, concise instructions at the outset promotes a smooth testing experience and enhances their performance.

Take-home quizzes. Some teachers opt for take-home quizzes, which students can complete outside class. These quizzes are often administered with an online quizzing system, via a document submitted online, or turned in on paper. Take-home or online quizzes are the options used with online classes. Take-home quizzes allow flexibility and convenience but may not always promote active learning.

Grading

Quizzes can be broadly categorized into two types based on grading methods: machine-graded and manually graded.[11]

Machine grading suits objective question types such as multiple-choice, multiple-selection, true or false, and matching questions. Machine-graded quizzes are generally easier to create and can efficiently evaluate student performance. The most significant benefit of machine-graded quizzes is they do not need a human to grade them. You can then create reusable quizzes, especially when using test banks. Students can practice repeatedly without impacting an instructor's time.

Manual grading is often necessary for subjective responses like short answers or essays and for paper-based quizzing. This grading method is challenging to scale and can be time-consuming.

A Scantron testing tool is an alternative way to grade paper-based, multiple-choice assessments. It uses paper answer sheets. Students fill in appropriate bubbles on paper answer sheets A scanning device reads and scores the responses.

Conclusion

Good quiz delivery improves the learning environment for educators and students. By planning things like timing, format, and grading, instructors can save time and make quizzes more useful.

Quiz delivery tips help educators spend less time on grading and answering questions while assisting students to feel more confident and ready to learn. Clear instructions and fair quizzes make a big difference.

When used well, quizzes become more than just tests—they help students grow and succeed.

Quick Quiz

Take a quick quiz to wrap up this chapter on quiz delivery.

9.1. Which of the following is a key factor to consider when deciding the timing of a quiz?

a) Availability of teaching assistants.

b) Students' alertness levels.

c) The length of the lecture.

d) The number of questions on the quiz.

9.2. What is one potential disadvantage of take-home quizzes compared to in-class quizzes?

a) They are less convenient for students.

b) They do not promote active learning as effectively.

c) They are more expensive to administer.

d) They are harder to grade manually.

9.3. Which quiz delivery method is most suitable for incorporating multimedia elements like images or videos?

a) Paper-based quizzes.

b) Online quizzes.

c) Interactive polling methods.

d) Oral quizzes.

9.4. What is the primary benefit of machine-graded quizzes?

a) They encourage critical thinking.

b) They reduce instructor grading time.

c) They are easier to design than manually graded quizzes.

d) They allow for subjective question types.

9.5. Which of the following practices can help ensure a supportive atmosphere during quiz administration?

a) Limiting students' ability to ask questions.

b) Scheduling quizzes at the end of the day.

c) Providing clear written and oral instructions.

d) Keeping the test environment slightly cold to maintain focus.

1. *Guidebook for Air Force Instructors*, AFMAN 36-2236 (U.S. Air Force, 2003), https://www.angtec.ang.af.mil/Portals/10/Courses%20resources/afman36-2236.pdf?ver=2018-10-02-084122-173.

2. Chunliang Yang et al., "Frequent Quizzing Accelerates Classroom Learning," *In Their Own Words: What Scholars and Teachers Want You to Know about Why and How to Apply the Science of Learning in Your Academic Setting*, 2023, 190–99.

3. Robin Boyle-Laisure, "Didn't Cover That in Class? Low-Stakes Technique of Quizzing to the Rescue," *The Journal of the Legal Writing Institute* 27 (2023): 299–307.

4. Tamara Swenson and Brad Visgatis, "Providing Feedback in Moodle Question Bank Items," *Osaka Jogakuin University*, 2022, 203–24.

5. Ingrid AE Spanjers et al., "The Promised Land of Blended Learning: Quizzes as a Moderator," *Educational Research Review* 15 (2015): 59–74, https://doi.org/10.1016/j.edurev.2015.05.001.

6. Vilogini Chandra Segaran and Harwati Hashim, "'More Online Quizzes, Please!' The Effectiveness of Online Quiz Tools in Enhancing the Learning of Grammar among ESL Learners," *International Journal of Academic Research in Business and Social Sciences* 12, no. 1 (January 29, 2022): 1756–70, https://doi.org/10.6007/IJARBSS/v12-i1/12064.

7. Lukas K. Sotola and Marcus Crede, "Regarding Class Quizzes: A Meta-Analytic Synthesis of Studies on the Relationship between Frequent Low-Stakes Testing and Class Performance," *Educational Psychology Review* 33, no. 2 (2021): 407–26, https://doi.org/10.1007/s10648-020-09563-9.

8. Yang et al., "Frequent Quizzing Accelerates Classroom Learning."

9. *Guidebook for Air Force Instructors*.

10. Ibid., 268.

11. Swenson and Visgatis, "Providing Feedback in Moodle Question Bank Items."

Chapter Ten

Mastery Quizzing Considerations

Imagine a classroom where students are fully engaged, eager to test their understanding, and excited to learn from their mistakes. Mastery quizzing creates a dynamic environment where quizzes are more than just grades; they are tools to unlock deeper learning.

For college educators, the challenge is balancing fostering academic excellence and reducing student stress. Mastery quizzing offers a solution by blending frequent, low-stakes quizzes with growth opportunities. This approach doesn't just measure what students know; it actively helps them learn, understand, and retain knowledge over time.

This chapter will explore considerations needed to make mastery quizzing successful. Whether you're designing quizzes to build confidence or crafting a grading system that motivates students, you'll find practical strategies and insights here to empower your teaching.

Objectives

- Describe the principles and benefits of mastery quizzing and how it fosters active engagement and deeper learning among students.

- Identify effective grading strategies (e.g., specifications grading, additive grading) supporting mastery learning while minimizing student stress.

- Analyze the impact of frequent, low-stakes quizzing on student motivation, performance, and retention.

Learners

Quizzes are more than assessment tools. They are learning tools. Students can better understand course material by actively engaging with the content; mastery quizzing can provide this necessary active engagement.

The more students engage with with the material through instruction, content, etc., the better they will perform academically.[1] Practice and experience taking exams helps students prepare for subsequent exams.[2] The better learners prepare for an exam, the better they will perform.[3]

While I advocate for instructors to develop mastery quizzes, encouraging students to create their own quizzes is an effective learning strategy that students can control.[4] Students can either work individually or in teams to build question sets for study. Various technological tools, such as Quizlet, are available to generate quizzes. Students can even use advanced tools like ChatGPT to craft questions.

Grading

In mastery quizzing, we must consider the crucial aspect of grading. Exams and quizzes hold distinct roles in the educational process. Typically, exams bear significantly more weight than quizzes, and their importance is reflected in the weight of their grades.[5] However, grading presents particular challenges. Students often prioritize their grades over actual learning, necessitating a shift in focus toward learning itself.[6]

Students have been conditioned to associate actions with consequences in their academic journey. To motivate them, educators can either work to uncondition this behavior or continue using it to their advantage. For instance, in a flipped classroom, where students are expected to master content outside the classroom, incorporating class quizzes can assess their learning.[7] The Air Force Academy Prep School used this strategy, known as the "Thayer Method." It required completing homework and submitting it for grading before receiving the lesson. This promoted active engagement and learning.

Deciding whether quizzes should contribute to a student's grade is a critical choice. To encourage students to take quizzes seriously, they must know that these assessments somehow effect their grades.[8] Quizzes can be assigned point values, adhere to specifications grading, or count as participation. The key to motivating students is to create a connection between quiz performance and grades .

Let's consider different grading strategies.

Traditional Grading

Traditional grading is typically identified by providing single attempts, focusing on completion versus mastery, and is often more stressful.[9] High-stakes, summative exams punctuate the learning journey. This grading method does not motivate students to learn the content; instead, students focus more on earning the grade.[10]

Traditional grading can be both labor-intensive and challenging to apply consistently.[11] Grading nuances, such as distinguishing between an 87 and an 89, can prove daunting. This is where **specifications grading** shines, as it employs an all-or-nothing approach. There's no need to differentiate between minor grade variations; either students meet the requirements, or they don't. This simplifies the grading process and maintains its integrity.

Specifications Grading

Specifications grading is a unique approach to assessing student learning.[12] I prefer it. Specifications grading breaks down the learning objectives into distinct modules, each with its own set of assessments. These assessments are graded on a simple "go or no-go" basis, meaning students either meet the specified standard or don't yet. Typically, students do not receive partial credit.

In specifications grading, students typically have multiple opportunities to demonstrate their understanding. These assessments are usually low-stakes, meaning they don't weigh much in the overall course grade.[13] The assessments are formative. This approach aims to reduce stress among students, as they don't face the pressure of a single high-stakes assignment that could make or break their course performance. Research shows specifications grading has led to a decrease in failing grades.[14]

The key idea is to focus on individual learning objectives or small objective sets and design rapid assessments around them. Mastery quizzing is a prime example of this strategy. Students take quizzes repeatedly until they achieve the desired level of mastery. Students have ample opportunities to revise and improve their work. Although instructors may have to grade multiple times, regrading typically only extends to a few iterations. Students rarely attempt more than five times before mastering the skill.[15] With an automated quizzing system, the impact on the instructor's time is negligible.

Mastery learning and low-stakes quizzes can be integrated into the grading system to enhance student performance and higher grades. These quizzes may carry minimal weight in the overall grade or serve solely as formative tools for the class.[16] However, they should count somehow. For example, students earn full credit only upon achieving 100%, ensuring mastery before moving forward. Regardless of the grading method chosen, providing student feedback is crucial.[17] Participation points can be awarded for submitting answers or completing quizzes.

One of the most significant benefits of specifications grading is its positive impact on low-achieving students.[18] This approach allows them to revise and retake assessments until they achieve mastery, significantly improving their chances of success. In addition, it fosters a sense of engagement in their classes, motivating them to study and review more, ultimately leading to improved learning outcomes.[19]

Another advantage of specifications grading is its clarity to students and instructors. With a "go or no-go" system, it's easy to see who has met the standard and who hasn't.[20] Instructors can use this information to improve their teaching methods. Additionally, there's no need to determine partial scores.[21]

Specifications grading does come with challenges in addition to its many advantages. Students may procrastinate due to the knowledge of having multiple attempts, leading to potential time management issues.[22] Moreover, the number of quizzes students can take may increase if they fall behind or struggle initially.[23] In light of these challenges, instructors must take the lead in clearly communicating the specifications grading approach to students, as it can be different from what they're used to.[24]

One common frustration among students is the "all or nothing" aspect of specifications grading.[25] Some students believe their efforts should earn them partial credit. Lack of partial credit can lead to dissatisfaction.[26] Instructors should provide clear rubrics and address negative perceptions to motivate and support students effectively in addressing these challenges and ensuring the success of specifications grading.[27]

Specification grading strategies help students avoid cramming and ensure consistent engagement with the material.[28] Under specification grading, students perform equally or better in final exams than traditional grading.[29] This method also leads to a more uniform distribution of grades. Additionally, students seek more help, such as attending office hours, to enhance their understanding.

Effective Grading Strategies in Education

Various grading strategies and techniques can significantly impact a student's learning experience. One such strategy is the difference between **"best performance grade"** and **"target performance grade."** Another is the difference between **additive and subtractive grading**.

Best Performance Grade vs. Target Performance Grade

Best performance grade (BPG). This grading method focuses on the highest score a student achieves, regardless of how many attempts they make. Essentially, the student's highest score is the one recorded. This approach allows students to continually improve their grades until they reach their maximum potential.

Target performance grade(TPG). In contrast, the target performance grade sets a specific threshold, typically around 70%. Students can retake assessments until they achieve a score above this threshold, after which they cannot retake the test.

In one study, the instructor incentivized students by manually raising the grade to 90% if a student got over the TPG goal of 70% on the first attempt.[30] This did not affect acing the quiz. The raw score was reported to the student. If the student got 7 or 8 out of 10 on the second attempt, the instructor raised the grade to 80%. There was no grade inflation for the third attempt.

In another study, instructors experimented with the BPG out of three attempts and a TPG of 70%.[31] All students in the study received the content, did the readings, participated in the lectures, and attended classes. The treatment-one group received eight multiple-choice quizzes and was graded on their best performance out of three attempts for each quiz. The treatment-two group also received eight quizzes, but their access to retakes of each quiz was shut off once they achieved a target performance grade of 70%.

My variation on these grading methods is to award credit for quiz completion only when a student has achieved 100% on a quiz. I ask students to complete a mastery quiz each week. They can repeat it as often as they want until they ace it by the class's final deadline.

Each of these grading methods has its practical implications. In a study comparing the two, the BPG group had higher average scores than the TPG group, indicating students with multiple opportunities for improvement tend to perform better.[32] On the other hand, students generally preferred the TPG method, as it provided a clear target to reach, enhancing their focus and motivation.[33]

Regarding performance, the TPG group demonstrated a slight edge over the BPG group in-class quizzes, practice midterms, and practice finals.[34] However, this difference was insignificant except for the final exam, where the TPG group significantly outperformed the other. This study underscores the need to consider the grading method's influence on student performance, particularly in high-stakes assessments.

Another factor to consider is the effect of grading methods on attendance and completion rates. In the same study, the TPG group exhibited higher attendance and completion rates than the BPG group.[35] This suggests the TPG approach might encourage students to engage more actively in the course.

These grade strategies can be used with the adaptive release of subsequent course content.

Additive Grading vs. Subtractive Grading

Beyond the choice between BPG and TPG, educators also face decisions regarding grading philosophy, specifically additive and subtractive grading. This decision is crucial as it can significantly impact students' learning experience and mindset.

Subtractive grading. Subtractive grading is a traditional method often used in classrooms. It assumes students start with a perfect score of 100%, and they lose points as they make mistakes. Subtractive grading can be discouraging, as losing points may push students down to lower grades with no chance of recovery. It does not contribute to a growth mindset.

Additive grading. Additive grading often fosters a more optimistic mindset among students, as they believe there is always an opportunity to achieve the desired grade. Additive grading starts from zero, allowing students to continuously add points as they complete assignments or retake assessments. There is always an opportunity to improve. I use an additive grading approach. In my classes, students can retake assignments and quizzes as often as they like. I provide variety in assignments, so there are always ways to earn points.

Incentivize Participation

As educators, you have the power to ensure students engage with the quizzes throughout the course. By collectively making them worth at least one to two letter grades, you can motivate students to participate actively in the mastery quizzing strategy, empowering them to take control of their learning.

This strategy offers flexibility and adaptability, allowing you to tailor it to your course's needs.

Another strategy to consider is allowing students to drop a few of their lowest quiz grades.[36] This approach reduces test anxiety and acknowledges that some individuals may have occasional difficulties with test-taking. By offering this flexibility, educators create a more inclusive and supportive learning environment, promoting overall student success.

As we continue, we will explore more strategies and nuances to refine your approach. Mastery quizzing can significantly enhance your students' learning experiences and outcomes.

Grading in the context of mastery quizzing requires thoughtful consideration. Different grading approaches, such as specifications grading and low-stakes quizzes, can motivate students and foster learning. When selecting the most suitable grading strategy, weighing the benefits and drawbacks of methods like BPG and TPG is crucial. Equally important is whether to implement additive or subtractive grading, as this can significantly influence students' motivation and perspective. Ultimately, the grading strategy chosen should align with the educational goals and the specific needs of the students in their learning context. Regardless of the selected method, communicating how you will grade, providing feedback, and considering student well-being are essential in pursuing effective grading strategies.[37]

Building a Culture of Learning and Integrity in Mastery Quizzing

I recognize that cheating runs counter to the idea of lifelong learning. There are many books on cheating. I recommend James Lang's book *Cheating Lessons: Learning from Academic Dishonesty*. I could write a book on cheating, but I do not want to devote much time to the topic. Spending time and energy in an arms race to thwart cheaters saps the motivation to do what you love to do—teach. This is especially true in a mastery quizzing environment where quizzes are primarily a formative learning strategy. Instead, spend time and energy developing a learning culture. You can do this by improving your test banks.

Embracing Learning-Centered Assessment

As an educator, your role in mastery quizzing goes beyond preventing cheating—it's about creating an environment where learning thrives. Here's how you can shift your focus toward meaningful educational experiences:

- **Encourage deeper engagement**. Design quizzes challenging students to apply knowledge and solve problems.

- **Move beyond memorization**. Focus on comprehension and application rather than rote memorization. Naturally, this is dependent upon what you want students to learn. Sometimes, you want to develop foundational knowledge, such as learning definitions.

- **Cultivate intrinsic motivation**. Prioritize learning outcomes over grades to ignite student curiosity and commitment.

- **Foster a positive environment**. Celebrate understanding and growth to enhance the classroom atmosphere.

Establishing Clear Expectations

Clear expectations are crucial in preventing cheating and promoting a culture of academic integrity, especially in mastery quizzing. Creating a supportive environment with clear guidelines:

- **Define what constitutes cheating**. Start by clearly defining what constitutes cheating in your classroom or learning environment. Clarify behaviors constituting academic dishonesty.

- **Communicate consequences**. Discuss disciplinary actions for dishonest behavior.

- **Outline quiz procedures**. Detail rules and expectations for quiz conditions. Providing transparency in quiz procedures helps students understand the boundaries of acceptable behavior and reduces ambiguity that could lead to misunderstandings or ethical lapses.

- **Promote a culture of integrity**. Emphasize honesty's value in learning and personal growth.

Encouraging Ethical Learning Practices

Promoting ethical learning practices is essential for preventing cheating in mastery quizzing and cultivating a culture of academic integrity. Foster ethical behavior through engagement and support:

- **Emphasize learning value**. Shift focus from grades to learning benefits. Encourage students to view quizzes and assessments as opportunities to demonstrate their knowledge and skills rather than hurdles to overcome.

- **Foster a growth mindset**. Encourage students to see quizzes as part of their learning journey rather than a definitive measure of their abilities. Promote resilience and continuous improvement.

- **Create engaging assessments**. Design quizzes that are engaging, relevant, and aligned with learning objectives. Incorporate real-world applications, case studies, or problem-solving tasks that require students to apply their understanding in practical contexts.

- **Reinforce ethical behavior through role modeling**. Lead by example. Model honesty, fairness, and respect for intellectual property rights in your work and assignments. Show students that ethical conduct is valued and expected in academic settings.

Responding Ethically to Challenges

Addressing cheating incidents with fairness and educational intent:

- **Approach with fairness**. Investigate incidents without assumptions.

- **Private discussions**. Respectfully discuss concerns with involved students. Listen actively to their explanations and consider any mitigating factors contributing to the situation.

- **Focus on education**. Use incidents of cheating as educational opportunities for students to learn about the importance of academic integrity. Discuss the consequences of their actions on their learning.

- **Reinforce consequences**. Consistently enforce consequences for dishonesty.

- **Offer support**. Provide resources for academic improvement and ethical decision-making. Emphasize the importance of seeking help when struggling academically rather than resorting to dishonest practices.

Designing Effective Quizzes

Designing quizzes that promote learning and discourage cheating is crucial for maintaining academic integrity:

- **Emphasize critical thinking**. Craft questions requiring reasoning and problem-solving skills.

- **Vary question formats**. Mix question types to challenge students. Automated quizzes will require closed question types for automated grading. However, you can still vary question types.

- **Leverage technology**. For enhanced security, utilize online platforms and anti-plagiarism software. Online platforms can randomize question order and answer choices, making it harder for students to predict quiz content.

- **Establish clear expectations**. Define cheating clearly and communicate consequences consistently. Encourage students to take pride in their work and discourage cheating as a shortcut to success.

- **Provide feedback and support**. Offer constructive feedback on quiz performance to help students improve their understanding and study habits. Create opportunities for students to review their mistakes and learn from them.

Promoting Mastery and Understanding

Enhancing learning outcomes through mastery quizzing strategies.

- **Emphasize conceptual mastery**. Assess deep understanding rather than surface-level knowledge. Discourage cheating by prioritizing conceptual mastery.

- **Encourage critical thinking**. Challenge students to analyze and synthesize information.

- **Integrate real-world applications**. Connect learning to practical scenarios for relevance. Demonstrating the significance of their learning motivates students to invest in understanding the material rather than focusing on memorization or shortcuts.

- **Provide opportunities for reflection**. Incorporate reflective components into your quizzes where students can articulate their learning process and identify growth areas.

By prioritizing learning and integrity in mastery quizzing, educators create a more engaging educational experience and nurture a culture where students develop a genuine thirst for knowledge and a commitment to academic honesty. This approach prepares students for exams and lifelong success built on a foundation of understanding and integrity.

Test Anxiety

A psychology professor, Dr. Martinez noticed test anxiety was severely affecting her students' performance. She introduced a weekly "confidence quiz," designed to be ungraded but still cover essential concepts. Before each quiz, she led the class in a brief mindfulness exercise to calm their nerves. Over time, students began to view these quizzes as practice opportunities rather than assessments to fear. By the end of the semester, one of Dr. Martinez's students, Jake, shared, "I used to feel sick before exams, but now they just feel like another quiz. I can handle it."

Test anxiety, a significant hurdle for many students, can be managed effectively with the right strategies. Educators can help students overcome their fears and succeed academically by understanding the causes of anxiety and implementing supportive practices.

Test anxiety, a common issue among students, affects their ability to perform well in exams. It's the nervousness or fear one might fail or not meet expectations. Many students worry about their performance and how others perceive them.[38] This fear can result in physical symptoms of stress and can severely impact a student's confidence and self-esteem. In severe cases, it leads to a vicious cycle: fearing poor performance, performing poorly, and then fearing tests even more. This cycle can negatively affect grades, lead to depression, and reduce overall life satisfaction.

Test anxiety is particularly noticeable in subjects like mathematics, where it can reinforce a negative mindset and hinder performance.[39] One way to combat this is by distributing grades more evenly across different types of assessments, reducing the pressure on major exams.

The pressure to succeed in high-stakes exams, like the bar or medical licensing exams, can have significant consequences.[40] Failure may lead to financial burdens, the need for extra study time, or a sense of personal failure. This fear can further detract from the positive aspects of quizzing.

This anxiety can occur before, during, and even after the test, leading to a range of problems.[41]

Frequent Quizzing Reduces Anxiety

Contrary to some beliefs, frequent quizzes and practice tests can help reduce test anxiety.[42] Students feel less anxious as they become more familiar with testing formats and materials. Students can become overwhelmed when they only have one or two major tests. However, when quizzes are frequent and have lower stakes, they become part of a routine, reducing anxiety.[43]

Starting with easier tests and gradually increasing difficulty can build confidence and competence.[44] While the first attempt at a quiz may lead to higher anxiety, subsequent attempts tend to be less stressful. The more students prepare for an exam and understand the format and grading criteria, the less stress they will have over time. It reduces uncertainty or the unknown.

One significant advantage of mastery quizzing is its ability to spread anxiety over time.[45] Instead of facing the pressure of a single, high-stakes exam, students encounter multiple quizzes, reducing the overall stress. Studies have found that students prefer mastery grading over traditional methods, especially in learning math.[46] This approach lessens test anxiety by allowing students to retake assessments, reinforcing their understanding.[47]

Other Stress-Reducing Strategies

Combining mastery quizzing with other strategies can further reduce test anxiety. For example, one significant benefit of specifications grading is reducing student stress.[48] Students report feeling less anxious about exams and are more optimistic about their chances of success in a specifications grading environment. Clear parameters also reduce disputes over grades, as there's no room for arguing about partial points.[49]

Game-based quizzing also significantly reduces test anxiety.[50] By simulating the testing experience in a fun and stress-free manner, these tools help students acclimate to testing pressures. This approach provides test-taking benefits and alleviates the usual stress associated with exams.

Timing/Frequency

At the start of the term, Professor Diaz implemented daily 10-minute quizzes. His students grumbled initially, but they soon realized that consistent practice better prepared them for exams. During a feedback session, one student shared, "It's like learning to play an instrument—you get better with practice."

Time is a crucial factor to consider when using quizzes as an active learning tool. Consider the timing or frequency and when to administer the quiz. You can apply these factors together or independently depending on your course needs.

The frequency of quizzes in your teaching can significantly impact student learning and engagement. By carefully considering the timing, feedback, and strategies, you can create a more effective learning environment for your students. When done thoughtfully, frequent quizzing is a powerful tool for educators and learners alike.

Scheduling them at the right time and format can significantly impact the learning experience. Starting with a quiz at the beginning of class and providing time for review at the end can be a powerful tool for deepening understanding. Additionally, in-class quizzes offer higher learning benefits than take-home quizzes.

Let's first take a deeper look at frequency.

Frequency

When using quizzes as a learning tool, the question of how often to give them is crucial. Let's explore this topic in a more structured way. First of all, why does the frequency matter?

The frequent testing approach ties in with motivation theory. Regular testing keeps students motivated to stay current with the material through better attendance, study preparation, and allocating more time to study.[51] In my experience at the prep school, I focused on my studies because I knew I would face a test every other day. This consistent testing encouraged me to stay on top of my lessons.

Frequent testing helps students better assess their understanding and make necessary course corrections.[52] It also helps them measure their actual level of knowledge. Sometimes, students might overestimate their grasp of a subject, but frequent quizzing can provide a reality check.

Frequent quizzing also improves student engagement during lectures, reducing mind wandering and distractions.[53] Importantly, it has a more significant impact on lower-performing students, helping to narrow the achievement gap. More quizzes mean more opportunities for feedback.[54] This feedback helps students understand where they need to improve.

Deciding how often to quiz students is crucial. Options range from daily to monthly. Students can take quizzes independently for a grade or non-grade. You can administer quizzes at the beginning or end of classes.[55] Additionally, you must consider whether the quiz will be taken in class or at home, as this impacts the quiz format and delivery method.

You can expect better results when you incorporate quizzes into your classes more often.[56] Students should be able to take quizzes multiple times per week. Frequent quizzes can prevent students who find the material challenging from falling behind. These quizzes spread out the grading, giving students more chances to succeed.

When deciding on the frequency of quizzes, there are several factors to consider:[57]

- **Frequency.** How often will quizzes be provided to students?

- **Spacing interval**. Determine the time gap between quizzes, especially if you plan to revisit previous questions.

- **Lag time**. Consider the time between when learning occurs and when testing happens.

- **Assessment type**. Decide on the type of assessment and feedback you will provide.

- **Feedback**. Will feedback be provided or withheld from students? Research strongly encourages giving feedback.

At the Air Force Academy Prep School, students took an in-class quiz every other day. Quizzes occurred at the beginning of the class period and lasted 10-15 minutes. We were quizzed quite often, considering we had four academic classes daily. Instructors provided results and feedback the next day. This frequent quizzing had a positive impact on retention and learning. Research demonstrates that repeated testing is more effective than a single test.[58]

Timing

Regarding quizzes, timing plays a crucial role in enhancing the learning experience. Consider when to schedule a quiz in your class.[59] The ideal times are at the beginning or the end of the class or both.[60] Conducting quizzes at the beginning and end of a class enhances the learning experience.

Low-stakes quizzes can be used before the start of a lesson to help students recall information from a previous lesson.[61] You can also provide quizzes at the beginning of the class to review material that students should have read before class. These quizzes can also prime students for the lesson ahead.

Quizzes given at the end of class provide recall practice.[62] The quizzes focus on the key points of the lesson. Post-instruction quizzes, given after learning the material, enhance learning more than pre-instruction quizzes. The timing of quizzes can impact their effectiveness.

One effective strategy is to start your class with a quiz. Here's how it works:[63]

- Give students a quiz as soon as the class begins.

- Allow them to hold onto it throughout the class.

- At the end of the class, provide time for them to review and adjust their answers.

This approach assesses students' initial knowledge and encourages active engagement and learning during class. Students can reflect on what they've learned and make improvements, which can reinforce their understanding.

The duration of quizzing matters. Longer-term quizzing interventions yield stronger effects, whether within a single class or spanning multiple semesters.[64] Frequent testing and supportive feedback support long-term learning while reducing test anxiety.[65]

Conclusion

Mastery quizzing turns assessments into powerful learning tools. By blending frequent, low-stakes quizzes with strategies like specifications and additive grading, educators can reduce stress, improve retention, and foster growth. These methods emphasize learning over grades, motivating students to engage actively and develop lasting skills. By prioritizing integrity, clear expectations, and support, educators can create a culture where students thrive academically and beyond.

Quick Quiz

How well did you grasp the information in this chapter? Test your knowledge.

10.1. What is the primary goal of mastery quizzing?

a) To assign grades based on one-time performance.

b) To foster active learning and long-term retention.

c) To increase the difficulty of exams over time.

d) To reduce the number of quizzes students take.

10.2. Which grading strategy allows students multiple attempts to meet a specific standard?

a) Traditional grading.

b) Additive grading.

c) Specifications grading.

d) Subtractive grading.

10.3. How does frequent quizzing help reduce test anxiety?

a) By making quizzes harder over time.

b) By familiarizing students with testing formats.

c) By eliminating feedback on performance.

d) By replacing exams with quizzes.

10.4. What is a key benefit of additive grading?

a) It allows students to recover lost points by retaking quizzes.

b) It starts students with a perfect score of 100%.

c) It discourages students from attempting difficult tasks.

d) It prevents students from earning full credit.

10.5. Which of the following is NOT a recommended practice for mastery quizzing?

a) Emphasizing conceptual understanding over memorization.

b) Designing quizzes with varied question formats.

c) Prioritizing grades over learning outcomes.

d) Providing clear feedback and opportunities for improvement.

1. Abderrahim Mimouni, "Using Mobile Gamified Quizzing for Active Learning: The Effect of Reflective Class Feedback on Undergraduates' Achievement," *Education and Information Technologies*, no. Journal Article (2022), https://doi.org/10.1007/s10639-022-11097-2.

2. John E. Edlund, "Implementing Exam Wrappers," in *In Their Own Words: What Scholars and Teachers Want You to Know about Why and How to Apply the Science of Learning in Your Academic Setting* (Society for the Teaching of Psychology, 2023), 480.

3. Chunliang Yang et al., "Do Practice Tests (Quizzes) Reduce or Provoke Test Anxiety? A Meta-Analytic Review," *Educational Psychology Review* 35, no. 3 (2023): 1–26, https://doi.org/10.1007/s10648-023-09801-w.

4. Robin Boyle-Laisure, "Didn't Cover That in Class? Low-Stakes Technique of Quizzing to the Rescue," *The Journal of the Legal Writing Institute* 27 (2023): 299–307.

5. Nicolas Garzone, Tracey Howell, and Daniela Tirnovan, "Mastering Anxiety: The Effect of Mastery-Based Testing on Quantitative Literacy College Students' Anxiety Levels and Mindsets," *International Journal for Mathematics Teaching and Learning* 24, no. 1 (2023): 62–73.

6. Ella Tuson and Tim Hickey, "Mastery Learning and Specs Grading in Discrete Math," in *Proceedings of the 27th ACM Conference on Innovation and Technology in Computer Science Education Vol. 1* (Dublin, Ireland, 2022), 19–25.

7. Matthew Spencer, "Implementation of Competency-Based Learning in a Laboratory-Focused Analog Design Course," in *2022 ASEE Annual Conference & Exposition* (Minneapolis, MN, 2022), 17.

8. Lukas K. Sotola and Marcus Crede, "Regarding Class Quizzes: A Meta-Analytic Synthesis of Studies on the Relationship between Frequent Low-Stakes Testing and Class Performance," *Educational Psychology Review* 33, no. 2 (2021): 407–26, https://doi.org/10.1007/s10648-020-09563-9.

9. Sydney L. Noell et al., "A Bridge to Specifications Grading in Second Semester General Chemistry," *Journal of Chemical Education* 100, no. 6 (2023): 2159–65, https://doi.org/10.1021/acs.jchemed.2c00731.

10. Carlos Rojas and Gina M. Quan, "Mastery Grading in a Software Engineering Course," in *2023 ASEE Annual Conference & Exposition* (Baltimore Convention Center, MD, 2023).

11. Tuson and Hickey, "Mastery Learning and Specs Grading in Discrete Math."

12. Noell et al., "A Bridge to Specifications Grading in Second Semester General Chemistry."

13. Ibid., 2162.

14. Ibid., 2161.

15. Tuson and Hickey, "Mastery Learning and Specs Grading in Discrete Math."

16. Boyle-Laisure, "Didn't Cover That in Class?"

17. Ibid., 299.

18. Noell et al., "A Bridge to Specifications Grading in Second Semester General Chemistry."

19. Rojas and Quan, "Mastery Grading in a Software Engineering Course."

20. Tuson and Hickey, "Mastery Learning and Specs Grading in Discrete Math."

21. Noell et al., "A Bridge to Specifications Grading in Second Semester General Chemistry."

22. Tuson and Hickey, "Mastery Learning and Specs Grading in Discrete Math."

23. Ibid., 24.

24. Rojas and Quan, "Mastery Grading in a Software Engineering Course."

25. Ibid., 8.

26. Rojas and Quan, "Mastery Grading in a Software Engineering Course"; Noell et al., "A Bridge to Specifications Grading in Second Semester General Chemistry."

27. Noell et al., "A Bridge to Specifications Grading in Second Semester General Chemistry."

28. Justin J. Donato and Thomas C. Marsh, "Specifications Grading Is an Effective Approach to Teaching Biochemistry," *Journal of Microbiology & Biology Education* 24, no. 2 (2023): 1–9, https://doi.org/10.1128/jmbe.00236-22.

29. Ibid., 6.

30. Mark Lubrick and Bill Wellington, "Formative Learning Assessment with Online Quizzing: Comparing Target Performance Grade and Best Performance Grade Approaches," *Journal of Learning and Teaching in Digital Age* 7, no. 2 (2022): 297–306, https://doi.org/10.53850/joltida.1036295.

31. Ibid., 300.

32. Ibid., 303.

33. Ibid., 304.

34. Ibid., 305.

35. Ibid., 304.

36. Matthew T. Johnson et al., "Improving Student Preparation and Pass Rates in Flipped Multivariable Calculus with Low-Stakes, Daily Quizzes," *PRIMUS* 33, no. 7 (2023): 714–28, https://doi.org/10.1080/10511970.2022.2163329.

37. Noell et al., "A Bridge to Specifications Grading in Second Semester General Chemistry."

38. Yang et al., "Do Practice Tests (Quizzes) Reduce or Provoke Test Anxiety? A Meta-Analytic Review."

39. Garzone, Howell, and Tirnovan, "Mastering Anxiety."

40. Monir M. Almotairy et al., "Comprehensive Licensure Review and Adaptive Quizzing Assignments for Enhancement of End-of-Programme Exit Examination Scores in Saudi Arabia: A Quasi-Experimental Study," *BMJ Open* 13, no. 7 (2023): 1–7, https://doi.org/10.1136/ bmjopen-2023-074469.

41. Yang et al., "Do Practice Tests (Quizzes) Reduce or Provoke Test Anxiety? A Meta-Analytic Review."

42. Yang et al., "Do Practice Tests (Quizzes) Reduce or Provoke Test Anxiety? A Meta-Analytic Review"; Svitlana Mykytiuk et al., "Seamless Learning Model with Enhanced Web-Quizzing in the Higher Education Setting," *International Journal of Interactive Mobile Technologies* 16, no. 3 (2022): 4–19, https://doi.org/10.3991/IJIM.V16I03.27257.

43. Chunliang Yang et al., "Frequent Quizzing Accelerates Classroom Learning," *In Their Own Words: What Scholars and Teachers Want You to Know about Why and How to Apply the Science of Learning in Your Academic Setting*, 2023, 190–99.

44. Yang et al., "Do Practice Tests (Quizzes) Reduce or Provoke Test Anxiety? A Meta-Analytic Review."

45. Garzone, Howell, and Tirnovan, "Mastering Anxiety."

46. Ibid., 70.

47. Donato and Marsh, "Specifications Grading Is an Effective Approach to Teaching Biochemistry."

48. Tuson and Hickey, "Mastery Learning and Specs Grading in Discrete Math."

49. Rojas and Quan, "Mastery Grading in a Software Engineering Course."

50. Yang et al., "Do Practice Tests (Quizzes) Reduce or Provoke Test Anxiety? A Meta-Analytic Review."

51. Mykytiuk et al., "Seamless Learning Model with Enhanced Web-Quizzing in the Higher Education Setting."

52. Ibid., 9.

53. Yang et al., "Frequent Quizzing Accelerates Classroom Learning."

54. Sotola and Crede, "Regarding Class Quizzes."

55. Boyle-Laisure, "Didn't Cover That in Class?"

56. Sotola and Crede, "Regarding Class Quizzes."

57. Lubrick and Wellington, "Formative Learning Assessment with Online Quizzing."

58. Yang et al., "Frequent Quizzing Accelerates Classroom Learning."

59. Boyle-Laisure, "Didn't Cover That in Class?"

60. Yang et al., "Do Practice Tests (Quizzes) Reduce or Provoke Test Anxiety? A Meta-Analytic Review."

61. Judith Schweppe and Ralf Rummer, "Wrapping up Lessons With Closed-Book and Open-Book Tests," in *In Their Own Words: What Scholars and Teachers Want You to Know about Why and How to Apply the Science of Learning in Your Academic Setting* (Society for the Teaching of Psychology, 2023), 494–98, https://www.researchgate.net/profile/Logan-Fiorella/publication/369588588_Learning_by_Teaching/links/64234a8ca1b72772e431adec/Learning-by-Teaching.pdf#page=501.

62. Ibid., 497.

63. Boyle-Laisure, "Didn't Cover That in Class?"

64. Yang et al., "Frequent Quizzing Accelerates Classroom Learning."

65. Yang et al., "Do Practice Tests (Quizzes) Reduce or Provoke Test Anxiety? A Meta-Analytic Review."

Chapter Eleven

In-Class Activities

Research has shown that in-class activities like quizzing can significantly enhance student learning. Students who participated in in-class activities like attendance checks and short assignments tended to perform better in exams.[1] These activities also boost student attention, leading to improved academic performance. Let's briefly look at a collection of in-class activities that align well with mastery quizzing.

Objectives

- Understand the role of in-class activities in promoting mastery learning.

- Identify effective in-class strategies for engaging students in mastery quizzing.

- Evaluate the impact of in-class mastery quizzing activities on student learning outcomes.

Types of In-Class Activities

Attendance checks or concept checks. These in-class activities involve active participation, which isn't only about being present. It could be responding to a quick quiz question or participating in an online or face-to-face chat. These activities are brief, often taking just a few seconds. A concept check or quiz is a single question given at some point during a class to assess understanding of a concept recently taught in class.[2] Students paid more attention in class knowing a concept check was coming but did not know when it would occur.[3]

Instructors at the Air Force Academy Prep School widely used concept checks. In each class, each student was called upon to answer a question or solve a problem. This method of instruction turned out to be compelling, even though we found it stressful at the time.

Brief writing assignments. These assignments, limited to about five minutes, consist of a few sentences on a specific topic. Students can complete them on paper or through an LMS like Canvas.

Graded assignments with revision. Students submit work for grading and can revise and resubmit, enhancing learning through reflection and correction.[4]

Mastery quizzing. Our focus is on mastery quizzing. Mastery quizzes used for in-class assignments are short quizzes at the beginning of a class that focuses on what students will learn or review what they recently covered. The quiz could be a single question or consist of multiple questions. I recommend no more than ten questions for an in-class quiz. These quizzes can be easily set up in your LMS.

A single question can activate students' thinking and set a positive tone for the lesson. In one study, instructors informed students if there was to be an assessment.[5] Students could expect a single mastery question at the beginning of the class, a single concept check during class, or nothing. This study spanned multiple classes. The questions were associated with or tied to courses that used or did not use mastery quizzes or concept checks. Instructors use the class type and Bloom's taxonomy to code questions. Overall, students performed better on exams when given in-class activities.

Learning moment quiz. A learning moment quiz question covers one of the lecture objectives.[6] In a study, an instructor created online lectures. Each unit had three prerecorded lectures. Each lecture contained three learning moments:[7] A quiz question, a statement confirming understanding, or a question of understanding. Students who had taken learning moment quiz questions in a prerecorded lecture performed better on exam questions than students who were just asked if they understood the content. As the instructor created the summative exams, she added a question from each learning moment activity.

Here is an example of how instructors implemented these in-class activities in their study. They scheduled four activities on a random basis[8]. Each activity or assignment was worth 2.5 points. The activities included:

- No activity (control)

- Attendance check

- Brief writing assignments

- Mastery quizzes

They notified students of the activity type on the day of the assignment. All activities other than no activity resulted in improved exam performance.

Adaptive Learning

Adaptive learning is an educational approach that uses technology to tailor instruction to the individual needs of each learner. It's built on the idea that learners have different strengths, weaknesses, and preferences, so a one-size-fits-all approach to education may not be the most effective.

Here's how adaptive learning typically works:

1. **Assessment**. Adaptive learning starts with assessing the learner's current knowledge, skills, and learning preferences. This assessment can take many forms, including quizzes, exams, or interactive activities.

2. **Personalization**. Based on the assessment results, the adaptive learning system creates a personalized learning path for each student. This path addresses areas where students need the most help while building on their knowledge and skills.

3. **Feedback**. The adaptive learning system provides real-time feedback as the student progresses through the learning path. This feedback can take many forms, including hints or explanations for incorrect answers, praise for correct answers, and recommendations for further study.

4. **Adjustment**. The adaptive learning system continuously monitors the student's progress and adjusts the learning path accordingly. The system may provide additional practice or resources if the student struggles with a particular concept. If students master concepts quickly, the system may move them on to more challenging material.

Adaptive learning can be used in a wide range of educational settings. It's particularly well-suited to subjects where students' prior knowledge and abilities vary widely, such as math or language learning.

One key benefit of adaptive learning is it allows students to learn at their own pace and in their own way. By providing personalized instruction and support, adaptive learning can help students stay engaged and motivated, leading to better learning outcomes.

A notable example involves nursing students using an adaptive quizzing program called PrepU to prepare for comprehensive nursing exams.[9] This method proved effective for mastering content. It helped students measure their knowledge level and pinpoint areas where they needed more study, a common goal in formative learning.

Adaptive Quizzing

Adaptive quizzing is a valuable strategy within formative quizzing. It dynamically adjusts difficulty based on a student's performance.[10] The concept is straightforward: the subsequent questions become more challenging when students answer questions correctly. Conversely, if they struggle, the questions become simpler. This approach allows instructors to set an appropriate challenge level for each student.

You must explore your LMS to determine if you can create native adaptive quizzes. However, you should be able to develop adaptive learning modules based on quizzes or create a graduated level of quizzes with most LMSs.

Adaptive Release

Adaptive quizzing is a flexible and effective tool in the educator's arsenal. It aids personalized learning and offers a structured path to mastering complex subjects. You can set up adaptive release in a variety of configurations.

Review content before receiving a quiz. Instructors can set up "adaptive release triggers," requiring students to engage with specific content before attempting a quiz.[11] This approach can include a variety of milestones, such as a preliminary quiz. Based on performance in this initial assessment, students might bypass some content or be required to review it before proceeding to the main quiz.

Using quizzes as gates. Quizzes can also control access to more challenging quizzes or move on to new topics. This helps ensure students understand the material before proceeding.

Students adapt their learning and study strategies through multiple formative quizzes to achieve better results, particularly when encountering challenges.[12] Students also view adaptive quizzing positively, feeling it contributes to academic success.[13] Here is an example of an adaptive release approach.

One instructor administered graded quizzes in a scaffolding sequence for different modules:[14]

- Week 1 - Basic quiz (no prior instruction)

- Week 1-2 - Intermediate quiz

- Week 2-3 - Advanced quiz

To progress, students had to unlock the prior quiz successfully through adaptive learning techniques.

Retaking Quizzes

Research shows that students who take online quizzes with multiple attempts tend to perform better than those who only take one quiz in the classroom.[15] This suggests that the more students engage with testing, the better they perform academically.

Retaking a quiz is a straightforward concept. It involves allowing students to provide multiple attempts on a quiz, with the instructor's discretion regarding the number of attempts. The option to retake quizzes can be a valuable tool for both students and instructors.

Increased success rates. Allowing quiz retakes significantly impacts student success.[16] It enables more students to succeed in their courses, even if they initially struggled. The ability to revise their work and improve their grades is essential for learning.[17]

Improved learning. Students appreciate the flexibility of the opportunity to retake quizzes.[18] It allows them to work on the content in focused blocks of instruction, set their schedules for retaking the exam, and concentrate on areas where they need improvement.[19] This adaptability enhances their learning experience.

Implementing quiz retakes has its challenges. The most significant challenge is the additional workload on both students and instructors.

Here are some strategies to consider:

Automation: Whenever possible, automate the process of quiz retakes. This reduces the administrative burden on instructors and ensures a smoother experience for students.

Unlimited attempts. Practice quizzes should be set up for unlimited attempts. It is up to the instructor to determine whether they are graded.[20] There should be no penalty for failure. Grade on participation or mastery if a grade is needed.[21]

Time constraints. Consider setting time limits for quiz retakes.[22] For example, students must complete a retake within a week of the initial attempt. This prevents the process from dragging on throughout the course. Most LMSs allow you to set the number of allowed attempts and a deadline for quiz completion.

Open Notes

Dr. Miller experimented with open-note quizzes in his history class. He encouraged students to focus on organizing their notes rather than memorizing facts. Surprisingly, exam scores improved, not because students relied on notes during quizzes but because they had developed better study habits through preparing them.

It's crucial to define the criteria clearly when organizing a quiz. For instance, you might decide whether students can use additional materials like textbooks or notes during the quiz. These criteria vary, ranging from closed-book (no aids allowed) to open-note exams. Research indicates there is a difference in subsequent exam performance.

Advantages of Open Notes

Open-note exams mirror real-world situations more closely.[23] Individuals often have access to various resources to solve problems in professional settings. Open notes can be invaluable for students who struggle with memory or recalling fine details. Additionally, using notes can decrease the likelihood of cheating and reduce test anxiety. However, it's important to note that open-note quizzes aren't inherently easier. They can be designed to be challenging and thought-provoking.

Studies have shown mixed results with open-note exams.[24] In some cases, students using open notes did not perform better than those with closed notes. This could be due to a lack of preparation, as students might over-rely on their notes instead of studying thoroughly. To address this, it's essential to:[25]

- **Explain the concept**. Clearly define what open-note exams entail in class and in the syllabus.

- **Emphasize effective note-taking**. Teach students how to take useful notes, emphasizing that it's not about writing down everything but capturing key points and ideas.

- **Promote good study habits**. Encourage spaced learning and note retrieval techniques to help students prepare effectively.

- **Organize Notes**. Guide students on how to review and organize their notes efficiently.

- **Retrieval Practice**. Explain the effects of retrieval practice and how it interplays with open and closed note exams.[26]

In a study, students were allowed only handwritten notes during the exam and prohibited from using printed materials or textbooks.[27] This method might add an extra challenge for those who struggle with handwriting, raising the question of whether typed notes should also be permitted.

Closed Book

Closed book is another possibility. For example, in a study, students took a 10-minute quiz with 2-3 open-ended questions after each classroom lesson. The control group was allowed to use their books during the quiz, while the experimental group had to take the quiz without using their books. In the eighth week, the students were given a surprise quiz.[28]

Students who completed low-stakes closed-book quizzes at the end of each class performed significantly better than those who took open-book quizzes.[29]

Students who answered closed-book questions first and then used their resources to check answers or work on hard questions outperformed both closed-book and open-book quiz takers on exams.[30]

Exam Wrapper

An **exam wrapper** is a reflective tool students use to assess their performance on exams or other assessments. It typically involves answering questions about the exam experience, such as:[31]

- What study strategies did you use to prepare for the exam?

- How much time did you need to prepare for the exam?

- How did you manage your time during the exam?

- What study activities did you use?

- Which questions did you find most challenging, and why?

- Why did you miss the questions that you did?

- Did you encounter any surprises on the exam?

- How confident were you in your answers?

- What could you have done differently to better prepare for the exam?

- What will you do differently in future exams based on this experience?

- What are ways the instructor could have assisted you better?

Reflecting on these questions can help students gain insight into their study habits, test-taking strategies, and areas for improvement. Students can use exam wrappers individually, or teachers can incorporate them into classroom activities to promote metacognition and self-assessment skills. Instructors can add these questions to the end of exams or assign them as a separate activity. It is up to the instructor whether or not to grade them. An appropriate grade could be for simply completing the question.

Researchers have found using exam wrappers can significantly improve student performance. In one study, the experimental group completed all exams, reviewed their answers, and completed and turned in exam wrappers. The students received their exam wrappers from their instructor a week before an exam to use them for review.[32] Students who used them performed better than those who did not. In a subsequent study, all scores improved when all students received and used exam wrappers.

Incentivizing Learning

Sometimes, you need to incentivize students to leave their comfort zone and try something more challenging or to do more. Here are some ideas to try.

A key consideration is how to motivate students to undertake additional work. One strategy could be offering extra credit for those who excel in advanced material. This approach encourages all students to master at least the intermediate level while providing an incentive for tackling more challenging content.

Another strategy to consider is implementing a token system.[33] Students can earn retake tokens by excelling in review content, typically distributed through the LMS. These tokens can then be used to retake quizzes.

Implementing Mastery Quizzing Success Tips

Mastery quizzing is an effective active learning strategy that enables students to assess their knowledge level, identify gaps, and adjust their learning strategies accordingly. This method demonstrates students' progress and helps make the learning process more transparent and effective. Here are success tips to help with the implementation of this strategy. These considerations should guide your approach to quizzing.

Communication is key. Communicate what you are doing. Instructors underestimate the amount of communication needed to secure buy-in.[34] Students have many and various concerns. For example, students struggle with exams because they do not know how to prepare or understand their format.[35] Students want to know how to succeed when encountering a new grading system. Communicate the change to students to increase success.[36] Student perception in getting buy-in to a learning strategy: if they believe it works, they will support it.[37] Explain the reason for giving quizzes and the frequency to improve performance.[38]

In one study, instructors held discussion sessions to help students better understand mastery grading.[39] Students were asked about their grading system preferences and to justify their opinions.

Communicate your high standards for each quiz. Approaches such as transparent assignment design ensure students understand what you expect.

Instructors are crucial in helping students manage test anxiety and successfully implement mastery quizzing. Here is a reminder of other effective strategies:

- **Low-stakes quizzes**. Incorporating ungraded or low-stakes quizzes can make testing less intimidating.[40] Quizzes should matter, but not too much. They should be about 10-25% of the grade.

- **Multiple attempts**. Allowing students to retake quizzes can reduce pressure and improve learning.

- **Gamification**. Making quizzes fun and engaging can alleviate anxiety.

- **Transparent assignment design**. Explaining assignments and expectations can help students feel more prepared.[41]

- **Practice exams**. Providing quizzes that mimic the exam can help students get used to the format and content, reducing anxiety.[42]

- **Make quizzes automated**. Use computerized quizzes for easier scoring and feedback.

- **Mandatory participation**. Quizzes should be required, not optional.

- **Use the best scores**. Grading based on the highest quiz score is a common and effective practice.

- **Provide good feedback**. Let students know what they got wrong and where to find the correct answers.

- **Use simple question types**. Stick to multiple-choice, matching, or true or false questions for easy grading.

- **Use test banks wisely**. Have a large pool of questions and randomize them to keep quizzes fresh.

- **Frequency**. Aim for at least one weekly quiz covering a whole chapter or specific concepts. Distribute your quizzes to reinforce learning over time, such as giving quizzes immediately after instruction, a week later, and a month later.[43]

Conclusion

Mastery quizzing is a powerful tool for helping students learn and grow. By using in-class activities that encourage practice, reflection, and collaboration, teachers can create an environment where students feel supported and challenged. These activities help students strengthen their understanding, identify areas where they need more work, and build confidence in their abilities.

When done well, mastery quizzing not only improves learning but also makes the classroom more engaging and fun. It shifts the focus from just getting the right answer to truly understanding the material. By combining clear goals, thoughtful questions, and interactive activities, teachers can inspire students to reach their full potential.

Remember, learning is a journey, and mastery quizzing is one way to make that journey meaningful and rewarding for everyone involved.

Quick Quiz

Close this chapter with a quick knowledge check.

11.1. What is the primary purpose of in-class mastery activities?

a) To fill time during lessons.

b) To reinforce learning through active engagement.

c) To reduce the need for assessments.

d) To allow students to work independently.

11.2. Which of the following is an example of an effective in-class mastery activity?

a) Requiring students to silently read their textbooks.

b) Conducting quizzes that allow peer discussion and feedback.

c) Assigning multiple-choice questions for homework.

d) Grading students solely on lecture attendance.

11.3. How can in-class mastery quizzing activities help identify student knowledge gaps?

a) By providing immediate feedback on student responses.

b) By focusing only on correct answers.

c) By using high-stakes assessments exclusively.

d) By discouraging collaborative learning.

11.4. What is a key characteristic of effective in-class mastery activities?

a) They promote memorization of facts without context.

b) They encourage interaction and discussion among students.

c) They focus on individual performance without collaboration.

d) They are only administered at the end of a course module.

11.5. Which approach best supports active learning during in-class activities?

a) Allowing students to skip quizzes they find challenging.

b) Incorporating questions that require application and analysis.

c) Using only true/false questions to save time.

d) Reducing opportunities for student participation.

1. Jeffrey S. Nevid, Luke H. Keating, and Shari Lieblich, "Effects of In-Class Engagement Activities in Online Synchronous Classes," *Scholarship of Teaching and Learning in Psychology* 8, no. 4 (2022): 304, https://doi.org/10.1037/stl0000312.

2. Ibid., 308.

3. Ibid., 310.

4. Lisa Michael and Irene-Angelica Chounta, "Quizzes and Eggs: Exploring the Impact of Course Design Elements on Students' Engagement," in *In Proceedings of the 15th International Conference on Computer Supported Education (CSEDU 2023)*, 2023, 25–34, https://doi.org/10.5220/0011745000003470.

5. Nevid, Keating, and Lieblich, "Effects of In-Class Engagement Activities in Online Synchronous Classes."

6. Lou Ann Griswold, "The Value of Quizzing Students to Support Transfer of Learning," in *In Their Own Words: What Scholars and Teachers Want You to Know about Why and How to Apply the Science of Learning in Your Academic Setting* (Society for the Teaching of Psychology, 2023), 481–87.

7. Ibid., 482.

8. Nevid, Keating, and Lieblich, "Effects of In-Class Engagement Activities in Online Synchronous Classes."

9. Hillary Parcell et al., "Evaluating the Effect of Pre-Exam Adaptive Quizzing on Nursing Student Exam Scores," *Nursing Education Perspectives* 43, no. 6 (December 2022): 100–102, https://doi.org/10.1097/01.NEP.0000000000000988.

10. Ibid., E100.

11. Almotairy et al., "Comprehensive Licensure Review and Adaptive Quizzing Assignments for Enhancement of End-of-Programme Exit Examination Scores in Saudi Arabia."

12. Sotola and Crede, "Regarding Class Quizzes."

13. Parcell et al., "Evaluating the Effect of Pre-Exam Adaptive Quizzing on Nursing Student Exam Scores."

14. Joshua K. Strakos et al., "A Learning Management System-Based Approach to Assess Learning Outcomes in Operations Management Courses," *The International Journal of Management Education* 21, no. 2 (2023): 1–9, https://doi.org/10.1016/j.ijme.2023.100802.

15. Lubrick and Wellington, "Formative Learning Assessment with Online Quizzing."

16. Noell et al., "A Bridge to Specifications Grading in Second Semester General Chemistry."

17. Rojas and Quan, "Mastery Grading in a Software Engineering Course."

18. Carlos Perez and Dina Verdin, "Mastery Learning in Undergraduate Engineering Courses: A Systematic Review," in *2022 ASEE Annual Conference & Exposition*, 2022.

19. Noell et al., "A Bridge to Specifications Grading in Second Semester General Chemistry."

20. Strakos et al., "A Learning Management System-Based Approach to Assess Learning Outcomes in Operations Management Courses."

21. Steven C. Pan et al., "Using Online and Clicker Quizzes to Learn Scientific and Technical Jargon," in *In Their Own Words: What Scholars and Teachers Want You to Know about Why and How to Apply the Science of Learning in Your Academic Setting* (Society for the Teaching of Psychology, 2023), 473–80.

22. Perez and Verdin, "Mastery Learning in Undergraduate Engineering Courses."

23. Carol Holstead, "In Praise of Open-Note Exams," The Chronicle of Higher Education, September 5, 2023, https://www.chronicle.com/article/in-praise-of-open-note-exams.

24. Ibid.

25. Ibid.

26. Schweppe and Rummer, "Wrapping up Lessons With Closed-Book and Open-Book Tests."

27. Holstead, "In Praise of Open-Note Exams."

28. Schweppe and Rummer, "Wrapping up Lessons With Closed-Book and Open-Book Tests."

29. Ibid., 496.

30. Ibid., 496.

31. Edlund, "Implementing Exam Wrappers."

32. Ibid., 490.

33. Noell et al., "A Bridge to Specifications Grading in Second Semester General Chemistry."

34. Rojas and Quan, "Mastery Grading in a Software Engineering Course."

35. Edlund, "Implementing Exam Wrappers."

36. Noell et al., "A Bridge to Specifications Grading in Second Semester General Chemistry."

37. Donato and Marsh, "Specifications Grading Is an Effective Approach to Teaching Biochemistry."

38. Pan et al., "Using Online and Clicker Quizzes to Learn Scientific and Technical Jargon."

39. Darryl Chamberlain Jr, "How One Instructor Can Teach a Large-Scale, Mastery-Based College Algebra Course Online," *PRIMUS*, 2023, 1–22.

40. Yang et al., "Do Practice Tests (Quizzes) Reduce or Provoke Test Anxiety? A Meta-Analytic Review."

41. Donato and Marsh, "Specifications Grading Is an Effective Approach to Teaching Biochemistry."

42. Yang et al., "Do Practice Tests (Quizzes) Reduce or Provoke Test Anxiety? A Meta-Analytic Review."

43. Yang et al., "Frequent Quizzing Accelerates Classroom Learning."

Chapter Twelve

Strategies

Exploring real-world applications of mastery quizzing can help you learn from successful implementations, gain insights into how mastery quizzing can be adapted to different settings, and understand the challenges and solutions encountered in real-world scenarios. Lessons learned will provide valuable guidance for those looking to implement mastery quizzing effectively. By the end of this chapter, you will be equipped with practical insights and inspiration to apply to your own educational or training contexts.

Objectives

- Evaluate real-world applications of mastery quizzing to understand their benefits and challenges in educational settings.

- Design and adapt mastery quizzing strategies to suit specific classroom environments and learning goals.

Examples of Employing Mastery Quizzes

The strategy I share in the last chapter is only one way to implement mastery quizzing in your classroom. Instructors worldwide have experimented with different elements of mastery quizzing. Here are some examples of manipulating different variables.

Varying number of questions, quizzes, and exams. Students completed three multiple-choice exams in one study, each with 15 questions.[1] Instructors used Respondus to lock down the quizzes. In another study, instructors gave students three quizzes and two exams.[2] The quizzes and exams had 3-4 questions. Students had 30-40 minutes to complete a quiz and 50 minutes to complete an exam.

Setting passing thresholds. One instructor built 200-question test banks for each chapter of a psychology course and created mastery quizzes from these test banks. Students needed to score 80% or higher to pass a quiz. They had to try again if they did not meet the threshold. These quizzes were a substantial part of their grade, up to 25%.

Replacement assignments. In another study, unique mastery quizzes could replace failed weekly quizzes.[3] Many students took advantage of these quizzes. These mastery quizzes served as part of a currency system. Nearly 22% of the students completed mastery quizzes, but many did not earn the "A."

Lecture support. Students took a quiz three times online:[4]

- Before the first lecture

- Before the second lecture

- After both lectures

Feedback on missed questions was provided immediately after each quiz. Students only received credit for completing each quiz.

Optional quizzes. Assignments were mandatory in one course, and quizzes were optional.[5] Those who focused primarily on assignments performed lower (below the mean) than those who completed the quizzes.

Deployment methods. An instructor experimented with different methods for deploying quizzes:[6]

- Online quizzes within the LMS

- Clicker quizzes

Flipped Instruction

Flipped instruction, a form of blended learning, is a teaching method that reverses the traditional classroom model.[7] It harmoniously combines out-of-class and in-class instruction. This approach, especially when paired with mastery quizzing, provides a balanced educational experience catering to diverse learning preferences and needs. It makes learning more interactive and engaging and allows instructors to spend more time on competency-based activities, thus enhancing the overall educational experience.

Instead of listening to lectures in class and doing homework at home, students watch lectures or engage with content at home and then participate in active learning exercises in the classroom. This method effectively utilizes classroom time for interactive learning, allowing for immediate feedback and assistance from instructors or peers.

Mastery quizzing seamlessly complements flipped instruction. In this approach, students complete quizzes in the classroom, providing a practical tool for assessing understanding and reinforcing learning. This method helps quickly identify and address misconceptions, thus ensuring a better grasp of the subject matter.

Administering a short quiz at the beginning of class could set the stage for a comprehensive review session. The quiz could assess understanding of assigned "homework" or previously reviewed material. It could also prepare students for what is to come in their homework sessions.

As discussed throughout this book, you have many options for administering the quiz. You could distribute the quiz on paper or digitally. You could assess individual effort along with group effort. You could project the quiz one question at a time and debrief each answer. There are many options available. One of the benefits of integrating quizzing into a flipped instruction session is the immediate feedback you could provide to improve understanding and mastery.

Benefits of Flipped Instruction

Mastery quizzing can transform flipped instruction by fostering a more efficient, engaging, and effective learning environment that naturally aligns with students' preferred active learning principles.

- **Enhanced preparation and performance**. Students engaged in flipped instruction tend to be better prepared, complete assignments more diligently, and often perform better in exams.[8]

- **Efficiency in learning**. Studies have shown that students in flipped instruction environments spend less time on course activities in and out of class than in traditional settings, making it a more efficient approach.[9]

- **Reduced failure rates**. Flipped instruction has successfully reduced failure rates by employing active learning strategies and enabling timely correction of misunderstandings.[10]

- **Preference among students**. Most students who have experienced flipped instruction prefer it over traditional methods, indicating its effectiveness and appeal.[11]

In flipped instruction, where students do most of their studying at home, it's common to see a drop in engagement over time as students lose interest in doing the required at-home work.

Teachers need to use strategies like regular quizzes, diverse materials (such as videos, articles, and podcasts), and short, focused instructional videos to keep students engaged in flipped instruction.

Vocabulary

Learning new vocabulary is essential in every academic discipline. Although challenging, regular vocabulary quizzes are an effective way to build a strong foundation in any subject. Vocabulary quizzes are vital for students to learn new words, especially in subjects like science and business, which often introduce thousands of new terms.[12] These quizzes help students memorize and understand these terms, which is crucial for success in these fields. Teachers have observed the advantages of vocabulary quizzes transcend the boundaries of a single course. Students carry the knowledge they acquire into future classes, applying the terms accurately across various subjects. This enduring application of learning underscores the lasting impact of this method.

We learned hundreds of words at the Air Force Academy Prep School every few weeks. Regular quizzes on these words significantly boosted my vocabulary. This method proved to be an effective way of learning and retaining new terms. Vocabulary quizzes are valuable for building students' language and enhancing their understanding of course material.[13]

Studies have shown the effectiveness of vocabulary quizzes. In one investigation, students took quizzes on specific terms every other week, and their recall of these terms was tested in major exams.[14] The results were compared to periods without quizzes. Another study examined how well students understood and used these terms in conceptual exam questions. In both cases, students who regularly took vocabulary quizzes performed significantly better in defining and applying terms in context.

Teachers should consider incorporating low-stakes quizzes in their classrooms to aid vocabulary learning.[15] These can be traditional quizzes or interactive ones, like clicker quizzes. One investigator created online 16-question quizzes using fill-in-the-blank and short answer questions to test vocabulary knowledge.[16] Each quiz covered 25-27 terms. The key is to offer students multiple chances to encounter new words and to build upon their knowledge over time.[17] Quizzes should cover new and previously learned terms, reinforcing the students' growing vocabulary.

A great way to create vocabulary lists and quizzes is through ChatGPT. This tool can be a valuable resource for students and teachers, helping them develop engaging and educational quizzes that foster long-term learning and understanding.

In the chapter on quiz design (chapter 8), I shared detailed instructions for developing questions with ChatGPT. You can create vocabulary lists and quizzes by providing open educational resources like an open textbook or other instructional content to ChatGPT and directing it to make the appropriate output.

Language Learning

Using mastery quizzing for language learning builds upon the strategies for learning vocabulary. Building extensive test banks that scaffold vocabulary, allows students to practice and assess their knowledge repeatedly. There are many ways to present questions:

- Present the word, and students choose the correct definition

- Present the definition, and students choose the correct word

- Provide fill-in-the-blank questions to increase difficulty

These adaptable strategies allow you to cater to different learning preferences and levels of proficiency. You can also increase the difficulty level by presenting all information in the targeted language, providing a flexible approach to language learning.

Grammar is essential to language learning.[18] There are ten categories of language grammar mistakes:

- Punctuation

- Word choice

- Spelling

- Verb formation

- Plurals

- Prepositions

- Verb tense

- Clause structure

- Subject/verb agreement

You can employ all the question development strategies to build targeted test banks focused on each element. You can then create a quick quiz to focus on a gap you observe in your classroom.

Learning grammar is considered challenging and tedious.[19] Quizzing tools can make it more engaging while reducing the level of anxiety that tends to be associated with language learning.

Let me take a moment to mention **Krashen's Affective Filter**. People often exhibit a level of anxiety when learning something new. This is especially true when learning a language. Most people want to be understood and do not want to feel foolish. When practicing a language, especially in the beginning, people are not understood well and can feel ridiculous. Krashen's Affective Filter is the emotional and psychological factors that can impede language learning.[20] However, through repeated quizzing, students develop confidence when they demonstrate their understanding of new vocabulary or language structure.

I use two programs to improve my language skills (Dutch): **Duolingo** and **LingQ**. While each works differently, they rely heavily on quizzing as a core feature to reinforce learning.

Duolingo: Building vocabulary through repetition. Duolingo offers a variety of exercises to test my ability to recognize, translate, and use words in context. It presents phrases where I must select the correct word or translate sentences. The app also provides optional practice sessions focused on vocabulary, allowing me to review and reinforce what I've learned. It delivers these activities in multiple formats, helping me encounter and process the material differently, enhancing retention.

LingQ: Contextual learning through stories. LingQ takes a slightly different approach by embedding vocabulary within short stories. As I read, I identify unfamiliar words. These words are stored in a personalized vocabulary repository. From this repository, the program generates review quizzes. These quizzes vary in format, including matching words to their meanings, selecting the correct word to complete a sentence, and translating from English into the target language. This variety keeps the learning process engaging and adaptive.

One of LingQ's standout features is its adaptiveness. Words I struggle with appear repeatedly until I demonstrate mastery. Once I've learned a word, it gradually cycles out of active review. However, I can always revisit the repository to refresh my memory.

Both programs offer unique and effective ways to build language skills. Combining Duolingo's structured practice with LingQ's contextual learning, I can see words in multiple settings and reinforce my understanding through repetition and application.

Math

Historically, mathematics has been challenging for students and instructors for many reasons. Instructors are challenged with developing robust test banks for repeated student practice. Math courses often serve as gatekeeping courses for different degree programs. For example, the US Air Force Academy would like to graduate at least 50% of students in the STEM fields, but a high percentage drop from STEM due to academic performance.[21] This is primarily due to multivariate Calculus. Many students lack confidence in their math ability and then suffer from test anxiety, which in turn degrades their performance.

Creating online math courses takes more time and energy because of the complexity of mathematical formulas.[22] One study involving large-scale mastery-based Algebra courses highlights some of these challenges:

- Creating multiple assessments

- Grading multiple assessments

- Providing feedback and progress reports

- Conducting meetings with teaching assistants

- Learning new course structures

The first three challenges listed can be mitigated with strategies outlined in this book. Starting with specific learning objectives, create questions focusing on the learning objective and supply feedback at the question level. Place each question in an appropriate test bank. Once you develop test banks, you can rapidly create randomly generated quizzes students can use repeatedly. In addition to creating unique problems, you can build formula questions, which allow you to develop vast test banks based on a formula and a set of variables.

Here is an example of some of these principles in action. Instructors built exams with specific parameters in mind in a Calculus study.[23] They built quizzes and exams with randomized questions. Each question was either fill-in-the-blank or multiple-choice. Quizzes were cumulative throughout the course. Feedback was provided after the quiz closed. The final exam included one question per learning objective. The objectives were organized based on mass versus spaced practice questions.

You should not hesitate to build a challenging yet supportive quizzing system. It may not make you popular with students, but it will help them be successful as they advance. This observation emerged from another research study conducted at the Air Force Academy. In one study focusing on Calculus I, students were randomly assigned to their sections.[24] Each class received the same syllabus, exam, and post-course evaluation. The only difference was the instructor. Students were randomly assigned to Calculus II at the end of the course. The results of the study were

- Students who performed strongly in Calculus I and rated their instructor favorably performed poorly in Calculus II

- Students who performed poorly in Calculus I and rated their instructor harshly performed better in Calculus II.

The lesson is not to punish hard instructors when they may have long-term favorable effects on performance.

In another study, students had to demonstrate algebra mastery by completing 12 modules (eight core and four advanced).[25] Students could choose from eight advanced modules.

The process for distributing module quizzes included the following:[26]

- Determine the 1st module on which students are testing.

- Provide one of three versions of the quiz. The quiz had ten multiple-choice questions, and students had 60 minutes to complete it.

- Students then ask for the second module.

- Provide one of three versions of the quiz. The quiz had ten multiple-choice questions, and students had 60 minutes to complete it.

- Students had to submit scratch paper recording their problem-solving strategies as part of the assessment process.

- Students also signed an academic integrity statement, reinforcing the importance of ethical conduct in their academic work.

Instructors tracked the results in an Excel spreadsheet. They returned graded results to students and updated the grade book in the LMS.

While the initial plan was successful regarding student performance, the instructor made other observations and adjustments to the course. The instructor developed a solution website with a script where students entered their grades to determine which module to complete next because they needed help deciding on which module to test.[27]

The instructor also increased the number of progression tests by reducing the number of modules tested.[28] This made providing retakes easier. In the new arrangement, students must complete at least eight progress quizzes. Students preferred this new arrangement. Finding a balance through experimentation will help improve mastery quizzing results. You will have to find your balance.

Conclusion

Mastery quizzing is a powerful tool that can transform the way students learn. By focusing on active engagement, regular practice, and immediate feedback, it helps students build confidence and retain knowledge over the long term. Whether used in flipped instruction, game-based platforms, or traditional classrooms, mastery quizzing offers flexibility and benefits that can fit different teaching styles and learning goals.

The examples and strategies in this chapter show how mastery quizzing can work in real-world settings. From building strong test banks to helping students overcome anxiety, these methods can inspire educators to create better learning experiences. By experimenting with these ideas, teachers can find the right balance to help their students succeed.

Remember, mastery quizzing isn't just about taking tests—it's about creating a supportive, engaging environment where students feel encouraged to learn and grow. Use the lessons from this chapter to try new approaches and make a lasting impact in your classroom.

Quick Quiz

Challenge yourself with a quick quiz to close this chapter.

12.1. Which of the following is a primary advantage of mastery quizzing in education?

a) It increases reliance on short-term memory.

b) It discourages regular feedback to students.

c) It enhances long-term retention and understanding.

d) It reduces the need for instructors to track progress.

12.2. In the context of flipped instruction, mastery quizzes are most effective when:

a) Students take them only at the end of the course.

b) They are used to assess and reinforce understanding during classroom sessions.

c) They focus solely on rote memorization of facts.

d) They are optional for all students to complete.

12.3. Which of the following is NOT a common feature of game-based quizzing platforms like Quizizz?

a) Incorporation of timers and game boards.

b) Providing multimedia elements in quizzes.

c) Mandatory use of group quizzes over individual quizzes.

d) Immediate feedback on quiz performance.

12.4. In mastery quizzing, which method helps reduce student anxiety while enhancing their confidence in language learning?

a) High-stakes final exams.

b) Immediate feedback and repeated practice.

c) Introducing advanced-level content immediately.

d) Focusing only on theoretical language concepts.

12.5. What is a recommended practice for building robust test banks for math mastery quizzes?

a) Using only prewritten questions from textbooks.

b) Creating formula-based questions with variable inputs.

c) Limiting the number of questions to a few static options.

d) Avoiding cumulative quizzes throughout the course.

1. Jeffrey S. Nevid, Luke H. Keating, and Shari Lieblich, "Effects of In-Class Engagement Activities in Online Synchronous Classes," *Scholarship of Teaching and Learning in Psychology* 8, no. 4 (2022): 304, https://doi.org/10.1037/stl0000312.

2. Jeremy L. Hsu et al., "Investigating the Influence of Assessment Question Framing on Undergraduate Biology Student Preference and Affect," *CBE—Life Sciences Education* 22, no. 4 (December 2023): ar45, https://doi.org/10.1187/cbe.22-12-0249.

3. Sydney L. Noell et al., "A Bridge to Specifications Grading in Second Semester General Chemistry," *Journal of Chemical Education* 100, no. 6 (2023): 2159–65, https://doi.org/10.1021/acs.jchemed.2c00731.

4. Steven C. Pan et al., "Using Online and Clicker Quizzes to Learn Scientific and Technical Jargon," in *In Their Own Words: What Scholars and Teachers Want You to Know about Why and How to Apply the Science of Learning in Your Academic Setting* (Society for the Teaching of Psychology, 2023), 473–80.

5. Lisa Michael and Irene-Angelica Chounta, "Quizzes and Eggs: Exploring the Impact of Course Design Elements on Students' Engagement," in *In Proceedings of the 15th International Conference on Computer Supported Education (CSEDU 2023)*, 2023, 25–34, https://doi.org/10.5220/0011745000003470.

6. Pan et al., "Using Online and Clicker Quizzes to Learn Scientific and Technical Jargon."

7. Matthew Spencer, "Implementation of Competency-Based Learning in a Laboratory-Focused Analog Design Course," in *2022 ASEE Annual Conference & Exposition* (Minneapolis, MN, 2022), 17; Matthew T. Johnson et al., "Improving Student Preparation and Pass Rates in Flipped Multivariable Calculus with Low-Stakes, Daily Quizzes," *PRIMUS* 33, no. 7 (2023): 714–28, https://doi.org/10.1080/10511970.2022.2163329.

8. Johnson et al., "Improving Student Preparation and Pass Rates in Flipped Multivariable Calculus with Low-Stakes, Daily Quizzes."

9. Ibid., 723.

10. Ibid., 715.

11. Ibid., 723.

12. Pan et al., "Using Online and Clicker Quizzes to Learn Scientific and Technical Jargon."

13. Robin Boyle-Laisure, "Didn't Cover That in Class? Low-Stakes Technique of Quizzing to the Rescue," *The Journal of the Legal Writing Institute* 27 (2023): 299–307.

14. Pan et al., "Using Online and Clicker Quizzes to Learn Scientific and Technical Jargon."

15. Ibid., 477.

16. Ibid., 474.

17. Ibid., 477.

18. Vilogini Chandra Segaran and Harwati Hashim, "'More Online Quizzes, Please!' The Effectiveness of Online Quiz Tools in Enhancing the Learning of Grammar among ESL Learners," *International Journal of Academic Research in Business and Social Sciences* 12, no. 1 (January 29, 2022): 1756–70, https://doi.org/10.6007/IJARBSS/v12-i1/12064.

19. Ibid., 1758.

20. Ibid., 1760.

21. Johnson et al., "Improving Student Preparation and Pass Rates in Flipped Multivariable Calculus with Low-Stakes, Daily Quizzes."

22. Darryl Chamberlain Jr, "How One Instructor Can Teach a Large-Scale, Mastery-Based College Algebra Course Online," *PRIMUS*, 2023, 1–22.

23. Keith B. Lyle et al., "Spaced Retrieval Practice Imposes Desirable Difficulty in Calculus Learning," *Educational Psychology Review* 34 (2022): 1–14, https://doi.org/10.1007/s10648-022-09677-2.

24. David J. Epstein, *Range: Why Generalists Triumph in a Specialized World* (New York: Riverhead Books, 2019).

25. Chamberlain Jr, "How One Instructor Can Teach a Large-Scale, Mastery-Based College Algebra Course Online."

26. Ibid., 876.

27. Ibid., 877.

28. Ibid., 880.

Chapter Thirteen

The Mastery Quizzing Strategy

Imagine a classroom where students aren't just trying to survive until the next exam but actively working towards mastering the material week by week. This chapter is about making that vision a reality through mastery quizzing, an approach that transforms quizzes from mere checkpoints into powerful learning tools. By focusing on incremental learning objectives, carefully designed quizzes, and providing detailed feedback, you can create a dynamic learning environment that encourages students to achieve true understanding.

We'll start by exploring aligning your quiz content with well-defined course learning outcomes. From there, we'll delve into how to construct engaging, real-world questions that challenge students at every cognitive level. Whether designing weekly quizzes or planning for comprehensive midterms and finals, this chapter offers a step-by-step guide to ensuring that your assessments support and reinforce the learning journey.

Objectives

- Identify the key components of developing effective quizzes aligned with course learning outcomes and objectives.

- Design a flexible test bank and exam blueprint to align assessments with course goals and objectives.

Establishing the Foundation

Creating effective quizzes for your course begins with a solid foundation: your course learning outcomes. These outcomes define what you want students to know or be able to do by the end of the course. Learning outcomes are typically broad. They should be refined into specific, measurable learning objectives. Taking the time to develop these will set a strong foundation for your course.

Start with learning objectives. Learning objectives identify the key concepts or skills students need to achieve. To support this process, consider the course materials you'll use—whether they are vendor-provided textbooks, open educational resources, or curated content. Carefully review the material to determine what students should know or be able to do by the end of the course.

Creating Questions

With your learning objectives in place, you can begin crafting questions. Generative AI tools like ChatGPT can assist in developing questions aligned with different levels of Bloom's Taxonomy. This ensures your questions scaffold learning, systematically progressing from lower-level to higher-level cognitive skills.

Create questions. Create a set of questions for each learning objective targeting various difficulty levels. When writing these questions, it's helpful to organize them in a spreadsheet, assigning each learning objective a unique identifier (e.g., LO1, LO2). This system makes it easy to track and reference questions during test creation.

Add real-world context. Enhance your questions by framing them in real-world scenarios. For example, present students as scientists, experts, or other appropriate roles. This contextual framing makes the questions more engaging and helps students connect course content to practical applications.

Provide detailed feedback. For each question, include specific feedback for both correct answers and distractors. This feedback should explain why an answer is correct or incorrect and, ideally, point students to relevant learning materials for further review. Detailed feedback supports learning by clarifying misunderstandings and reinforcing key concepts.

Build a flexible test bank. Organize your questions into a test bank categorized by learning objectives and levels of difficulty. A well-structured test bank allows you to create tests or quizzes with randomized questions covering all necessary objectives. This flexibility enables a variety of test permutations, ensuring a comprehensive assessment of student learning.

Optimizing for bulk upload. When crafting questions, consider the file format required by your LMS. Many LMS platforms allow for bulk uploads, so generating questions in the correct format can save significant time. Generative AI tools can assist with this process, but reviewing and refining the output is essential.

Additionally, you can incorporate pre-existing question banks from vendors or open-source resources. Students can also generate questions for your learning objectives. This would show them the relationship between assessment and the learning objectives. Regardless, it's crucial to vet these questions for quality and relevance and to add feedback where necessary.

Ideally, you create questions for each learning objective for your entire course before the course even starts. However, I recognize most courses are not built ahead of time and are only one or two weeks ahead of the students.

Building Your Exam Blueprint

Creating quizzes is a critical part of effective course design. To ensure your quizzes align with your course goals and enhance learning, starting with an exam blueprint is helpful. This tool lets you plan every quiz detail, from content to format, making the development process more streamlined.

Structuring your quizzes. First, think about how quizzes will fit into your course. Will you provide a quiz weekly, as part of each module, or at other intervals? For example, in a 16-week course, you might schedule a weekly quiz. Alternatively, if your course is divided into larger modules, you may need multiple quizzes within each module to cover the material effectively.

When planning, consider the cognitive levels you want to assess. Will your questions focus on foundational knowledge, like recalling facts, or more advanced skills, like applying concepts? Use Bloom's Taxonomy as a guide to ensure you are challenging students appropriately.

Designing with purpose. Your exam blueprint is a document that should specify the following:

1. **Learning objectives**. What skills or knowledge should the quiz assess? For each objective, assign a weight or points to reflect its importance.

2. **Question types**. Decide whether to use multiple-choice, true or false, short answer, or other formats. Automated quizzes often work best with closed-ended questions, such as multiple-choice or fill-in-the-blank, to streamline grading.

3. **Question distribution**. Determine the number of questions drawn and their point values for each objective.

Building the Quiz

Once your blueprint is ready, use it as a guide to develop the quiz in your LMS. Write clear instructions specifying key details.

- **Time limits**. How much time will students have to complete the quiz?

- **Attempts**. Can students retake the quiz? If so, how many times?

- **Randomization**. Draw questions randomly from a test bank to ensure each attempt provides a unique experience.

Leveraging test banks. Organizing questions into **test banks** based on learning objectives allows for efficient quiz creation. For example, if your blueprint highlights Learning Objective 5, you can pull questions from that corresponding test bank. Keep quizzes concise, with 10–15 questions, to maintain focus and avoid overwhelming students.

Using an exam blueprint ensures your quizzes are well-structured, purposeful, and aligned with course goals. This not only makes the building process smoother but also enhances the learning experience for students.

Deploying the Quizzes

Mastery quizzes are powerful tools for reinforcing learning and ensuring long-term retention. Here is a strategy for implementing these quizzes effectively in a 16-week course. By following these steps, you encourage students to achieve mastery of the material while maintaining their engagement and motivation.

Weekly quizzes with a "go or no-go" standard. Imagine a course where students complete a quiz each week. The quizzes are set to a "go or no-go" standard, meaning students can take them as many times as they need until they achieve a perfect score. Credit for the quiz is awarded only when they reach 100%.

Tracking completion may require maintaining a simple spreadsheet or another tracking system to log students' progress. The repetition helps reinforce learning, and the emphasis on mastery motivates students to understand the material fully.

Making quizzes count. To ensure students prioritize these quizzes, consider making their overall quiz performance a significant part of their final grade. This could be 10% to 20% of the course grade—equivalent to one or two letter grades. This structure encourages students to invest the necessary time to achieve mastery.

Building and randomizing test banks. The quiz questions should be drawn randomly from a well-structured test bank. For additional reinforcement, include questions from previous weeks in each subsequent quiz. This cumulative approach ensures students retain material from earlier in the course.

For instance, you can organize your test banks as follows:

1. **Week 1**: A standalone test bank for the week.

2. **Week 2**: A test bank that includes new material and some questions from Week 1.

3. **Week 3**: A combined test bank with questions from Weeks 1 and 2 and the new material for Week 3.

Continue this process throughout the course, building a more extensive test bank incorporating all questions from previous weeks. While this requires more upfront effort, it encourages students to stay engaged with earlier material and prevents them from forgetting key concepts.

Administration and grade tracking. When students achieve 100% on a quiz, promptly record their score in the grade book. Maintaining a separate grade category or column in your grading system for these quizzes is helpful. This transparency allows students to track their progress and feel accomplished as they master the course content.

By Week 16, students will have completed a series of cumulative quizzes reinforcing their knowledge and promoting long-term retention. This method requires careful planning, but the student learning and engagement payoff is well worth the effort.

Midterm and Final Examinations

Creating a midterm or final exam follows a similar process to building a weekly quiz, with a few key differences. The main distinction is the scale and scope of the exam. While a weekly quiz might focus on 10 to 15 questions, midterms and finals often require a more extensive set of questions, typically ranging from 25 to 50 or more. These exams also draw from a broader range of learning objectives, allowing for a more comprehensive assessment of student understanding.

Developing a robust exam blueprint. First, use the test banks you've already established for each learning objective. These should include questions at varying difficulty levels—beginning, intermediate, and advanced. This variety ensures the exam challenges students appropriately while aligning with their preparation level.

Consider incorporating open-ended questions in addition to multiple-choice or other objective formats for midterms and finals. Open-ended questions can provide deeper insights into student understanding and encourage critical thinking.

Encouraging continuous engagement. One key advantage of this approach is its ability to keep students engaged throughout the course. Weekly quizzes serve as a foundation, allowing students to practice and master the material incrementally. By the time they face the midterm or final, they've already interacted with most of the content multiple times.

This method also allows students to revisit previous quizzes as study aids. For example, if the midterm is scheduled for Week 8, students can review and retake quizzes from Weeks 1 through 7. Since these quizzes are part of their learning strategy rather than one-and-done assessments, they serve as valuable tools for reinforcing knowledge.

Structuring the midterm or final exam. Unlike weekly quizzes, midterms and finals are limited to a single attempt. However, students should have ample time to prepare through practice quizzes. This ensures fairness while maintaining the rigor of the exam. Randomly drawing questions from a well-organized test bank also prevents predictability, encouraging students to stay on top of their studies.

Benefits of a strategic approach. This strategy promotes active learning and long-term retention. Rather than cramming or relying on short-term memory, students are encouraged to engage with the material consistently. By revisiting content and practicing with randomized questions, they build a stronger and more comprehensive understanding of the subject.

Incorporating this approach into your teaching will help students perform better on exams and foster a deeper appreciation for the subject matter. Let me know how this strategy works for you!

Quick Quiz

Close this chapter with a quick knowledge check.

13.1. What is the first step in creating effective quizzes for a course?

a) Choosing the quiz format.

b) Developing a test bank.

c) Refining course learning outcomes into specific objectives.

d) Randomizing questions in the quiz.

13.2. How does aligning questions with Bloom's Taxonomy benefit students?

a) It reduces the complexity of the quiz.

b) It ensures questions scaffold learning from basic to advanced levels.

c) It eliminates the need for a test bank.

d) It allows for a single level of cognitive skill assessment.

13.3. Why is it essential to include detailed feedback for quiz questions?

a) To provide students with the correct answers automatically.

b) To reinforce key concepts and clarify misunderstandings.

c) To reduce the number of questions needed in a quiz.

d) To save time during grading.

13.4. What is the primary purpose of an exam blueprint?

a) To simplify the creation of randomized questions.

b) To organize questions based on their difficulty levels.

c) To plan quiz content, structure, and alignment with course objectives.

d) To ensure quizzes are graded fairly.

13.5. What is a recommended strategy for promoting long-term retention through quizzes?

a) Allowing students to skip quizzes.

b) Using a "go or no-go" standard with cumulative weekly quizzes.

c) Limiting quizzes to a single attempt.

d) Removing older material from subsequent quizzes.

Appendix A: Glossary

Active learning. Active learning is an instructional approach that engages students in the learning process through activities and discussions rather than passively receiving information. Examples include group work, quizzing, problem-solving tasks, discussions, and hands-on activities. Active learning improves comprehension and retention by involving students directly in their learning.

Adaptive learning. Adaptive learning is a personalized educational approach that uses technology to adjust the learning experience based on the individual student's needs, progress, and performance. Adaptive learning systems collect data on student performance and adapt the content, pace, and difficulty level accordingly, providing a customized learning path for each student.

Blended learning. Blended learning is a teaching method that combines online lessons with traditional in-person classes. In this approach, students can learn at their own pace using online resources while also getting face-to-face help from teachers in the classroom. This mix allows for more flexible and personalized learning, helping students better understand the material.

Burn-down chart. A burn-down chart is a concept that originates in project management. It helps teams in projects, especially in Agile methods like Scrum, to see how much work is getting done over time. It's like a graph with time on one side and the amount of work left to do on the other. As the project goes on, the line on the graph should go down, showing progress toward finishing all the work by the end. It helps teams know if they're on track and need to make changes to meet their goals. I have adapted this for classes I have taught to help students stay on track.

Exam/test. An exam, or examination, is a more comprehensive assessment that evaluates a learner's knowledge, skills, and understanding over a broad range of material, usually covering multiple units, an entire course, or a significant portion of the curriculum. They are often summative assessments measuring the cumulative learning and proficiency of the student. Exams tend to be high-stakes, contributing substantially to the final grade. Exams can include various question types, such as multiple-choice, essays, short answers, and practical tasks.

Exam blueprint. An exam blueprint, also known as a test blueprint or assessment blueprint, is a detailed outline or plan that specifies the content and structure of an examination. It is a road map for creating assessments that accurately measure a student's knowledge and skills in a particular subject area.

Exam wrapper. An exam wrapper is a reflective exercise that students can use to evaluate their performance.[1] It is a meta-cognition exercise that either supplements an assessment or is part of the actual assessment. An exam wrapper typically questions a student's exam preparation strategies.

Feedback. Feedback involves giving students information about their performance on individual questions, including what they got right or wrong and why. This feedback helps students understand their mistakes, learn the correct information, and improve their knowledge and skills for future assessments.

Flipped instruction. Flipped instruction, or the flipped classroom model, involves learning new content at home through videos, readings, or other resources and then applying that knowledge in class through activities, discussions, and problem-solving. This approach shifts the focus from lecture-based instruction to active, student-centered learning during class.

Formative exam. A formative exam is an assessment conducted during learning to monitor student progress, provide ongoing feedback, and guide instructional strategies. The primary purpose of formative exams is to identify areas where students may need additional support or improvement. These assessments are typically low-stakes, meaning they have little or no impact on the overall grade. Instead, they enhance the learning experience by allowing educators and students to identify strengths and weaknesses in real time.

Learning objective. A learning objective is a specific, measurable statement that defines what students are expected to learn and be able to do by the end of a lesson, unit, or course. Learning objectives guide instructional design, teaching strategies, and assessments, ensuring educational activities align with desired outcomes. They often follow the criterion objective format (standard or behavior, condition, criteria) and focus on observable behaviors or skills.

Mastery grading. Mastery grading evaluates students based on their understanding of the material rather than just giving them a grade for completing assignments or tests. In this system, students work on a topic until they fully understand it or "master" it before moving on to the next topic. This approach helps ensure that students learn the material, not just memorize it for a test.

Mastery learning. Mastery learning is an instructional strategy based on the belief that all students can achieve a high level of understanding if given enough time and the right support. In this approach, students must demonstrate mastery of a topic before moving on to the next. This often involves frequent formative assessments and opportunities for revision and improvement.

Mastery quizzing. Mastery quizzing involves frequent, low-stakes quizzes designed to assess students' understanding of specific concepts. These quizzes are typically used in a mastery learning framework, allowing students to retake quizzes until they achieve a high level of proficiency. The focus is on learning and mastery rather than grades.

Passive learning. Passive learning involves students receiving information from an instructor without active engagement or interaction. Traditional lecture-based teaching is a common example. In passive learning, students typically listen, take notes, and memorize information, but there is little opportunity for interaction, discussion, or hands-on activities.

Quiz. A quiz is a short assessment designed to measure a learner's understanding of specific concepts or topics covered within a short time frame, such as a single class, a chapter, or a few lessons. Quizzes are formative assessments containing a subset of questions from a larger test bank to provide immediate feedback and guide further instruction. They are usually low-stakes, meaning they do not significantly impact the overall grade but serve to reinforce learning and identify areas needing improvement.

Retaking. Retaking exams allows students to retryan assessment they have previously taken. This opportunity is often provided to improve their scores and demonstrate a better understanding of the material. Retaking exams will contain different questions aligned with the same learning objectives as the previous quiz. The conditions for retaking exams, such as the number of allowed attempts and the effect on final grades, vary depending on the institution or instructor's policies.

Specifications grading. Specifications grading is an assessment system where students are graded based on whether they meet specified criteria for assignments and exams. Instead of traditional point-based grades, students receive pass/fail or satisfactory/unsatisfactory marks for meeting clearly defined standards. This method aims to reduce grade inflation and focus on mastery of learning objectives.

Summative exam. A summative exam is an assessment conducted at the end of an instructional period to evaluate student learning, knowledge, proficiency, and academic achievement. It is a high-stakes assessment, meaning it significantly impacts the overall grade. The primary purpose of summative exams is to measure the extent to which students have achieved the learning objectives and to provide a comprehensive evaluation of their performance.

Test bank. A test bank is a collection of exam questions and answers educators use to create tests and quizzes. These questions are typically organized by chapter, topic, or objective and can cover various types of questions, such as multiple-choice, true/false, short answer, essay, and matching. Educators create test banks or use textbook publisher materials.

---

1. John E. Edlund, "Implementing Exam Wrappers," in *In Their Own Words: What Scholars and Teachers Want You to Know about Why and How to Apply the Science of Learning in Your Academic Setting* (Society for the Teaching of Psychology, 2023), 480.

Appendix B: Writing Learning Objectives with ChatGPT

Here are ChatGPT prompts based on Bloom's Taxonomy for writing learning objectives for each skill level. Add the specific number of objectives in place of the <X>. For example, "write 3 learning objectives for ..."

Remembering Level Prompt

Write <X> learning objectives for a <course subject> course at the remembering level of Bloom's Taxonomy using verbs like Cite, Define, Describe, Draw, Enumerate, Identify, Index, Indicate, Label, List, Match, Meet, Name, Outline, Point, Quote, Read, Recall, Recite, Recognize, Record, Repeat, Reproduce, Review, Select, State, Study, Tabulate, Trace, Write

Understanding Level Prompt

Write <X> learning objectives for a <course subject> course at the understanding level of Bloom's Taxonomy using verbs like Add, Approximate, Articulate, Associate, Characterize, Clarify, Classify, Compare, Compute, Contrast, Convert, Defend, Describe, Detail, Differentiate, Discuss, Distinguish, Elaborate, Estimate, Example, Explain, Express, Extend, Extrapolate, Factor, Generalize, Give, Infer, Interact, Interpolate, Interpret, Observe, Paraphrase, Picture graphically, Predict, Review, Rewrite, Subtract, Summarize, Translate, Visualize

Applying Level Prompt

Write <X> learning objectives for a <course subject> course at the applying level of Bloom's Taxonomy using verbs like Acquire, Adapt, Allocate, Alphabetize, Apply, Ascertain, Assign, Attain, Avoid, Back up, Calculate, Capture, Change, Classify, Complete, Compute, Construct, Customize, Demonstrate, Depreciate, Derive, Determine, Diminish, Discover, Draw, Employ, Examine, Exercise, Explore, Expose, Express, Factor, Figure, Graph, Handle, Illustrate, Investigate, Manipulate, Modify, Operate, Personalize, Plot, Practice, Predict, Prepare, Price, Process, Produce, Project, Provide, Relate, Round off, Sequence, Show, Simulate, Sketch, Solve, Subscribe, Tabulate, Transcribe, Translate, Use

Analyzing Level Prompt

Write <X> learning objectives for a <course subject> course at the analyzing level of Bloom's Taxonomy using verbs like Analyze, Audit, Blueprint, Breadboard, Break down, Characterize, Classify, Compare, Confirm, Contrast, Correlate, Detect, Diagnose, Diagram, Differentiate, Discriminate, Dissect, Distinguish, Document, Ensure, Examine, Explain, Explore, Figure out, File, Group, Identify, Illustrate, Infer, Interrupt, Inventory, Investigate, Layout, Manage, Maximize, Minimize, Optimize, Order, Outline, Point out, Prioritize, Proofread, Query, Relate, Select, Separate, Subdivide, Train, Transform

Evaluating Level Prompt

Write <X> learning objectives for a <course subject> course at the evaluating level of Bloom's Taxonomy using verbs like Appraise, Assess, Compare, Conclude, Contrast, Counsel, Criticize, Critique, Defend, Determine, Discriminate, Estimate, Evaluate, Explain, Grade, Hire, Interpret, Judge, Justify, Measure, Predict, Prescribe, Rank, Rate, Recommend, Release, Select, Summarize, Support, Test, Validate, Verify

Creating Level Prompt

Write <X> learning objectives for a <course subject> course at the creating level of Bloom's Taxonomy using verbs like Abstract, Animate, Arrange, Assemble, Budget, Categorize, Code, Combine, Compile, Compose, Construct, Cope, Correspond, Create, Cultivate, Debug, Depict, Design, Develop, Devise, Dictate, Enhance, Explain, Facilitate, Format, Formulate, Generalize, Generate, Handle, Import, Improve, Incorporate, Integrate, Interface, Join, Lecture, Model, Modify, Network, Organize, Outline, Overhaul, Plan, Portray, Prepare, Prescribe, Produce, Program, Rearrange, Reconstruct, Relate, Reorganize, Revise, Rewrite, Specify, Summarize

Appendix C: Writing Questions with ChatGPT

Bloom's Taxonomy Targeted

Here are example prompts for each question type, incorporating Bloom's Taxonomy for variety. Please add the specific subject in place of [Subject].

Multiple-Choice Questions

- **Knowledge level.** "Create a multiple-choice question to test students' recall of the key concepts in [Subject]. Provide four options, with one correct answer."

- **Comprehension level.** "Design a multiple-choice question that assesses students' understanding of the main ideas in [Subject]. Include four answer choices, with one being correct."

- **Application level.** "Generate a multiple-choice question where students need to apply principles from [Subject] to a new situation. Include four possible answers, one of which is correct."

- **Analysis level.** "Write a multiple-choice question that requires students to analyze a scenario related to [Subject] and choose the best course of action. Provide four options, with one correct answer."

- **Evaluation level.** "Create a multiple-choice question that asks students to evaluate the effectiveness of different strategies or approaches in [Subject]. Provide four choices, with one correct answer."

True/False Questions

- **Knowledge level.** "Generate a true/false question that checks students' recall of basic facts in [Subject]."

- **Comprehension level.** "Design a true/false question that assesses students' understanding of concepts explained in [Subject]."

- **Application level.** "Write a true/false question where students must apply a concept from [Subject] to a specific example or scenario."

- **Analysis level.** "Create a true/false question that requires students to analyze a statement or scenario in [Subject] and determine its validity."

- **Evaluation level.** "Develop a true/false question that asks students to evaluate the accuracy or effectiveness of a method or idea in [Subject]."

Matching Questions

- **Knowledge level.** "Create a matching question to test students' recall of terms and their definitions in [Subject]. Provide a list of terms and a corresponding list of definitions."

- **Comprehension level.** "Design a matching question that assesses students' understanding by having them match concepts with examples in [Subject]."

- **Application level.** "Write a matching question where students match principles or theories from [Subject] with real-life applications or scenarios."

- **Analysis level.** "Generate a matching question that requires students to analyze different components or elements of a process in [Subject] and match them correctly."

- **Evaluation level.** "Develop a matching question that asks students to evaluate different approaches or methods in [Subject] by matching them with their respective outcomes or impacts."

Fill-in-the-Blank Questions

- **Knowledge level.** "Create a fill-in-the-blank question that tests students' recall of key terms or facts in [Subject]."

- **Comprehension level.** "Design a fill-in-the-blank question that requires students to demonstrate their understanding of concepts in [Subject] by completing sentences with appropriate terms."

- **Application level.** "Write a fill-in-the-blank question where students apply their knowledge of [Subject] to fill in missing information in a scenario."

- **Analysis level.** "Generate a fill-in-the-blank question that asks students to analyze a situation in [Subject] and complete the statement with the correct conclusion."

- **Evaluation level.** "Develop a fill-in-the-blank question that requires students to evaluate information or a scenario in [Subject] and provide the missing term or phrase."

Short Answer Questions

- **Knowledge level.** "Create a short answer question that asks students to list or describe key facts about [Subject]."

- **Comprehension level.** "Design a short answer question that requires students to explain a concept or idea from [Subject] in their own words."

- **Application level.** "Write a short answer question where students need to apply a principle from [Subject] to solve a problem or address a scenario."

- **Analysis level.** "Generate a short answer question that asks students to analyze a case study or situation related to [Subject] and provide a detailed response."

- **Evaluation level.** "Develop a short answer question that requires students to evaluate the effectiveness of a strategy or approach in [Subject] and justify their answer."

Essay Questions

- **Knowledge level.** "Create an essay question that asks students to summarize the main points of [Subject]."

- **Comprehension level.** "Design an essay question that requires students to explain the significance of a major concept in [Subject] and its implications."

- **Application level.** "Write an essay question where students must apply their understanding of [Subject] to a real-world problem or scenario and propose a solution."

- **Analysis level.** "Generate an essay question that asks students to analyze a complex issue or topic within [Subject] and break it down into its component parts."

- **Evaluation level.** "Develop an essay question that requires students to evaluate the effectiveness or impact of a policy, theory, or method in [Subject] and provide evidence to support their evaluation."

Modify and expand upon these prompts based on your students' specific needs and learning outcomes. You may also want to indicate the level of difficulty.

Learning Objective Targeted

Here are similar examples with a placeholder for the learning objective.

Multiple-Choice Questions

- **Knowledge level.** "Create a multiple-choice question to test students' recall of the key concepts related to [Learning Objective]. Provide four options, with one correct answer."

- **Comprehension level.** "Design a multiple-choice question that assesses students' understanding of the main ideas related to [Learning Objective]. Include four answer choices, with one being correct."

- **Application level.** "Generate a multiple-choice question where students need to apply principles from [Learning Objective] to a new situation. Include four possible answers, one of which is correct."

- **Analysis level.** "Write a multiple-choice question that requires students to analyze a scenario related to [Learning Objective] and choose the best course of action. Provide four options, with one correct answer."

- **Evaluation level.** "Create a multiple-choice question that asks students to evaluate the effectiveness of different strategies or approaches related to [Learning Objective]. Provide four choices, with one correct answer."

True/False Questions

- **Knowledge level.** "Generate a true/false question that checks students' recall of basic facts related to [Learning Objective]."

- **Comprehension level.** "Design a true/false question that assesses students' understanding of concepts related to [Learning Objective]."

- **Application level.** "Write a true/false question where students must apply a concept from [Learning Objective] to a specific example or scenario."

- **Analysis level.** "Create a true/false question that requires students to analyze a statement or scenario related to [Learning Objective] and determine its validity."

- **Evaluation level.** "Develop a true/false question that asks students to evaluate the accuracy or effectiveness of a method or idea related to [Learning Objective]."

Matching Questions

- **Knowledge level.** "Create a matching question to test students' recall of terms and their definitions related to [Learning Objective]. Provide a list of terms and a corresponding list of definitions."

- **Comprehension level.** "Design a matching question that assesses students' understanding by having them match concepts with examples related to [Learning Objective]."

- **Application level.** "Write a matching question where students match principles or theories related to [Learning Objective] with real-life applications or scenarios."

- **Analysis level.** "Generate a matching question that requires students to analyze different components or elements of a process related to [Learning Objective] and match them correctly."

- **Evaluation level.** "Develop a matching question that asks students to evaluate different approaches or methods related to [Learning Objective] by matching them with their respective outcomes or impacts."

Fill-in-the-Blank Questions

- **Knowledge level.** "Create a fill-in-the-blank question that tests students' recall of key terms or facts related to [Learning Objective]."

- **Comprehension level.** "Design a fill-in-the-blank question that requires students to demonstrate their understanding of concepts related to [Learning Objective] by completing sentences with appropriate terms."

- **Application level.** "Write a fill-in-the-blank question where students apply their knowledge related to [Learning Objective] to fill in missing information in a scenario."

- **Analysis level.** "Generate a fill-in-the-blank question that asks students to analyze a situation related to [Learning Objective] and complete the statement with the correct conclusion."

- **Evaluation level.** "Develop a fill-in-the-blank question that requires students to evaluate information or a scenario related to [Learning Objective] and provide the missing term or phrase."

Short Answer Questions

- **Knowledge level.** "Create a short answer question that asks students to list or describe key facts related to [Learning Objective]."

- **Comprehension level.** "Design a short answer question that requires students to explain a concept or idea related to [Learning Objective] in their own words."

- **Application level.** "Write a short answer question where students need to apply a principle related to [Learning Objective] to solve a problem or address a scenario."

- **Analysis level.** "Generate a short answer question that asks students to analyze a case study or situation related to [Learning Objective] and provide a detailed response."

- **Evaluation level.** "Develop a short answer question that requires students to evaluate the effectiveness of a strategy or approach related to [Learning Objective] and justify their answer."

Essay Questions

- **Knowledge level.** "Create an essay question that asks students to summarize the main points related to [Learning Objective]."

- **Comprehension level.** "Design an essay question that requires students to explain the significance of a major concept related to [Learning Objective] and its implications."

- **Application level.** "Write an essay question where students must apply their understanding related to [Learning Objective] to a real-world problem or scenario and propose a solution."

- **Analysis level.** "Generate an essay question that asks students to analyze a complex issue or topic related to [Learning Objective] and break it down into its component parts."

- **Evaluation level.** "Develop an essay question that requires students to evaluate the effectiveness or impact of a policy, theory, or method related to [Learning Objective] and provide evidence to support their evaluation."

Modify these prompts based on your students' specific learning objectives and outcomes.

Appendix D: Question Development Formula

Here are the essential steps to develop questions and build robust quizzing databases.

1. Write clear learning objectives. (Chapter 5 – Question Design)

2. Define key concepts or skills students need to achieve objectives. (Chapter 5 – Question Design)

3. Develop questions meeting learning objectives. (Chapter 5 – Question Design)

4. Enhance questions with real-world context. (Chapter 5 – Question Design)

5. Write feedback for both incorrect and correct answers. (Chapter 6 – Feedback)

6. Include a naming convention to classify each question. (Chapter 7 – Test Banks)

7. Add the question to the appropriate test bank. (Chapter 7 – Test Banks)

8. Develop an Exam Blueprint (Chapter 8 – Quiz Design)

9. Build quizzes using the test bank. (Chapter 8 – Quiz Design)

Appendix E: Accessibility Checklist

Accessible Quiz Design Checklist for Educators

Use this checklist to ensure your quizzes are accessible to all students.

Technology and Platform

- The quiz platform supports *assistive technologies* (screen readers, magnifiers, etc.).

- The quiz is fully *navigable using a keyboard* (no mouse required).

- The quiz works well on *all devices*, including phones and tablets.

Text and Content

- Text is written in *clear, plain language* with no jargon.

- Fonts are easy to read (e.g., sans-serif) and at least *12–14 points* in size.

- Text strongly contrasts with the background (e.g., black text on white).

- Any images or diagrams include *descriptive alt text*.

Timing and Flexibility

- No strict time limits or *extra time* is available upon request.

- Students can pause and return to the quiz if needed.

Question Design

- Questions are *consistent in structure* across the quiz.

- Instructions are clear and easy to follow.

- Feedback is meaningful and helps students understand their responses.

Visual Design

- Colors are not the only way to convey information (e.g., "select the red button" also includes a label).

- The quiz avoids flashing or flickering content that could cause seizures.

- Visual content is easy to interpret, even for students with visual impairments.

- Visual elements have enough contrast to be interpreted clearly.

Input and Interaction

- Students can complete the quiz using a *keyboard, mouse, or touch*.

- Input elements (checkboxes, dropdowns, etc.) are *labeled clearly* for screen readers.

- Open-ended questions allow students to use *voice-to-text* tools if needed.

Audio and Video

- Videos include *captions* and/or *transcripts*.

- Audio content has a *transcript* or written alternative.

- Students can adjust the *volume and playback speed* for multimedia.

Accommodations

- The quiz offers *extended or unlimited time* for students who need it.

- Alternative formats (e.g., printable quizzes) are available upon request.

Testing and Feedback

- Students with diverse needs and abilities have tested the quiz.

- Feedback from users has been incorporated to address accessibility barriers.

Legal and Ethical Considerations

- The quiz complies with *WCAG 2.1 guidelines* or other relevant accessibility standards.

- Accessibility features demonstrate *care and inclusion*, ensuring all students can participate fully.

By following this checklist, you can design quizzes that are inclusive, fair, and accessible, helping all students succeed in your classroom.

Appendix F: Exam Blueprint Example

Example: Science Test Blueprint with Learning Objectives Alignment

Exam Overview:

- Total Points: 100

- Duration: 90 minutes

Section 1: Biology (40 points)

- 10 Multiple-Choice Questions (2 points each)

  - Learning Objectives:

    - LO1: Describe the structure and function of cells.

    - LO2: Explain the process of photosynthesis.

    - LO3: Understand the basic principles of genetics.

- 5 Short Answer Questions (4 points each)

  - Learning Objectives:

    - LO4: Identify major human body systems and their functions.

    - LO5: Classify living organisms based on taxonomy principles.

Section 2: Chemistry (40 points)

- 5 Multiple-Choice Questions (3 points each)

  - Learning Objectives:

    - LO6: Define elements and compounds and differentiate between them.

    - LO7: Describe common chemical reactions and their applications.

- 5 Short Answer Questions (5 points each)

  - Learning Objectives:

    - LO8: Explain the properties of acids and bases.

    - LO9: Analyze periodic table trends and their significance.

Section 3: Physics (20 points)

- 5 Multiple-Choice Questions (2 points each)

  - Learning Objectives:

    - LO10: Understand fundamental concepts of forces and motion.

    - LO11: Explain different forms of energy and their conversions.

- 2 Essay Questions (5 points each)

  - Learning Objectives:

- LO12: Apply principles of electricity and magnetism to everyday examples.

- LO13: Describe the function and applications of simple machines.

Exam Grading:

- Multiple-Choice: 45 points

- Short Answer: 45 points

- Essays: 10 points

- Total: 100 points

Appendix G: Chapter-end Quiz Answers

Chapter 1: My Story with Quizzes

1.1. What role did quizzes play in the author's experience at the Air Force Academy Preparatory School?

- **Answer**: b) They were a primary method for regular assessment and preparing for exams.

- **Correct Answer Feedback**: "That's correct! Quizzes were a primary method for regular assessment and preparing for exams, fostering active learning and reducing test anxiety."

- **Incorrect Answer Feedback**: "Not quite. The quizzes at the Air Force Academy Preparatory School were integral to regular assessment and preparing for exams, emphasizing active engagement with the material."

1.2. Which of the following best describes the author's preparation for advancement exams in the Air Force?

- **Answer**: c) Using test banks and answering hundreds of questions nightly.

- **Correct Answer Feedback**: "That's correct! Using test banks and answering hundreds of questions nightly helped the author identify weaknesses and consistently improve."

- **Incorrect Answer Feedback**: "Not quite. The author's preparation involved rigorous practice with test banks and answering hundreds of questions nightly to build competence and reduce errors."

1.3. What deficiency did the author observe in higher education regarding quizzes and exams?

- **Answer**: b) Insufficient formative quizzes for practice.

- **Correct Answer Feedback**: "That's correct! The author observed a lack of formative quizzes for practice, which limited opportunities for active learning and preparation."

- **Incorrect Answer Feedback**: "Not quite. The main deficiency in higher education was the insufficient use of formative quizzes, which are essential for practice and preparation."

Chapter 2: Key Concepts

2.1. What is the primary goal of mastery learning?

- **Answer: b)** To ensure students achieve a high level of understanding before advancing.

- **Correct Answer Feedback**: "That's correct! Mastery learning ensures that students achieve a high level of understanding before progressing, fostering deeper learning and retention."

- **Incorrect Answer Feedback**: "Not quite. The goal of mastery learning is to ensure students fully understand and master a topic before moving to the next, rather than rushing through or solely focusing on grades."

2.2. Which of the following is a key feature of mastery quizzing?

- **Answer: b)** Multiple attempts to achieve mastery.

- **Correct Answer Feedback**: "That's correct! Multiple attempts to achieve mastery are a cornerstone of mastery quizzing, allowing students to refine their understanding and improve over time."

- **Incorrect Answer Feedback**: "Not quite. One of the key features of mastery quizzing is multiple attempts to achieve mastery, which gives students the opportunity to learn from their mistakes and deepen their understanding."

2.3. What psychological principle explains why students retain information better when they quiz themselves regularly?

- **Answer: b)** The testing effect.

- **Correct Answer Feedback**: "That's correct! The testing effect explains how active retrieval through quizzing significantly enhances memory retention and learning."

- **Incorrect Answer Feedback**: "Not quite. The testing effect is the principle that quizzing oneself regularly improves retention by reinforcing memory through active retrieval."

2.4. How does spaced repetition improve learning outcomes?

- **Answer: c)** By reviewing material at increasingly spaced intervals to strengthen memory.

- **Correct Answer Feedback**: "That's correct! Spaced repetition strengthens memory by reviewing material at gradually increasing intervals, promoting long-term retention."

- **Incorrect Answer Feedback**: "Not quite. Spaced repetition involves reviewing material at spaced intervals, allowing information to be consolidated over time and improving retention."

2.5. Which of the following describes active recall?

- **Answer: b)** Actively retrieving learned information to strengthen neural connections.

- **Correct Answer Feedback**: "That's correct! Active recall involves actively retrieving learned information, which strengthens neural connections and promotes deeper learning."

- **Incorrect Answer Feedback**: "Not quite. Active recall is the process of actively retrieving information from memory, rather than passively reviewing material, to reinforce learning."

Chapter 3: Why Quizzing?

3.1. Which of the following is a primary benefit of low-stakes quizzing?
- **Answer:** c) Improving performance through active engagement with material.

- **Correct Answer Feedback:** "That's correct! Low-stakes quizzing enhances performance by actively engaging students with the material, promoting better retention and understanding."

- **Incorrect Answer Feedback:** "Not quite. Low-stakes quizzing primarily improves performance by encouraging active engagement with the material, rather than focusing on stress or reducing content."

3.2. How do mastery quizzes help students succeed in summative exams?
- **Answer**: b) By aligning questions with learning objectives and encouraging repeated practice.

- **Correct Answer Feedback:** "That's correct! Mastery quizzes align with learning objectives and provide repeated practice, which boosts student performance in summative exams."

- **Incorrect Answer Feedback:** "Not quite. Mastery quizzes are effective when they align with learning objectives and encourage repeated practice, which supports success in summative assessments."

3.3. What is one major challenge of implementing a mastery learning strategy?
- **Answer**: c) Teachers must dedicate significant time to setup and administration.

- **Correct Answer Feedback:** "That's correct! Implementing mastery learning requires significant time for setup and administration, which can be challenging but rewarding."

- **Incorrect Answer Feedback:** "Not quite. The primary challenge of implementing a mastery learning strategy is the time and effort teachers must dedicate to setup and administration."

3.4. Why are formative quizzes particularly useful for instructors?

- **Answer:** b) They provide immediate data to identify misconceptions and adapt teaching strategies.

- **Correct Answer Feedback:** "That's correct! Formative quizzes provide immediate data, helping instructors identify misconceptions and adapt their teaching strategies effectively."

- **Incorrect Answer Feedback:** "Not quite. Formative quizzes are particularly useful because they offer immediate data to identify misconceptions and adapt teaching strategies accordingly."

3.5. Which statement best describes the relationship between quizzing and student motivation?

- **Answer:** b) Quizzing motivates students to prepare, engage actively, and improve study habits.

- **Correct Answer Feedback:** "That's correct! Quizzing motivates students by encouraging preparation, active engagement, and the development of better study habits."

- **Incorrect Answer Feedback:** "Not quite. Quizzing enhances student motivation by encouraging preparation, active engagement, and improved study habits, rather than solely stressing students or being ineffective."

Chapter 4: Technology

4.1. What is one primary advantage of using digital quizzing platforms?

- **Answer:** b) They provide instant feedback.

- **Correct Answer Feedback:** "That's correct! Digital quizzing platforms allow students to learn from their mistakes immediately and adjust their understanding in real time."

- **Incorrect Answer Feedback:** "Not quite. The primary advantage of digital quizzing platforms is their ability to provide instant feedback, enabling quick corrections and better retention."

4.2. Which of the following is NOT a benefit of learning management systems (LMS)?

- **Answer:** c) Limited scalability.

- **Correct Answer Feedback:** "That's correct! Learning management systems are designed to be scalable, accommodating various class sizes and learning needs."

- **Incorrect Answer Feedback:** "Not quite. LMS platforms are known for their scalability, among other benefits like customizable layouts and detailed grade reporting."

4.3. What feature is common in student response systems (SRS)?

- **Answer:** c) Use of electronic clickers or polling apps for real-time interaction.

- **Correct Answer Feedback:** "That's correct! Student response systems often use clickers or apps to facilitate immediate interaction and engagement in the classroom."

- **Incorrect Answer Feedback:** "Not quite. A common feature of SRS is the use of electronic clickers or polling apps for real-time interaction and immediate feedback."

4.4. Which game-based quizzing tool is known for its leaderboard feature to promote competition?

- **Answer:** b) Kahoot!

- **Correct Answer Feedback:** "That's correct! Kahoot! is widely recognized for its leaderboard feature, which fosters a competitive and engaging learning environment."

- **Incorrect Answer Feedback:** "Not quite. Kahoot! stands out for its leaderboard feature, which motivates students through friendly competition."

4.5. How do game-based quizzing applications like Quizizz improve student engagement?

- **Answer:** b) By incorporating multimedia elements and competitive features.

- **Correct Answer Feedback:** "That's correct! Quizizz enhances engagement by integrating multimedia and competitive features to make learning interactive and fun."

- **Incorrect Answer Feedback:** "Not quite. Game-based quizzing applications like Quizizz improve engagement by combining multimedia elements and a competitive atmosphere."

Chapter 5: Question Design

5.1. Which of the following best describes the purpose of a learning objective?

- **Answer:** b) To describe observable behaviors that indicate learning has occurred.

- **Correct Answer Feedback:** "That's correct! Learning objectives articulate observable behaviors that signify learning, helping educators and students track progress effectively."

- **Incorrect Answer Feedback:** "Not quite. The purpose of a learning objective is to describe observable behaviors that indicate learning has occurred, rather than just providing lesson plans or assessment strategies."

5.2. What are the three main components of a well-written learning objective?

- **Answer:** b) Performance, Condition, Criterion.

- **Correct Answer Feedback:** "That's correct! Performance, condition, and criterion form the essential framework for clear and actionable learning objectives."

- **Incorrect Answer Feedback:** "Not quite. A well-written learning objective includes performance (what to do), condition (under what circumstances), and criterion (the standard for success)."

5.3. Which question type is best suited for assessing higher-order thinking skills according to Bloom's Taxonomy?

- **Answer:** c) Short answer or essay questions.

- **Correct Answer Feedback:** "That's correct! Short answer or essay questions are ideal for assessing higher-order thinking, such as analysis and evaluation."

- **Incorrect Answer Feedback:** "Not quite. To assess higher-order thinking skills like analysis and evaluation, short answer or essay questions are more effective than simpler formats like multiple-choice."

5.4. What is the primary goal of mastery quizzing?

- **Answer:** b) To encourage students to retake quizzes for full understanding.

- **Correct Answer Feedback:** "That's correct! Mastery quizzing motivates students to retake quizzes until they achieve complete understanding, reinforcing their learning."

- **Incorrect Answer Feedback:** "Not quite. The primary goal of mastery quizzing is to encourage students to retake quizzes to deepen their understanding, not just to grade them or assess memorization."

5.5. Why should instructors avoid negative-worded questions in quizzes?

- **Answer:** b) They often increase student confusion and reduce performance

- **Correct Answer Feedback:** "That's correct! Negative-worded questions can lead to confusion and negatively impact student performance."

- **Incorrect Answer Feedback:** "Not quite. Negative-worded questions often confuse students, which can lower their performance and hinder effective assessment."

Chapter 6: Feedback

6.1. What is the primary purpose of feedback in mastery quizzing?

- **Answer:** c) To help students understand their mistakes and improve their performance.

- **Correct Answer Feedback:** "That's correct! Feedback in mastery quizzing is designed to help students identify and learn from their mistakes, guiding them toward better performance."

- **Incorrect Answer Feedback:** "Not quite. The main goal of feedback in mastery quizzing is to help students understand their errors and make improvements, not just to reinforce correct answers or prepare for summative assessments."

6.2. Why is it important to include explanations for incorrect answers in feedback?

- **Answer:** b) It bridges the gap between current knowledge and desired understanding.

- **Correct Answer Feedback:** "That's correct! Providing explanations for incorrect answers helps students see where they went wrong and connects their current knowledge to the learning objectives."

- **Incorrect Answer Feedback:** "Not quite. The purpose of explaining incorrect answers is to help students understand the reasoning behind their mistakes and how to achieve the correct understanding."

6.3. What is a potential drawback of providing immediate feedback during quizzes?

- **Answer:** a) It creates a dependency on the feedback.

- **Correct Answer Feedback:** "That's correct! Immediate feedback can sometimes lead to students relying on it too much, rather than developing independent problem-solving skills."

- **Incorrect Answer Feedback:** "Not quite. While immediate feedback can enhance engagement, it risks creating a dependency on feedback, which might hinder independent learning."

6.4. Which of the following is a benefit of reflective class feedback?

- **Answer:** b) It provides students with detailed explanations through group discussions.

- **Correct Answer Feedback:** "That's correct! Reflective class feedback fosters deeper understanding through detailed explanations and collaborative group discussions."

- **Incorrect Answer Feedback:** "Not quite. The benefit of reflective class feedback lies in engaging students in discussions and providing comprehensive explanations to clarify misconceptions."

6.5. How can instructors encourage students to use automated feedback effectively?

- **Answer:** b) By teaching students how to interpret and apply feedback early in the term.

- **Correct Answer Feedback:** "That's correct! Teaching students to understand and use automated feedback early ensures they can make the most of the learning opportunities it provides."

- **Incorrect Answer Feedback:** "Not quite. Instructors should focus on helping students learn how to interpret and apply feedback from the beginning, enabling them to improve consistently."

Chapter 7: Test Banks

7.1. What is the primary purpose of a test bank?

- **Answer:** b) To collect and organize quiz questions for educational assessments.

- **Correct Answer Feedback:** "That's correct! Test banks are designed to organize and store quiz questions effectively, facilitating their use in educational assessments."

- **Incorrect Answer Feedback:** "Not quite. The main goal of a test bank is to collect and organize quiz questions for assessments, not to store textbooks or track attendance."

7.2. How can instructors use Bloom's Taxonomy in test banks?

- **Answer:** b) To create questions tailored to different cognitive levels.

- **Correct Answer Feedback:** "That's correct! Bloom's Taxonomy helps design questions that target various cognitive skills, from basic recall to critical thinking."

- **Incorrect Answer Feedback:** "Not quite. Instructors use Bloom's Taxonomy to design questions at different cognitive levels, enriching the learning experience."

7.3. What is a key benefit of using generative AI in test bank creation

- **Answer:** c) It helps generate a variety of questions quickly and efficiently.

- **Correct Answer Feedback:** "That's correct! Generative AI accelerates question creation and offers diverse, well-structured options."

- **Incorrect Answer Feedback:** "Not quite. The key benefit of generative AI is its ability to quickly and efficiently generate diverse questions, not to replace evaluations or instructors."

7.4. Which strategy helps reduce the workload when updating test banks?

- **Answer:** b) Sharing test banks among instructors.

- **Correct Answer Feedback:** "That's correct! Sharing test banks fosters collaboration, reduces duplication, and streamlines updates."

- **Incorrect Answer Feedback:** "Not quite. Sharing test banks among instructors helps standardize and expand resources, reducing the workload."

7.5. Why is organizing test banks by difficulty levels important?

- **Answer:** b) To allow for flexibility in creating quizzes that scaffold from basic to complex knowledge.

- **Correct Answer Feedback:** "That's correct! Organizing by difficulty allows instructors to design quizzes that build from foundational to advanced knowledge."

- **Incorrect Answer Feedback:** "Not quite. Organizing test banks by difficulty provides flexibility to create assessments that progress from basic to complex levels."

Chapter 8: Quiz Design

8.1. Which of the following best defines formative assessments?

- **Answer:** c) Assessments designed to provide feedback and enhance learning during the instructional process.

- **Correct Answer Feedback:** "That's correct! Formative assessments are designed to provide feedback and enhance learning during the instructional process, helping students improve and refine their knowledge."

- **Incorrect Answer Feedback:** "Not quite. The purpose of formative assessments is to enhance learning by offering timely feedback and practice, not merely to grade or evaluate at the end of a course."

8.2. What is one benefit of the "backward testing effect?"

- **Answer:** b) It improves retention of previously studied material.

- **Correct Answer Feedback:** "That's correct! The 'backward testing effect' strengthens retention of previously studied material, making it easier to recall in the future."

- **Incorrect Answer Feedback:** "Not quite. The 'backward testing effect' primarily helps improve retention of earlier material, rather than simplifying concepts or focusing on future content."

8.3. Which principle is critical to effective quiz design?

- **Answer:** b) Providing timely and detailed feedback to learners.

- **Correct Answer Feedback:** "That's correct! Effective quiz design involves providing timely and detailed feedback to help learners understand their progress and address areas for improvement."

- **Incorrect Answer Feedback:** "Not quite. The most critical principle of effective quiz design is providing timely and detailed feedback, which supports continuous learning and improvement."

8.4. What is the primary purpose of mastery quizzing?

- **Answer:** c) To support ongoing learning through practice and feedback.

- **Correct Answer Feedback:** "That's correct! Mastery quizzing is designed to support ongoing learning by providing opportunities for practice and feedback, reinforcing understanding over time."

- **Incorrect Answer Feedback:** "Not quite. The primary purpose of mastery quizzing is to promote continuous learning and mastery through regular practice and constructive feedback."

8.5. How can the naming of assessments influence student perceptions?

- **Answer:** a) It reduces anxiety and makes assessments seem less intimidating.

- **Correct Answer Feedback:** "That's correct! Naming assessments thoughtfully, like calling them 'mastery quizzes,' can reduce anxiety and create a more supportive learning environment."

- **Incorrect Answer Feedback:** "Not quite. The naming of assessments can significantly reduce student anxiety and make assessments feel more approachable and less intimidating."

Chapter 9: Quiz Delivery

9.1. Which of the following is a key factor to consider when deciding the timing of a quiz?

- **Answer:** b) Students' alertness levels.

- **Correct Answer Feedback:** "That's correct! Scheduling quizzes when students are most alert can improve their performance and confidence."

- **Incorrect Answer Feedback:** "Not quite. Timing matters because students perform better when quizzes are scheduled during their peak alertness, such as in the morning."

9.2. What is one potential disadvantage of take-home quizzes compared to in-class quizzes?

- **Answer:** b) They do not promote active learning as effectively.

- **Correct Answer Feedback:** "That's correct! In-class quizzes actively engage students and encourage better retention of material."

- **Incorrect Answer Feedback:** "Not quite. Take-home quizzes are more flexible but often fail to encourage the same level of active learning as in-class quizzes."

9.3. Which quiz delivery method is most suitable for incorporating multimedia elements like images or videos?

- **Answer:** b) Online quizzes.

- **Correct Answer Feedback:** "That's correct! Online quizzes allow for the integration of multimedia elements, making them engaging and versatile."

- **Incorrect Answer Feedback:** "Not quite. Online quizzes are best suited for incorporating multimedia, as they offer flexibility and interactive options unavailable in traditional formats."

9.4. What is the primary benefit of machine-graded quizzes?

- **Answer:** b) They reduce instructor grading time.

- **Correct Answer Feedback:** "That's correct! Machine grading saves instructors significant time, especially for large classes."

- **Incorrect Answer Feedback:** "Not quite. The main advantage of machine-graded quizzes is their ability to efficiently save time on grading."

9.5. Which of the following practices can help ensure a supportive atmosphere during quiz administration?

- **Answer:** c) Providing clear written and oral instructions.

- **Correct Answer Feedback:** "That's correct! Clear instructions help students feel prepared and reduce unnecessary confusion during quizzes."

- **Incorrect Answer Feedback:** "Not quite. Providing clear written and oral instructions is essential for creating a supportive and effective quiz environment."

Chapter 10: Mastery Quizzing Considerations

10.1. What is the primary goal of mastery quizzing?

- **Answer:** b) To foster active learning and long-term retention.

- **Correct Answer Feedback:** "That's correct! Mastery quizzing focuses on helping students engage deeply with the material and retain knowledge over time."

- **Incorrect Answer Feedback:** "Not quite. The goal of mastery quizzing is to foster active learning and long-term retention, not just grading or reducing assessments."

10.2. Which grading strategy allows students multiple attempts to meet a specific standard?

- **Answer:** c) Specifications grading.

- **Correct Answer Feedback:** "That's correct! Specifications grading gives students opportunities to demonstrate mastery through multiple attempts."

- **Incorrect Answer Feedback:** "Not quite. Specifications grading is the method that lets students meet standards through repeated attempts, ensuring mastery."

10.3. How does frequent quizzing help reduce test anxiety?

- **Answer:** b) By familiarizing students with testing formats.

- **Correct Answer Feedback:** "That's correct! Frequent quizzing helps students become comfortable with testing formats, reducing anxiety over time."

- **Incorrect Answer Feedback:** "Not quite. Frequent quizzing reduces test anxiety by familiarizing students with the testing process, not by eliminating feedback or making quizzes harder."

10.4. What is a key benefit of additive grading?

- **Answer:** a) It allows students to recover lost points by retaking quizzes.

- **Correct Answer Feedback:** "That's correct! Additive grading motivates students by allowing them to continuously improve their scores."

- **Incorrect Answer Feedback:** "Not quite. Additive grading helps students recover lost points through retakes, fostering a growth mindset."

10.5. Which of the following is NOT a recommended practice for mastery quizzing?

- **Answer:** c) Prioritizing grades over learning outcomes.

- **Correct Answer Feedback:** "That's correct! Mastery quizzing focuses on learning and growth rather than prioritizing grades."

- **Incorrect Answer Feedback:** "Not quite. Mastery quizzing emphasizes learning outcomes, feedback, and understanding, not simply achieving grades."

Chapter 11: In-Class Activities

11.1. What is the primary purpose of in-class mastery activities?

- **Answer:** b) To reinforce learning through active engagement.

- **Correct Answer Feedback:** "That's correct! In-class mastery activities are designed to actively engage students and reinforce their learning in real-time."

- **Incorrect Answer Feedback:** "Not quite. The primary purpose of in-class mastery activities is to reinforce learning through active engagement, not just to fill time or focus on individual work."

11.2. Which of the following is an example of an effective in-class mastery activity?

- **Answer:** b) Conducting quizzes that allow peer discussion and feedback.

- **Correct Answer Feedback:** "Well done! Quizzes with peer discussion and feedback effectively engage students and deepen their understanding."

- **Incorrect Answer Feedback:** "Incorrect. Effective in-class mastery activities, like peer-discussion quizzes, are interactive and provide immediate feedback to enhance learning."

11.3. How can in-class mastery quizzing activities help identify student knowledge gaps?

- **Answer:** a) By providing immediate feedback on student responses.

- **Correct Answer Feedback:** "Correct! Providing immediate feedback allows both students and instructors to identify and address gaps in understanding."

- **Incorrect Answer Feedback:** "Not quite. The key to identifying knowledge gaps is providing immediate feedback on student responses to guide improvement."

11.4. What is a key characteristic of effective in-class mastery activities?

- **Answer:** b) They encourage interaction and discussion among students.

- **Correct Answer Feedback:** "That's right! Encouraging interaction and discussion fosters a collaborative learning environment that enhances mastery."

- **Incorrect Answer Feedback:** "Incorrect. Effective in-class mastery activities promote interaction and discussion rather than focusing solely on individual performance or memorization."

11.5. Which approach best supports active learning during in-class activities?

- **Answer:** b) Incorporating questions that require application and analysis.

- **Correct Answer Feedback:** "Correct! Questions that require application and analysis help students engage with the material on a deeper level."

- **Incorrect Answer Feedback:** "Not quite. Active learning is best supported by incorporating questions that challenge students to apply and analyze their knowledge, rather than focusing solely on rote memorization or limited participation."

Chapter 12: Strategies

12.1. Which of the following is a primary advantage of mastery quizzing in education?

- **Answer:** c) It enhances long-term retention and understanding.

- **Correct Answer Feedback:** "That's correct! Mastery quizzing enhances long-term retention and understanding by encouraging regular practice and feedback."

- **Incorrect Answer Feedback:** "Not quite. The primary advantage of mastery quizzing is its ability to improve long-term retention and understanding, not short-term memory or reducing instructor involvement."

12.2. In the context of flipped instruction, mastery quizzes are most effective when:

- **Answer:** b) They are used to assess and reinforce understanding during classroom sessions.

- **Correct Answer Feedback:** "That's correct! Using mastery quizzes during classroom sessions helps assess and reinforce understanding in real time, making learning more interactive."

- **Incorrect Answer Feedback:** "Not quite. Mastery quizzes are most effective when used to assess and reinforce understanding during classroom sessions, not just at the end of a course or for rote memorization."

12.3. Which of the following is NOT a common feature of game-based quizzing platforms like Quizizz?

- **Answer:** c) Mandatory use of group quizzes over individual quizzes.

- **Correct Answer Feedback:** "That's correct! While Quizizz offers many features like timers and multimedia elements, it does not mandate group quizzes over individual quizzes."

- **Incorrect Answer Feedback:** "Not quite. Game-based quizzing platforms like Quizizz often include timers, multimedia, and immediate feedback but do not require group quizzes over individual ones."

12.4. In mastery quizzing, which method helps reduce student anxiety while enhancing their confidence in language learning?

- **Answer:** b) Immediate feedback and repeated practice.

- **Correct Answer Feedback:** "That's correct! Immediate feedback and repeated practice are key to reducing anxiety and building confidence in language learning."

- **Incorrect Answer Feedback:** "Not quite. Reducing student anxiety and enhancing confidence in language learning are best achieved through immediate feedback and repeated practice."

12.5. What is a recommended practice for building robust test banks for math mastery quizzes?

- **Answer:** b) Creating formula-based questions with variable inputs.

- **Correct Answer Feedback:** "That's correct! Creating formula-based questions with variable inputs allows for a wide range of unique problems to support mastery."

- **Incorrect Answer Feedback:** "Not quite. To build robust test banks for math mastery quizzes, it's important to create formula-based questions with variable inputs, rather than relying on static options or prewritten textbook questions."

Chapter 13: The Mastery Quizzing Strategy

13.1. What is the first step in creating effective quizzes for a course?
- **Answer:** c) Refining course learning outcomes into specific objectives.

- **Correct Answer Feedback:** "That's correct! Refining course learning outcomes into specific objectives lays the groundwork for designing targeted and effective quizzes."

- **Incorrect Answer Feedback:** "Not quite. The first step in creating effective quizzes is refining course learning outcomes into specific objectives to ensure alignment with the course's overarching goals."

13.2. How does aligning questions with Bloom's Taxonomy benefit students?
- **Answer:** b) It ensures questions scaffold learning from basic to advanced levels.

- **Correct Answer Feedback:** "That's correct! Aligning questions with Bloom's Taxonomy helps structure learning progressively, guiding students from foundational knowledge to higher-order thinking skills."

- **Incorrect Answer Feedback:** "Not quite. Aligning questions with Bloom's Taxonomy benefits students by scaffolding their learning from basic to advanced levels, fostering a deeper understanding of the material."

13.3. Why is it essential to include detailed feedback for quiz questions?
- **Answer:** b) To reinforce key concepts and clarify misunderstandings.

- **Correct Answer Feedback:** "That's correct! Detailed feedback is crucial for reinforcing key concepts and helping students address misunderstandings effectively."

- **Incorrect Answer Feedback:** "Not quite. Providing detailed feedback reinforces key concepts and clarifies misunderstandings, ensuring that students learn from each quiz attempt."

13.4. What is the primary purpose of an exam blueprint?

- **Answer:** c) To plan quiz content, structure, and alignment with course objectives.

- **Correct Answer Feedback:** "That's correct! An exam blueprint is a strategic tool for planning quiz content, structure, and ensuring alignment with course objectives."

- **Incorrect Answer Feedback:** "Not quite. The primary purpose of an exam blueprint is to plan quiz content, structure, and alignment with course objectives, ensuring a comprehensive assessment strategy."

13.5. What is a recommended strategy for promoting long-term retention through quizzes?

- **Answer:** b) Using a "go or no-go" standard with cumulative weekly quizzes.

- **Correct Answer Feedback:** "That's correct! A 'go or no-go' standard with cumulative weekly quizzes reinforces learning and promotes long-term retention."

- **Incorrect Answer Feedback:** "Not quite. Using a 'go or no-go' standard with cumulative weekly quizzes ensures consistent reinforcement of material, aiding long-term retention."

Appendix H: Downloadable Resources and Mentioned Links

Here is a list of URLs for each of the downloadable resources mentioned in this book along with other referenced links:

- *Mastery Through Quizzing* Resources Folder
  https://tubarksblog.com/MQResources

- Appendix B: Writing Learning Objectives with ChatGPT
  https://tubarksblog.com/MQLearningObjectives

- Appendix D: Writing Questions with ChatGPT
  https://tubarksblog.com/MQQuestions

- Appendix F: Exam Blueprint Example
  https://tubarksblog.com/MQBlueprint

- Chapter 5: New York Institute of Technology's Canvas Exam Converter
  https://tubarksblog.com/MQQTIConverter

Did You Find a Typo?

Hey there, awesome reader!

First off, huge thanks for picking up this book.

Many folks have already combed through its pages, but pesky typos can be sneaky little things, and sometimes they manage to play hide-and-seek with even the keenest eyes. If you spot any, I'd be incredibly grateful if you could give me a heads-up! Not only will you be helping me fine-tune this masterpiece, but you'll also be ensuring that future readers get an even smoother experience.

Just head on over to https://tubarksblog.com/typo and let me know. Together, we can make this book the best it can be!

Happy reading and happy typo hunting!

Also By

More Books From Stan Skrabut

80 Ways to Use ChatGPT in the Classroom: Using AI to Enhance Teaching and Learning
Evernote: A Success Manual for College Students
Mastery Through Quizzing: An Active Learning Approach for Today's Classroom
Read to Succeed: The Power of Books to Transform Your Life and Put You on the Path to Success
Strategies for Success: Scaling Your Impact As a Solo Instructional Technologist and Designer
tubarksblog.com/my-books

About the Author

Stan Skrabut is a card-carrying lifelong learner who has spent his career helping people and organizations achieve improved performance. He is a scholar, teacher, author, veteran, martial artist, and avid reader. Throughout his working life, he has changed roles and responsibilities countless times. He worked as a guard, organizational trainer, instructional technologist, webmaster, systems programmer, lecturer, and director. He uses informal learning, especially reading, to improve himself and his teams. His interest in informal learning inspired his dissertation, *Study of Informal Learning Among University of Wyoming Extension Educators*.

He lives with his wife and dog in Rhode Island. Nomadic in nature, he loves to travel and has lived in Germany, Belgium, Holland, Turkey, and various locations across the United States. His number one passion is helping others achieve their goals.

Scan the QR code to join me on my learning journey as I explore the world of teaching and learning.

Connect with Stan online:

- tubarksblog.com/newsletter

- facebook.com/StanSkrabutAuthor

- tubarksblog.com/podcast

Acknowledgments

Writing a book is never a solo endeavor. I am deeply grateful to everyone who contributed to this journey.

First, my heartfelt thanks go to my wife and partner, **Bernadette van der Vliet**. She reviewed countless drafts and provided invaluable design recommendations that enhanced each version of this book. Her artistic talent brought the cover to life and created stunning marketing images. She makes me—and this book—look better. I can never thank her enough.

I also place my full trust in **Wendy Picard**, whose thoughtful editing and patience helped refine this manuscript. Her keen eye and expertise elevated this book in ways I deeply appreciate.

A special thank you to my beta readers, whose insights and feedback strengthened this book. Many of their suggestions shaped the final version. Thank you, **Alan Adams, Camille Napier Bernstein, Jenn Buckley, Amanda Gibson, Kathleen Gradel, Nikki Vassallo, and Dawn Walker-Elders**.

I am also grateful to my advance review team for helping spread the word. Their enthusiasm and outreach played a crucial role in getting this book into readers' hands. Thank you, **Alan Adams, Abdullah Alotaibi, Tim Arnold, Camille Napier Bernstein, Bob Cook, Kevin Corcoran, Reda Othman, Thom Powell, Stacey Stearns, and Dawn Walker-Elders**.

To everyone who supported this journey—thank you. Your encouragement made all the difference.

www.ingramcontent.com/pod-product-compliance
Lightning Source LLC
Chambersburg PA
CBHW071718120626
46550CB00001B/282